ASTROLOGICAL SECRETS
OF
FRIENDSHIP, LOVE AND MARRIAGE

By the same authors:

- ASPECTS IN VEDIC ASTROLOGY
- ASTROLOGY AND YOU
- BODY READING
- NUMEROLOGY FOR ALL
- PALMISTRY FOR ALL
- PREDICTIVE ASTROLOGY OF THE HINDUS
- THE SOLAR RETURN OR VARSHAPHAL
- अंकविद्या (ज्योतिष)
- जातक-पारिजात (२ भाग)
- जातकादेश मार्ग-चन्द्रिका
- फलदीपिका (भावार्थबोधिनी)
- भारतीय लग्न-सारिणी
- त्रिफला (ज्योतिष)
- सुगम ज्योतिष प्रवेशिका
- हस्तरेखा विज्ञान

Astrological Secrets of Friendship, Love and Marriage

GOPESH KUMAR OJHA
ASHUTOSH OJHA

MOTILAL BANARSIDASS PUBLISHERS
PRIVATE LIMITED • DELHI

ISBN: 978-81-208-3562-7

MOTILAL BANARSIDASS
41 U.A. Bungalow Road, Jawahar Nagar, Delhi 110 007
8 Mahalaxmi Chamber, 22 Bhulabhai Desai Road, Mumbai 400 026
203 Royapettah High Road, Mylapore, Chennai 600 004
236, 9th Main III Block, Jayanagar, Bangaluru 560 011
Sanas Plaza, 1302 Baji rao Road, Pune 411 002
8 Camac Street, Kolkata 700 017
Ashok Rajpath, Patna 800 004
Chowk, Varanasi 221 001

PREFACE TO THE REVISED EDITION

मकरन्दं पिबन्भृङ्गो गन्धान् नापेक्षते यथा।
नादासक्तं सदा चित्तं विषयं न हि काङ्क्षति ॥ 42 ॥
बद्धः सुनादगन्धेन सद्यः संत्यक्तचापलः । 42½

Just as भौंरा (a large black honey bee) while drinking honey does not care for the smell, similarly the *'Chitta'** which is all time engrossed into the enchantment of '*Nada*', does not desire the gratification of the senses: it is so engulfed into the ecstasy of the '*Nada*' that it has lost its wandering nature.

(*Nadabindopanishad:* sl. 42, 42½)

The importance of Love, Friendship and Marriage in life can never be over emphasized. The Man-Woman relationship as a friend, lover or spouse is significant. But what is the factor that where one man is successful the other is not. Is he the incarnation of '*Kamadev*'† or does he know the art of '*Vashikaran*'††?

We do not think so. It is the placement of stars. All this and more is described in the present book. It deals with the hidden and secret principles of Astrology as related to one's Love life.

There are several books. These tell us of how to be successful in relationships and love or books like 'Kamasutra' or 'The Joy of Sex' which deal with the performances or try to remove ignorance. There was a time when even speaking of love was '*taboo*'. But all this has changed.

---

* Consciousness, thought, intelligence, Brahman.

† Cupid: The God of Love.

†† To control others; to subdue the will of others so they act as per the desire of one who has control on them.

It is all in our Stars, in our horoscopes, in the placements of Planets and the periodic influences of directions and transits that we are passing through; that our life takes shape. By this statement we are not advocating *Fatalism*. We in the East do not believe in 'What has to be has to be'. The theory of *Karma* is threefold and the main thing it emphasizes is that by good actions the past can be eliminated. Control on the mind, by prayers and precautions, the Destiny can be changed. If *Fatalism* would be real it would bind all our lives into a frigid mould from which none can escape. It would bring the World to standstill and paralyze all activities. The Scriptures do not support this. Even *'Koran'* which at bottom so very fatalistic counsels him who wants to go to sleep to hobble his horse. If what has to be has to be then the *Prophet Mohammed* would have told his disciples to beware of theft?

The present book describes the mysteries, i.e. the hidden Astrological Secrets of Love, Friendship and Marriage and when the effects would fructify.

There is a separate chapter which deals exclusively with the female horoscopes. Women have their superiority and their hold on men have no parallel. Most *wars have been fought for or on account of women* like the ones for Sita, Draupadi, or Helen of Troy whose beauty had been compared to *the Evening Air and thousand of Stars*.

> "Thou art fairer than Evening Air
> clad in the beauty of a Thousand Stars
>
> ....
>
> Sweet Helen make me immortal with a kiss".

('Dr. Faustus' by Marlowe)

The *Adi Shankara* who started on his pilgrimage to defeat the pandits in the northern India in debates to prove the superiority was a worshipper of Brahma. He took to 'sannyasa' at the age of twelve. "Aham Brahmasmi" viz. I am the Brahma the lord of creation, Near 'Varanasi' he suffered from dysentary and was taking rest under the shadow of a tree when a young girl came to see him. She asked him where he was travelling to.

On being told that he is going to North Bihar and Kashmir to defeat the pandits in debates. The young girl smiled and said to him "Those pandits are very learned and you should first try to defeat me so as to have a practice". Shankara replied 'Mother I am weak. I have no 'Shakti' (strength) even to speak-so how can I enter into a 'Vada-Vivad' (discussion) with you.

Hearing him say so the young woman laughed and said if you have no 'Shakti' then why are you a proponent of 'Brahma'? Why do you not worship 'Shakti'? Then and there Adi Shankara realized that 'the Goddess Mother' has come in person to show him the right path of worship suitable for his needs.

He turned to the worship of Shakti and the first shloka that he said in "Saundarya Lahari"—*The Wave of Bliss* was:

शिवः शक्त्या युक्तो यदि भवति शक्तः प्रभवितुं
न चेदेवं देवो न खलु कुशलः स्पन्दितुमपि।
अतस्त्वामाराध्यां हरिहर विरिञ्चादिभिरपि
प्रणन्तुं स्तोतुं वा कथमकृतपुण्यः प्रभवति ॥ 1 ॥

Shiva is able to create only when he is united with Shakti; otherwise the Deva cannot even move about. Therefore, is it possible for those who have not done good Karma either to worship or praise thee that art worshipped by Hari, Hara, Brahma and others.

How correctly it describes that there is no fruition all alone. [The Absolute Brahman of itself cannot do anything. The creative potency is generated by its union with Shakti. A seed has to have earth, water, air, or fire to change and this is where man and woman play the first stage in the order of evolution.]

This book has been updated and revised thoroughly. Appendices and Glossary of the two parts viz., the Western and the Hindu, have been clubbed together. Certain chapters have been rearranged, combined and expanded so that the book becomes complete in itself.

— Ashutosh Ojha

H.No. 1952
Sector IV HUDA
Gurgaon (Haryana), India
aojha@vsnl.com

PREFACE TO THE FIRST EDITION

Perhaps I owe a few words, by way of apology, for bringing out this book, when already many books by eminent authors are in the market. My explanation is: So far as I am aware there is no book dealing exclusively with this subject and in the manner I have done. Mention may be made in this connection of *Astrology and Marriage* by Sepharial—a book containing fifty-nine pages, which enunciates some basic principles of Astrology in relation to married happiness. But to my mind that book, though very interesting, touches only the outline of the subject and a desire is created in the mind of the reader, to know more, and delve deeper into the study of this fascinating subject. This is no doubt a tribute to the eminent author, because, as I have stated, it has been successful in creating an interest in the subject. Then, there is another book *Successful Marriage* by Pharos. This is, comparatively speaking, a voluminous book closely printed and covering about 218 pages. But this deals only with the influence of 'Sun', according as the Sun is in one Zodiacal sign or the other, at the time of birth. Even the subject of matching the horoscopes— astrological judgment depending upon planetary configurations—how far a particular male would have successful marriage with a particular female—has been limited to the influence of the 'sign' in which the 'Sun' is.

So that, this book—though no doubt of immense interest to the layman—is of little use to the astrologer who, while acknowledging the superior influence of the mighty Sun, considers its influence on the married life and happiness as just one of the many factors and not *the* factor.

Then, there are a number of eminent authors, dealing fully with the entire subject of astrology, casting a horoscope and delineation of it, who have—most of them—based their structures on the ptolemic foundation. These eminent authors have dealt with all aspects of life—health, wealth, brethren, home, parents, children, married happiness, business, position and activity, friends, journeys to foreign land, incarceration, imprisonment and a list of other subjects which touch some department or other of human life.

Had I attempted such a thing, the present volume would have become too bulky and would have entirely defeated the very purpose which has been kept in view.

The purpose is twofold:

(a) To keep exclusively within the limits of the subject-matter which comes under 'Love and Marriage' and thus confine the study to human emotions and affairs dealing with this department of life alone.

Thus, if a planet, say in the seventh House, denotes influence on marriage, business partnerships, etc. or again if a planet in a particular sign gives certain sex-propensities as well as disease, the discussion here has been confined to marriage and sex propensities alone, because the other matter should be considered under business or health. Many readers would no doubt consider that procreation of children is a corollary of marriage and as such some interested readers had appreciated this book better, if that matter also had been allotted its rightful place in this book. But with that line of argument, many more subjects would have claimed simultaneous attention and my effort to confine the study to one subject alone would have been defeated. That would have made the volume bulky and at the same time taken away that simplicity of arrangement—which is the special feature of this book.

(b) To explain what I mean by 'simplicity of arrangement' I must refer the readers to the contents of the book. Look to the contents of Part I. You have the influence of the

(1) Sun in twelve signs; (2) Sun in twelve houses; (3) Moon in twelve signs; (4) Moon in twelve houses; (5) Mars in twelve signs; (6) Mars in twelve houses and so on.

Now, if an astrologer or even a layman who knows something about signs and houses and aspects wants to ascertain the specific influence, he can commence looking up with Sun's influence in a particular sign and then Sun's influence in a particular house. There are twelve signs and twelve houses. One need confine his attention to Sun's influence in the particular sign in the horoscope under enquiry. Then one may safely skip the pages dealing with Sun's influence in other signs. Similarly, one may look up the required effect of the Sun's house position in the particular house the Sun is situated and leave the other pages. One may next proceed with the Moon in a similar manner and then with Mars and Mercury and so on. This arrangement has been made to facilitate summing up influences.

It is true that in a horoscope the influences are not isolated, but synthetic *i.e.*, a particular effect is not the result of one planet alone—much less the effect of a planet's 'sign' position only or 'house' position only. But how to know the cumulative effect, unless one knows the individual effect ? The art of synthesis is the most delicate art—of blending similar and dissimilar influences and arriving at the resultant influence. It requires prudence and knowledge and experience but above all, one must know what one is synthesising. Unless one knows the component forces how can one know the resultant force ?

It happens many a time that when a particular horoscope is being examined some points are missed. In the present volume all component or individual effects have been carefully classified, grouped and arranged, so that one has not to hunt in all directions— to find the effect of any particular influence, either due to sign or house or aspect or any other factor. Thus, this book affords the same facility as a classified catalogue, so that one knows where one would find what one is looking for and can directly put his finger in the right place.

It is this arrangement, which I may be permitted to state is the 'key-note' or the very special feature, which no doubt would save a lot of time and energy, which one has usually to expend in looking through the various standard texts.

Another consideration, which has prompted me to bring out this book is to make available to the readers the principles and practice of Western as well as Hindu Astrology in one single volume. There are many books in English dealing with Principles of Western Astrology. There are yet others which deal with the subject matter only from Hindu point of view, *i.e.* embodying and employing only those principles which have been dealt with in Hindu Astrology. It has been my good fortune to study and admire the salient features of both the systems. On one hand, I attach importance to the tropical Zodiac, which regulates Sunrise and Sunset, durations of day and night, climate, seasons, crops and so many geographical and other influences having a bearing on the flora and the fauna and it would be but natural to presume that it exerts influence in similar manner in regard to human beings also, and the 'Kalapurush' must have a constant analogy to the moveable Zodiac, on the other, believing as I do in stellar influence, I have deep and abiding faith in the influence of the ambient—containing billions and billions of stars. The Sanskrit texts are all one in regard to the influence of the fixed stars and 'nakshatra Vidya' or the 'knowledge of the fixed stars', is the foundation of Hindu astrology. Not only the Vedic texts but the greatest and the first epic of the Hindus, the Valmiki Ramayana, written many centuries before Christ refer to the natal star 'nakshatra' of Dasharath having been afflicted by Sun, Mars and Rahu (northern node of the Moon).

This same epic, written many centuries before Christ also mentions the phenomenon of earth's movement round the Sun. In modern times, even eminent Western astrologers like Mr. Cyril Fagan, Mr. E.V. Robson, Mr. W.J. Tucker, Mr. D.A. Bradley and others have recognised the importance of the Sidereal Zodiac. In the Hindu system not only the division of the Zodiac, but the Dasha System (Directions) is based upon fixed constellations. So, to my mind, any system which does not take cognisance of the 'immoveable' or fixed Zodiac would be incomplete.

So, the first difference between the two systems is of the moveable or fixed Zodiac. The second difference between the two systems is that of application by aspects. The third major difference is of Directions. Besides, there are other differences in the two systems, which are already well-known to the students of astrology. And to others, those who are beginners, the matter would gradually unfold itself, as they go through these pages.

I have purposely not mixed one system with the other. That would have only confused the issue. Besides, it would not have been fair to of the systems to break it, in order to fit in with the other.

I hope the readers would enjoy this volume and also derive much help from it. I can divide the readership into two sections—those who believe in this ancient science of astrology and those others who do not believe in it. To the first, I need say nothing for they have no doubt experienced the great truth which the mystic influence of the occult hides from the common man.

To others I need only say that there is no mystery about astrology. It is as clear and simple as any other branch of science. The mighty Sun gives us heat and light. Even a layman understands these two phenomena. But the various other elements, which are directly attributable to Sun's rays can be detected only by an analysis and examination of Sun's rays by means of a spectroscope. No wonder, therefore, that Sun's rays have other properties, which have not been so far tested by our modern scientific instruments. So far—but what instrument would be more sensitive and susceptible to those influences than the human body itself ?

What is this phenomenon which aggravates or abates the diseases according to whether Moon is full or half or a quarter? What is the cycle that produces physical changes in women periodically? What has the influence of Moon to do with the lunatics ? Why particular ailments are more troublesome in the morning and increase and decrease with the heat of Sun? If the eyesight can be affected so favourably or adversely by the heat and light of Sun, if the pulmonary troubles can be traced to have direct and certain connection with Moon; there is no reason to disbelieve that Sun and Moon and other heavenly bodies give out from their bodies other energies or substance which when emitted and passed through so many stratospheres of ether, air and other gases affect human bodies and spirit in a peculiar way. Our ignorance of the magnitude and nature of the beneficent Jupiter or the malignant Saturn of the markedly martial Mars or the luxuriously benign Venus should not shut our eyes to the prepondering influence that these planets exert over our minds and spirit and shape our destinies both directly and indirectly—directly by wielding power as potential agents and indirectly through the instrumentality of our very selves, whose all actions are conceived, dictated and guided by our spirit.

The horoscope of a man is nothing more than the plotting of the different planets in their respective positions at the time of the native's birth. The positions of the planets decide the fate of man; his life, his wealth, brothers and sisters, parents, progeny, ailments and enemies, love affairs, wife or husband, prosperity, income and practically every other thing that touches a man's interest can be predicted with fair accuracy.

But the book would be incomplete if we discussed only the good and evil influences that the planets exert over the human emotion, without suggesting some definite steps to counteract the evil influences at work. The science loses its practical value— as a useful weapon to safeguard one's marital interests and conjugal happiness. One great thing that should never be lost sight of is the psychological and the physiological relationship between the sexes. I mean, the relationship of sex is not so simple as it looks on the surface. When two parties unite sexually a certain amount of 'give and take' takes place and the reactions are not only chemical, physical or biological but also ethical and psychological. In case of marriage or love affairs in general, some people are not affected as profoundly as others. Some regard it only as an advanced stage of flirtation while others sink their whole life and soul in a union. The repercussions of a sexual union are too varied to be catalogued, and we can assume in a general way that the destiny of many a man or woman is so intricately woven with the marital relationship that their whole being swings in a pendulum, as it were, under the forces that attract or repel. The psychological effect of marriage or union in any other way has, of late, formed the subject-matter of much enlightened discussion. And the benefits or otherwise that flow from the right or wrong union cannot be overlooked in our consideration of the career that is shaped so subtly yet inevitably by affairs of love.

It has been said by an eminent writer (perhaps Freud) that the whole energy can be resolved and its component parts found to be sexual in their fundamental character. The energy that works wonders in the realm of art or education is more often than not frittered away in idle gestures of love and loyalty towards one's partner. The essentially martial man capable of being a Hitler or Mussolini often diverts his energies in a channel where they flow with full vigour but achieve nothing. And yet it remains a problem to solve, how best we can choose our partners so that we may mitigate the evil influences and find ourselves best suited to each other, to go hand in hand higher up in the path of advancement and ultimately reach our goal.

To take up the question directly, can we not so devise our partnerships in marriage that we may counteract all the evil influences and enhance the benign ones. In one word: is there a thing like suitability, adaptability or compatibility in marriage from the astrological point of view? A medical man would at once say that age, nationality, health, heredity; etc. are the factors that govern the suitability of marriage between the parties. The science of astrology is nothing but advanced knowledge of the system of which the elementary principles alone are taken into consideration by the doctor.

When the doctor examines a young man and a young woman intending to marry, he would see whether any of the two suffer from any congenital defects or contagious disease and whether they are physically suited to each other. Not so the astrologer. The doctor cannot say whether a man who has excellent lungs and perfect blood pressure would after ten years suffer from phthisis or be a victim to some wasting, devastating disease. The astrologer can—if Moon and Venus are ill-placed, if the lords of the first and the sixth houses are weak and afflicted and in unfavourable positions—declare that the man in whom no bacteria can be found today and who has apparently all the symptoms of good health will at a particular time be a patient of and succumb ultimately to T.B.

A healthy couple with absolutely no trace of impurity of blood will be declared suitable partnership by a physician but not so by an astrologer who knows that Mars, the planet presiding over heat and blood, if afflicted, ill-placed and evilly aspected shall give rise to impurities of blood and eruptions and boils and wounds that may prove fatal. Saturn governs frigidity and the unimpaired influence of Venus endows a man with extra passion. Moon is a cold luminary and if it is weak and afflicted at the time of birth, would give the native little stamina.

But we are here not judging the isolated values of the good or evil influence of planets in a horoscope. We are considering the law of relativity. A and B are two men, C and D are two women. A, B, C and D have all some favourable and some unfavourable features in their horoscopes. But it is possible to say astrologically that the marriages of a A and C and of B and D may prove a boon and a blessing while the other combination of A and D and B and C may result in cat and dog life, domestic devastation or even death. It is for judgment of this aspect that the chapters on "mutual harmony" have been added. I would, however, invite attention of the readers to one, important aspect in the science of prediction. While assessing the strength of the stars and their influence on human emotions or overt acts, one should not lose sight of the environment and the effects of individual efforts. The Hindu scriptures lay emphasis again and again on the place (native land and attending circumstances at the time of birth), time (the epoch, e.g. conditions in 20th century civilisation are widely different from those in 18th or 19th century) and the background of family, education, moral standards and other circumstances of the individual whose horoscope is under scrutiny. I have come across many good astrologers—who though well-read, do not attach sufficient weight to the above three factors. (Times, country, background of the Individual). So, I want to invite specific attention to the above. The aphorisms based on Western Astrology are more applicable to Western society than to orthodox Hindu Society. In matters of chastity, standards differ from country to country and from time to time. In one society, flirtation may be a routine part of life, while in another it may be considered shocking sacrilege. So, readers are requested not to jump to conclusions but thoroughly weigh the various factors, before arriving at any definite conclusion.

The laws in relation to marriage have undergone radical changes. At one time, in certain communities plurality of wives was a common feature among the rich; today monogamy has come to stay. So, the factors which would have brought about plurality of marriages would reveal only secret affairs.

When I was writing this book, it was at one stage my intention to give some example horoscopes. But the obvious delicacy which became a difficulty was that if I had given the horoscopes, my clients would have easily identified these as being their horoscopes and I could not have possibly commented upon the moral character or love-affiliations or otherwise which formed the special features of their lives. So, I leave it to the readers to pick and choose horoscopes of individuals, men and women of their acquaintance, and find for themselves the significant combinations of planets, referred to herein.

Another matter to which I would refer is that English authors use 'he' for Jupiter, Sun and Mars and 'she' for Venus and Moon. According to us, Hindus, Sun, Mars and Jupiter are masculine in astrological influence; Moon and Venus are feminine in the matter of astrological influence. Mercury is a male eunuch and Saturn is a female eunuch. But for purposes of grammar, all planets or 'grahas' are treated as masculine. So I have, generally used the pronoun 'it' instead of he or she for any planet.

I would be failing in my duty if I do not acknowledge the deep debt of gratitude which I owe to all the old authors, oriental as well as occidental because the present book is the product of my deep study of the older authors and I have with me 30 years of experience put in new bottles, what is undoubtedly old, very old, coming down centuries and centuries.

In a subject like astrology it is really difficult to contribute something new. Our labours would be amply repaid if we study the old maxims and apply them *mutatis mutandis* to the life around us.

August 1, 1959,
93, Daryaganj,
Delhi -110 007

PANDIT GOPESH KUMAR OJHA

CONTENTS

INTRODUCTION

This is primarily a book of astrology and would no doubt be consulted by people, who know ABC of Astrology—what is a horoscope, what is the rising sign—how it is calculated, what are the cusps of the houses—and what are the limits of 'house' on either side, how to determine the longitude of a planet and in which sign and which house to put it. These and several other matters are a little too technical for the layman to understand. Although some of the astrological words and phrases have been explained at the end, yet there are certain matters—preliminary to the study of this book with which the readers must become acquainted,to understand and appreciate the astrological maxims. Those who have been students of astrology and know how to make a horoscope or read it, would find nothing new in these preliminary pages because they are no doubt already familiar with the subject-matter that follows immediately. But others who have love for this science of astrology yet are not well versed in the technique of making a horoscope, would find the following instructions very helpful. To begin with, what is a horoscope ? Horoscope is the chart of the heavens—skies as it existed at the time of birth of a person and as seen or visualised from the place of birth.

It is impossible to put on paper the billions and billions of stars that occupy the skies; so the astrologer contents himself by putting in their respective positions the 9 stars and planets and the nodes of the Moon.

Technically, Sun and Moon are called the luminaries, while

Mars, Mercury, Jupiter, Venus and Saturn are called planets. In Hindu Astrology, as in common parlance, all are referred to as planets. Besides, these seven planets, Rahu and Ketu have also been assigned place of importance. In Hindu mythology, many interesting stories have been woven round the role of Rahu and Ketu, but we are not concerned with them here.

Rahu is the northern or the upper node of the Moon. It is not any planet—nor any visible phenomenon. It is the point where Moon's orbit cuts Earth's orbit. This is deemed to be a very sensitive point, as far as astrological influences are concerned. The point where Moon's orbit cuts Earth's orbit is, however, not a permanently fixed point but recedes. So the node of Moon or Rahu's longitude is constantly changing and in all ephemerides Rahu's or node's position is given in degrees and minutes like those of other planets.

Ketu is just another point 180° distant from Rahu. Once, therefore, the longitude of Rahu in degrees and minutes is known that of Ketu can be immediately calculated by adding or subtracting 180° from Rahu's longitude. So much about Rahu and Ketu. Just as these nodes of the Moon have been assigned place of importance in Hindu Astrology, so in Western Astrology, the influence of three new planets, Herschel, Neptune and Pluto is also taken into consideration.

In earlier Greek astrology or in early English astrology, these three planets did not figure, because they have been discovered, comparatively speaking only recently.

'Herschel' is also called 'Uranus'. In fact, Herschel is the name of the famous astronomer who discovered this planet, so it is called 'Herschel' also. In this book,we have given preference to the name 'Herschel' over its other name Uranus. Since these two planets are of recent discovery they could not possibly be referred to in Hindu astrology. But, now modern Hindu Astrologers have started giving consideration to the effect of these planets and we agree with them.

I have purposely omitted the influence of Pluto, because

the orbit of that planet is very erratic and nothing can be said with certainty about its influence on married life or love affairs. It stands to reason that it should also exert influence, if it is posited in the 5th, 7th, or 11th houses or conjoined with or in strong aspect with the lords thereof, but since inference in relation to these are still under discussion, I prefer to abstain rather than give doubtful instructions on the influence of Pluto in relation to love affairs or marriage.

How to Find Longitudes of Planets

Sun, Moon, Mars, Mercury, Jupiter, Venus and Saturn have been familiar from times immemorial and need no introduction. The planetary positions (or longitudes of planets) are given for 12 noon 'Greenwich Mean Time' (in Raphael's Ephemeris) for each day of the year. Suppose a person was born at New Delhi on the 11th December, 1915 at 1-30 P.M. Indian Standard Time. (I.S.T.) Now, as Indian Standard Time is 5 hours 30 minutes ahead of Greenwich Mean Time (G.M.T.) it would be 8 A.M. G.M.T. when it is 1-30 P.M. I.S.T. In order to fix the longitude of planets at 1-30 I.S.T., we have to find the position of planets at 8 A.M. G.M.T.

Now if you possess a copy of the Raphael's Ephemeris for 1915 (if you have not, you had better purchase, because the Ephemeris for the particular year is absolutely necessary to find the longitudes) please turn to pages 24-25 of the Ephemeris which give positions of planets for each day of December, 1915. In the left-hand column are given the days of the week and the dates. If you would look up the horizontal figures against 11 (*i.e.*, 11th December) you would find that the positions of planets as given therein are as follows:

Sun—in Sagittarius—18°-22′-17″

This is the longitude of Sun as at 12 G.M.T.

Now the position of Sun on 10th December, 1915 is given in the line against Date 10, which is Sagittarius 17°-21′-16″.

Thus the motion in 24 hours from 12 Noon G.M.T. on 10th

December, 1915, to 12 Noon G.M.T. on 11th December is:

18°-22′-17″
17°-21′-16″
1°- 1′ - 1″

1 degree 1 minute 1 second. Since this is the motion in 24 hours, the motion in 4 hours would be 0° -10′-10.17″ seconds approximately. Those who are familiar with the use of logarithms can compute very easily with the aid of logarithm tables but others who are not well versed in these can calculate by the rule of three, with which every student of arithmetic is well familiar. We have calculated motion in 4 hours, so that by deducting this from the longitude at 12 Noon G.M.T. we shall be able to find out Sun's longitude at 8 A.M. G.M.T.

Thus Sun's position at

12 Noon :	18° - 22′ - 17″
Deducting motion in 4 hours	0° - 10′ - 10.17″
Position at 8 A.M. would be in Sagittarius:	18° - 12′ - 6.83″

For purposes of convenience we leave the decimal points in seconds and we would be fairly approximate if we put Sun's longitude at 8 A.M. G.M.T. as 18°-12′-7″ . This corresponds to 1.30 P.M. Indian Standard Time. So if a person was born on 11th December, 1915 at New Delhi the position of Sun would be 18°-12′-7″ in Sagittarius. The above illustration has been given to explain how longitudes of planets for a particular day and for a particular time are found out. Just as longitude of Sun for a particular time has been worked, so also longitudes of other planets can be worked out.

Working as above we find that the longitudes of other planets at 8 A.M. G.M.T. or 1.30 P.M. I.S.T. would be as follows:

Moon	27°-23′-21″	in Aquarius.
Mars	27°-21′	in Leo.

Mercury	15°-35′-20″	in Sagittarius.
Jupiter	19°-48′	in Pisces.
Venus	10°-40′-30″	in Capricorn.
Saturn	14°-55′-40″	in Cancer.
Rahu	10°-50′-30″	in Aquarius.
Ketu	10°-50′-30″	in Leo.
Herschel	12°-45′-30″	in Aquarius
Neptune	2°-20′-10″	in Leo.

How to Find Declinations of Planets

The declinations of planets have been given on the same page of the Ephemeris and since declinations of planets are also for 12 Noon, they will have also to be calculated for the particular time. While calculating declinations it is quite sufficient if we calculate up to degrees and minutes only—calculation of seconds can be dropped.

By reference to Raphael's Ephemeris it would be found that the declinations of the planets would be as follows:

Sun 22° South 56′. Moon 13° South 21′. Mars 14° North 57′. Mercury 23° South 32°. Jupiter 5° South 16′. Venus 24° South 21′. Saturn 22′ North 6′. Herschel 17° South 37′. Neptune 19° North 21′.

The above illustration has been given by reference to Raphael's Ephemeris for the particular year. People in possession of other Ephemerides can similarly work out positions of planets by reference to them.

It is necessary to refer to one doubt, which may arise in the mind of an earnest student of astrology.

We have to find out the positions of the planets at 1.30 P.M. Indian Standard Time on 11th December, 1915. This time—1.30 P.M. I.S.T. corresponds to 8 A.M. G.M.T. This is true. But will the position of Sun be the same if seen at a particular moment from New Delhi, Greenwich or London ?

To this our reply is that longitudes of planets as given in Raphael's Ephemeris are Geocentric longitudes, that is *as looked at from the centre of Earth.*

It would make little difference in longitudes of planets, seen at a particular moment from New Delhi or Greenwich or London. This difference would be quite appreciable in case of Moon—because Moon is nearer to Earth. But most of the astrologers are agreed that Geocentric longitudes—being longitudes of planets as if viewed from the centre of Earth serve the purpose best, because as a result of planetary influences, the earth as a whole is affected. In others words, the planetary influences are Geocentric rather than Geographical (as seen from the surface of Earth). So the above doubt about there being any serious difference in planetary positions (computed for the Meridian of Greenwich and for other places) may be dismissed.

So we have known how longitudes of planets for a particular moment are calculated. The next point for calculation is the *exact point which is rising at the Eastern Horizon as seen from the place of birth*.

How to Find the Rising Sign or Lagna

In case of planetary positions we have for practical purposes omitted the difference in longitudes of places (as given in the Ephemeris for a particular meridian and the place of birth). *But in calculation of the point which is rising at the Eastern Horizon as seen from the place of birth, we have to attach the greatest importance to the locality or place of birth.*

For calculation of the particular point rising at the eastern horizon the following particulars are required:

(a) local mean time of birth,
(b) longitude and latitude of the birthplace,
(c) sidereal time at noon and
(d) table of houses for the latitude of birthplace.

Here the exact birth time is known, i.e. 1.30 P.M. Indian Standard Time. For longitude and latitude of the place of birth we refer to any good geographical Atlas, wherein the same are given.

The longitude of New Delhi is 77°-13′ East and the latitude of New Delhi is 28°-39′North. The local mean time of birth is calculated by converting the Indian Standard Time by adding to I.S.T., if the longitude of birthplace is east of 82°-30′ or subtracting from I.S.T., if the birthplace is west of 82°-30′.

Greenwich's longitude is 0°. Since the difference between Indian Standard Time and G.M.T. is 5 hours 30 minutes or 330 minutes, we find that the Indian Standard Time has been fixed for 82°-30′ by allowing a difference of 4 minutes for each degree of longitude.

The I.S.T. is for	82° -30′
Longitude of New Delhi	77° -13′
	5° -17′

Thus the difference for 5°-17′ (five degrees 17 minutes of longitude at the rate of 4 minutes for each degree) would be 21 minutes 8 seconds. Since New Delhi is west of 82°-30′ the local mean time of birth would be as follows:

Time of birth I.S.T.	1-30-0 P.M.
L.M.T. of birth for New Delhi	21-8
	1- 8-52

or say 13 hours 8 minutes 52 seconds P.M.

Sidereal time at Noon on birth date can be known at a glance from the Ephemeris.

In Raphael's Ephemeris, we find that the sidereal time for 11th December, 1915 Noon has been given as 17 hours 16 minutes 28 seconds.

The fifth and that too very essential thing is to have a table of houses for the latitude of the birthplace.

For this I recommend Raphael's Table of Houses for Northern Latitude from the Equator to 50° North, published by W. Foulsham & Co. Ltd.

Now we proceed to work as follows:

		Hrs. Mts. Sec.
(i)	Sidereal time at Noon* on birth date:	17 - 16 - 28
(ii)	Add time elapsed since Noon (this is obtained by deducting 12 from the local mean time of birth) thus:	1 - 8 - 52
		18 - 25 - 20

13 - 8 -52
12 - 0 - 0
1 - 8 -52

(iii)	Add at the rate of 10 secs. per hour for the duration obtained in (ii) above;	0 - 0 - 11
(iv)	Total:	18 - 25 - 31

This total is called sidereal time of birth or Right Ascension of the Meridian cusp. Now we require the table of Houses for the *Latitude* of the place of birth.

Referring to Raphael's Table of Houses, we find that we have table of Houses for Delhi latitude 28°- 40′ N. we find the following:—

Sidereal Time Hrs. Mts. Scs.	*Ascendant*
18- 21 - 48	7°– 46′ Aries.
18- 26 - 9	9°– 19′ Aries.

Thus we see that the exact figure of 18 Hrs. 25 Mts. 31 Secs.

* Many astronomers make correction in Sidereal time also, but since we are following Raphael here, we are not making that correction. This amounts to a few seconds depending upon longitude of the place.

for which we want to find the rising sign or the ascendant is not found here. But we find that at sidereal time 18 hours 21 Mts. 48 Secs. The rising sign was 7°-46′ Aries while at sidereal time 18 Hrs. 26 Mts. 9 Secs., the sign rising would be 9°-19′ Aries. Thus we find that in an interval of

Hrs.	Mts.	Secs.
18 -	26 -	8
18 -	21 -	48
0 -	4 -	21

4 minutes 21 secs., the ascendant progressed by

Deg.	Mts.
9 -	19
7 -	46
1 -	33

1 degree 33 minutes or say (60 plus 33) 93 minutes of arc. Since we know, the ascendant for 18 Hrs. 26 Mts. 9 Secs. and we have to find ascendant for 18 Hrs. 25 Mts. 31 secs., if we can deduct the progress for:

Hrs.	Mts.	Secs.
18 -	26 -	9
18 -	25 -	31
0 -	0 -	38

38 seconds of time from 9°-19′ Aries, we can know the exact degree and minute rising at 18 Hrs. 25 Mts. 31 Secs. Working by rule of three we find:

In 4 minutes 21 secs.

or

261 seconds: of time progress 93 Mts. of Arc.

In one seconds: 93/261.

In 38 seconds. $93 \times 38/261 = 14'$ Mts. of Arc. approx. Ascendant at 18 hrs. 25 Mts. 31 seconds would, therefore, be (9°-19′) - 14′=9°-5′ Aries. So 9°-5′ Aries will be the rising sign or the Ascendant or the cusp of the first house.

To Find Cusps of Other Houses

The next step is to find the cusps of the 2nd, 3rd, 4th, 5th, 6th, 7th, 8th, 9th, 10th, 11th and 12th houses. Again we have to refer to the table of houses.

For sidereal time 18 Hrs. 26 Mts. 9 seconds the cusps of the houses given therein are as follows. Making correction for the 10th cusp and leaving the others, as they are*:

Cusp of the	*Sign*	*Degree*
10th House	Capricorn	5°-46′
11th House	Aquarius	0°
12th House	Pisces	0°
2nd House	Taurus	15°
3rd House	Gemini	12°

It may, in passing, be mentioned here that the above is an approximate method because for a particular difference in sidereal time, the difference in the cusps of the various houses is not identical.

Thus, we have calculated the cusps of the 1st, 2nd, 3rd, 10th, 11th and 12th houses. What remains is the calculation of cusps of the other houses, which is (once the above has been done) very easy.

Add 180 degrees or six full signs to the cusp of the first house and you have the cusp of the 7th house. Add 180° or 6 signs to the cusp of the 2nd house and you have the cusp of the 8th house. Add 180° or six full signs (one sign has full 30 degrees) to the cusp of the 3rd house and you have the cusp of the 9th house. Add 180° or six signs to the cusp of the 10th house and you have the cusp of the 4th house. Add 180° or full six signs to the cusp of the 11th house and you have the cusp of the 5th house and add lastly six full signs or 180° to the cusp of the 12th house and you have the cusp of the 6th house.

* Since the cusps of the various houses (other than 10th and the Ascendant) given even in the Raphael's table of houses are up to degrees only, (minutes of arc have been left and rounded to degrees) we shall be fairly accurate if we follow the above method.

Working as above, the cusps of the other houses in the example horoscope, would be as follows:-

Cusps of the houses	*Sign*	*Degrees and Mts.*
7th	Libra	9°-5′
8th	Scorpio	15°
9th	Sagittarius	12°
4th	Cancer	5°-46′
5th	Leo	0°
6th	Virgo	0°

Now you can make the following chart*:

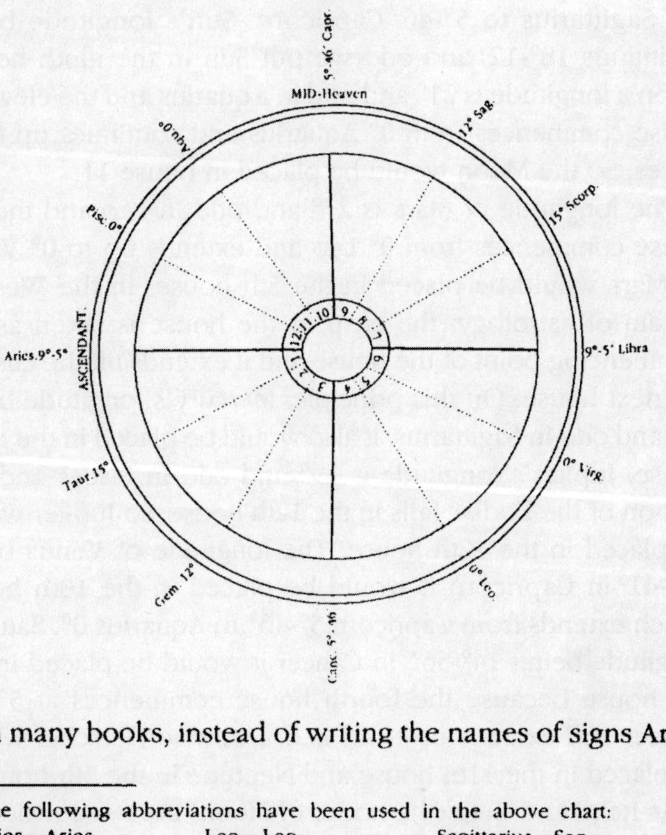

In many books, instead of writing the names of signs Aries,

* The following abbreviations have been used in the above chart:

Aries—Aries	Leo—Leo	Sagittarius—Sag.
Taurus—Taur.	Virgo—Virg.	Capricorn—Capr.
Gemini—Gem.	Libra—Libr.	Aquarius—Aqu.
Cancer—Canc.	Scorpio—Scorp.	Pisces—Pisc.

Taurus, Gemini, etc., they use symbols for these signs. But for those who are not practised to identify the symbols easily, the above method of writing out the names is the best.

Once the ascendant and the cusps of the houses are calculated and put in, the next stage is to put the planets in the various houses. By reference to longitudes of planets in the example horoscope worked out above we find that Sun's longitude was 18°-12'-6.83 secs. in the sign Sagittarius. Now, by reference to the birth chart, we find that Sagittarius 12° is on the cusp of the 9th house. The ninth house extends from 12° Sagittarius to 5°-46' Capricorn. Sun's longitude being Sagittarius 18°-12' and odd we put Sun in the ninth house. Moon's longitude is 21° and odd in Aquarius and the eleventh house commences from 0° Aquarius and continues up to 0° Pisces. So the Moon would be placed in house 11.

The longitude of Mars is 27° and odd in Leo and the 5th house commences from 0° Leo and extends up to 0° Virgo. So Mars would be placed in the 5th house. In the Western system of astrology, the cusp of the house is taken as the commencing point of the house and it extends till the cusp of the next house. On this principle, Mercury's longitude being 15° and odd in Sagittarius, it also would be placed in the ninth house. Jupiter's longitude is 19° and odd in Pisces and this section of the Zodiac falls in the 12th house, so Jupiter would be placed in the 12th house. The longitude of Venus being 10°-41' in Capricorn it would be placed in the 10th house which extends from Capricorn 5°-46' to Aquarius 0°. Saturn's longitude being 14°-56' in Cancer it would be placed in the 4th house because the fourth house commences at 5°-46' Cancer and extends up to 0° Leo. Likewise Herschel would be placed in the 11th house and Neptune in the 5th house.

As Rahu and Ketu (the nodes of Moon) are not considered in Western astrology, we have not put them in the birth chart here. The calculations of their longitudes would be useful when making a chart according to Hindu astrology.

Thus after putting the planets in the houses where they were at the time of the birth we obtain the following chart*:

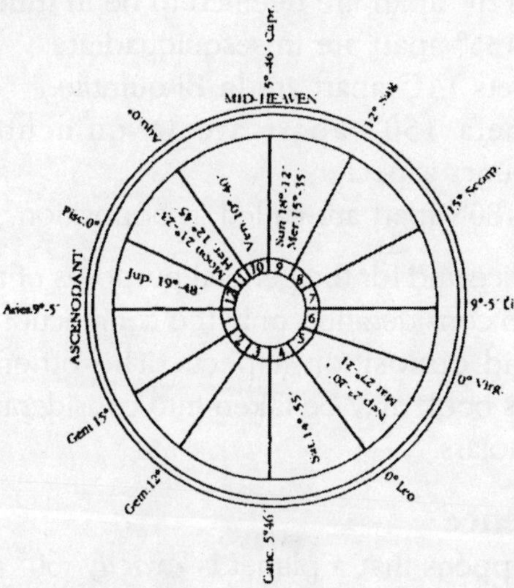

Sun is in the 9th house, Moon in 11th ,Mars in 5th, Mercury in 9th, Jupiter in 12th, Venus in 10th, Saturn in 4th, Herschel in 11th and Neptune in 5th. Thus completes the birth chart. What remains now is the aspect between the planets.

Aspects

In Western astrology the following aspects are taken into consideration:

(i) Planets in the same degree of longitude are considered in conjunction.

(ii) Planets 30° apart are called in semi-sextile aspect.

(iii) Planets 45° apart from each other are called in semi-square aspect.

(iv) Planets 60° apart from each other are called in sextile aspect.

(v) Planets 72° apart are in quintile aspect.

---

* The following abbreviations have been used in the chart:

Sun—Sun	Mercury—Mer.	Saturn—Sat.
Moon—Moon	Jupiter—Jup.	Herschel—Hers.
Mars—Mars	Venus—Ven.	Neptune—Nept.

(vi) Planets 90° apart from each other are considered as being in square aspect.
(vii) Planets 120° apart are deemed to be in trine aspect.
(viii) Planets 135° apart are in sesquiquadrate.
(ix) (a) Planets 144° apart are in Bi-quintile.
(b) Planets 150° apart are in quincunx or in conjunct aspect.
(x) Planets 180° apart are called in opposition.

In actual practice and for the general purposes of this book we may take into consideration only the conjunction, sextile, square, trine and opposition aspects. The other aspects referred to in this book may be taken into consideration only by advanced scholars.

Orbs of Influence

But it seldom happens that a planet is *exactly* 60° or 90° or 120° or 180° from the other. So a little margin is allowed. This margin is called 'orb' of influence. What this margin or 'orb' of influence should be, has been explained in the 'Glossary of Astrological and Technical Terms'—under aspects at the end of this book.

Thus the following aspects are formed in the example horoscope:

(a) The diffference between Sun and Moon is about 63° so they are in sextile aspect.
(b) The difference between Sun and Mars is 111°—so they are in trine aspect.
(Had it been nearer 120°— the aspect would have been strong, still we have included this.)
(c) The difference between Sun and Mercury is about 3°, so they are in conjunction.
(d) The difference between Sun and Jupiter is about 92°, so they are in square aspect.
(e) The difference between Sun and Herschel is 54°, so they are in sextile aspect.

Besides the above, Sun forms some aspects with Venus and Saturn also, but as we have here confined ourselves to the principal aspects, we prefer to omit them from our consideration. Having noted the principal aspects of Sun, we proceed to find the aspects Moon forms with other planets.

(f) The difference between the longitudes of Moon and Mars is about 186°, so they are in opposition.

(g) The difference between Moon and Mercury is about 66° so they are called in sextile.

(h) The difference between Moon and Herschel is about 9° so they are in conjunction.

Next coming to Mars we find that :

(i) Difference between Mars and Mercury is 108° (the exact trine is 120°—here the margin is too much, so we may omit this).

(j) The difference between Mars and Herschel is 165° and as opposition aspect is at 180° we may also omit this.

Now taking up Mercury we find that:

(k) The difference between Mercury and Jupiter is 94°, so there is square aspect.

(l) The difference between Mercury and Herschel is 57° so they are in sextile.

Taking up Jupiter, we find that difference between

(m) Jupiter and Venus is about 69°, so they are in 'weak' sextile aspect.

(n) The difference between Jupiter and Saturn in 115°, so they are in trine aspect.

Now taking up Venus we find that:

(o) Venus and Saturn are about 184° apart so they are in opposition aspect.

(p) Herschel and Neptune are about 170° apart, so they are in opposition.

Having gone through patiently and with deliberate care through the aspects formed between the various planets, we note our observations for purposes of reference in the following form*:

	Sun	*Moon*	*Mars*	*Mer.*	*Jup.*	*Ven.*	*Sat.*	*Her.*	*Nep.*
Sun	Sx.	Tr.	Cn.	Sqr.			Sx.		
Moon	Sx.		Op.	Sx.				Cn.	
Mars	Tr.	Op.							
Mercury	Cn.	Sx.			Sqr.			Sx.	
Jupiter	Sqr.			Sqr.			Tr.		
Venus							Op.		
Saturn					Tr.	Op.			
Herschel	Sx.	Cn.		Sx					Op.
Neptune								Op.	

So far we have dealt with the aspects based on distance between the longitudes of the two planets.

But besides longitudes we have to consider their declinations also.

Parallels

Whether the declinations of both the planets (between whom aspects are being considered) are Northern or Southern or one is Northern and the other is Southern is immaterial. If the degrees of Declination of the two planets are identical, they will be deemed to be in parallel.

Thus if Sun's declination is 22°-56′ South, any planet whose declination is about 22° or 23° would be deemed to be in parallel with Sun—it is immaterial whether the declination of that planet is 22° North or South. While considering the parallels of declination also, we have to allow some margin. Western astrologers generally allow margin of 1°. Thus, in the

---

* The following abbreviations have been used:
Cn=Conjunction; Op=Opposition; Sq=Square; Sx=Sextile; Tr=Trine.
Minor Aspects have been omitted.

example horoscope, the difference between the declinations of

(a) Sun and Mercury is 36′ so they are in parallel.
(b) Sun and Saturn is 50′ so they are in parallel.
(c) Mercury and Venus is 49′ so they are in parallel.

Two points may be emphasised in this connection:

When the two planets are just on the outside limits of the 'orbs' the aspect would be a weak one. But if the aspect is exact without allowing any margin) that aspect would be deemed a strong one.

But in some cases, even where an aspect appears to be weak due to their being on the border of the orbs, the aspect may become stronger due to the position of any planet aspecting both of them and having degrees in between the two.

Thus in the example horoscope the Orb or margin between Herschel and Mars is 15°, Herschel's degrees are 12° and those of Mars 27° but Sun aspects both of them and its degrees are 19°. So even the aspect of Mars and Herschel has been made stronger.

This is technically called, 'Transmission of lights' or acting of a third planet as a transmitter or communication between two planets. Another point to remember is that if three planets are so located, that two of them are equally distant from the third, this configuration also acts as a parallel.

We have so far dealt with the culcrelations pertaining to the Western type of horoscope. Now we deal with principles of Hindu Astrology and illustrate the differences between the two systems.

The first and the major difference in the matter of casting and judgment of the horoscope is that in Western Astrology, that point is regarded as point of commencement or 0° in the Zodiac, where Sun appears to be when it is exactly on the Equator at the spring Equinox (when day and night are equal). This point, however, recedes at the rate of about 50.25 seconds of arc every year, with the result that 0°Aries in Western Astrology is not a fixed point but is ever-changing.

In Hindu Astrology, the point of commencement or 0° Aries is a fixed point, the "Ashwini" Star. Being a fixed star in the Zodiac, its position does not change and Hindu astrologers have through ages commenced their 0° degree in the Zodiac from this point. There is no doubt that at one time the 0 degree of the western movable Zodiac and the Hindu Fixed Zodiac were identical but during centuries, that have elapsed, the difference or movement at the rate of about 50" per year has aggregated to about 23° with the result that while a Hindu astrologer calculating the position of Sun in the Fixed Zodiac would say that Sun is in 0° Aries, the western astrologer would say that it is in 23°-17' Aries. Similarly, with all other positions in Zodiac—whether it be the longitude of planets or degrees of the rising sign or cusp of any other house.

Now in order to convert a western type of horoscope into a horoscope according to Hindu system we have to proceed as follows:

First Step

Find out the precession of the Equinox on the date of birth.

As finding out nutation and precession of Equinoxes mathematically involves intricate knowledge of spherical trigonometry and acquaintance with higher mathematics. I am giving in the Appendix a table of precessions of Equinoxes on 1st January, each year, since 1900. Please see the appendix V. The readers will no doubt observe that the rate of procession and nutation is not uniform from year to year. In 60 years, from 1st January, 1900 to 1960, the precession has been about 50 minutes of arc. So the average for one year comes to about 50" per year. But once the exact precession is known on 1st January of the year of birth and on the 1st January of the next year, the exact precession can be worked for the birth date by applying rule of 3. Now readers are referred to the example horoscope in Introduction to Part I. We shall take the same date for furnishing a horoscope. According to the Appendix we find that on 1st January, 1915 precession was 22°-40'-26" and on 1st January, 1916 the precession was 22°-41'-21". So on 11th December, 1915 (about 20 days before 1st January) the precession was 22°-41'-18."

Second Step

Once the exact or very approximate precession is known, this has to be deducted from the longitudes of planets as well as from the cusps of the 1st and 10th houses, to arrive at longitudes in the fixed Zodiac or the Nirayan (Nirayan in Sanskrit means without precession of the Equinox) positions as followed in the Hindu Astrology.

Deduction is a simple matter, yet it is worked out below for better acquaintance with the procedure: Sun is 18° and odd in Sagittarius. Sagittarius is the ninth sign in the Zodiac, so Sun has completed 8 full signs and is traversing the ninth.

So we put as follows:

	Sign.	*Deg.*	*Min.*	*Sec.*
	8 -	18 -	12 -	6
Deducting Precession		22 -	41	-18
	7	25	30	48

which means that as counted from the 0° of the sidereal or stellar or the fixed Zodiac, Sun is in the 8th sign in 26th degree.

Similarly, deducting precession from the longitude of Moon in the movable or tropical Zodiac we find:

Sign.	*Deg.*	*Min.*	*Sec.*
10 -	21 -	23 -	21
	22 -	41 -	18
9	28	42	3

that in the fixed Zodiac Moon has traversed 28 degrees 42 minutes 3 seconds. Particular attention is invited to the number of sign which we have put above. Earlier Moon has been described as being in Aquarius, which is the eleventh sign. But here we have put only 10 as the number of sign. Why ? The explanation is very simple. Suppose a man is running a race. We speak of him as being in the eleventh mile, but while describing his exact position—the distance completed—suppose, he has completed 2 furlongs 10 yards we would put 10 miles 2 furlongs, 10 yards. So also the position of planets. Under the 'Sign' we put the number of signs completed.

Thus:

	Sign	*Deg.*	*Min.*	*Sec.*
Tropical longitude of Mars	4	- 27	- 21	
Deducting ayanansh		22	- 41	- 18
Sidereal longitude	4	4	39	42
Tropical longitude of Mercury	8	- 15	- 35	- 20
Deducting ayanansh		22	- 41	- 18
Sidereal longitude	7	22	54	2
Tropical longitude of Jupiter	11	- 19	- 48	
Deducting ayanansh		22	- 41	- 18
Sidereal longitude	10	27	6	42
Tropical longitude of Venus	9	- 10	- 40	- 30
Deducting ayanansh		22	- 41	- 18
Sidereal longitude	8	17	59	12
Tropical longitude of Saturn	3	- 14	- 55	- 40
Deducting ayanansh		22	- 41	- 18
Sidereal longitude	2	22	14	22
Tropical longitude of Rahu	10	- 10	- 50	- 30
Deductin g ayanansh		22	- 41	- 18
Sidereal longitude	9	18	9	12
Ketu	3	18	9	12

We have not calculated the positions of Herschel and Neptune in the sidereal Zodiac, because these have not been dealt with in Hindu Astrology.

Third Step

Now as we have reduced the Tropical Longitudes of planets to Sidereal Longitudes, so we have to find the sidereal longitudes of the cusps of the 1st and 10th houses.

Note. As the Ephemeris gives only degrees and minutes and omits seconds, we should also omit seconds in our calculations. I have given position up to seconds only to illustrate the method.

Tropical longitude of	*Sign*.	*Deg*.	*Min*.	Sec.
the first house	0 -	9 -	5 -	00
Deducting ayanansh		22	- 41 -	18
	11	16	23	42

(Since there are 12 signs in the Zodiac, we add 12 to the number of signs, when necessary for purposes of deduction).

Thus the sidereal longitude of the cusp of the first house or of the rising sign or the ascendant, by whatever name you are pleased to call it, is 11-16-23-42 or 16 degrees 23 minutes 42 seconds in the twelfth sign, *i.e.* Pisces.

Similarly, the sidereal longitude of the cusp of the 10th house would be worked out as follows:

Tropical longitude of cusp of the 10th house	9- 5-46-00
Deducting ayanansha	22-41-18
Sidereal longitude	8-13- 4- 42

Fourth Step

Having calculated the sidereal longitudes of the first and the tenth houses we place the planets as follows. First we draw a chart as given below putting the number of rising sign in the top centre.

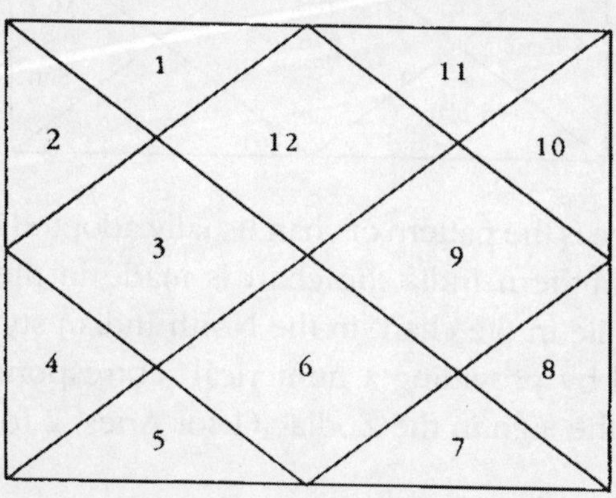

The sidereal longitude of the ascendant is 11-16°-23'-42", which mean that 11 signs have been completed and 12th sign is rising. So we put 12 in the top centre. The number 12 is just a symbol to denote that the 12th sign or Pisces is rising.

Now referring to the sidereal longitudes of Planets we have calculated above, Sun has completed 7 signs and is in 8th so we put Sun in the place where 8 is written; Moon has completed 9 signs and is in 10th, so we put Moon where 10 is. Similarly, Mars has completed 4 signs and is in 5th, so we put Mars in the sign no. 5. Mercury has completed 7 signs and is traversing 8th sign, so we put Mercury there. Jupiter has completed 10 signs and is running in the 11th so we put him in the 11th sign, Venus has completed 8 signs and is in the 9th sign, so we put it there; Saturn has completed 2 signs and is in 3rd, so we put it there. Rahu has completed 9 signs and is in the 10th, so we put it in sign 10; Ketu is always in opposition to Rahu so we put it in sign 4. So the birth chart is filled in as follows:

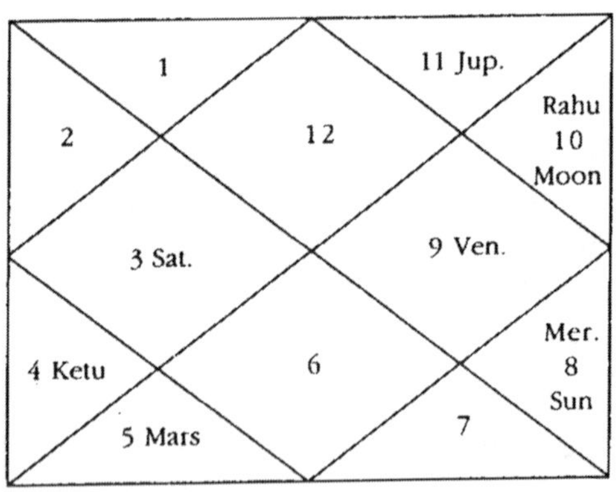

The above is the pattern of chart usually adopted in Northern India. In Southern India the chart is made in the following pattern. While in the chart, in the North Indian style, the sign is indicated by providing a numerical corresponding to the number of the sign in the Zodiac (1 for Aries, 2 for Taurus, 3

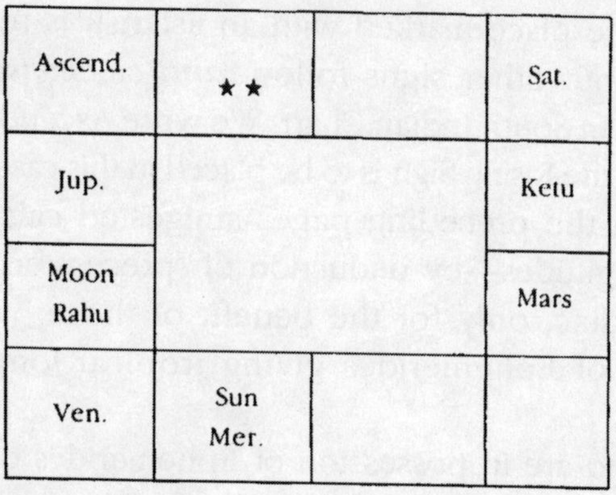

for Gemini and so on) in the South, the place marked with asterisks is always reserved for Aries and the succeeding signs counted clockwise refer to the succeeding signs in order.

Thus, the, sign in which Saturn is placed is number 3 as counted from the place marked with asterisks. So counting from Aries.......... Aries 1, Taurus 2, Gemini, 3 Saturn is in Gemini. Likewise the signs—the other planets are in—can be known by counting from the place marked with asterisks. Those who become a little practised get used to identify particular places with particular signs by merely glancing at the chart. In Bihar and Bengal the following figure is used for making the chart.

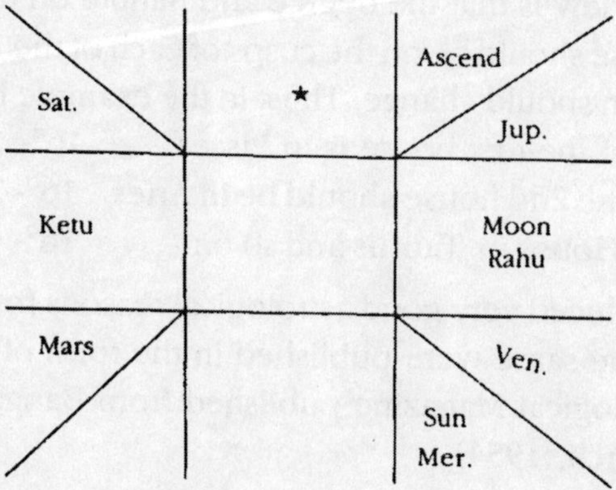

Here also the place marked with an asterisk is reserved for sign Aries, but other signs follow *anti-clockwise,* and not *clockwise* as in South Indian Chart. We write Ascendent, Lagna or 'L' where the Rising Sign is to be placed in this case, in Pisces.

I have in the preceding pages suggested calculation of sidereal longitudes—by deduction of 'precession' from the tropical Zodiac, only for the benefit of those, who are in possession of Ephemerides giving tropical longitudes of planets.

Those who are in possession of Ephemerides or (Sanskrit Panchangas) giving sidereal longitudes directly from the sidereal ephemerids without resorting to the circuitous course of calculating tropical longitudes and then converting them into sidereal ones.

Those who have only sidereal Ephemerides (almost all Hindu Panchangas give sidereal longitudes) can if they want tropical longitudes, do the same by the reverse process of adding precession of equinoxes or Ayanansha on birth date and obtain tropical longitudes.

Fifth Step

The chart according to Hindu Astrology has been made, as shown above. Now what remains is to calculate the cusps of the houses.

My own view is that the degree and minute on the cusp of the first house should be on the cusps of each of the 12 houses. Only the sign should change. Thus, in the example horoscope

if the cusp of the first house is in Pisces	16°- 23'- 42"
the cusp of the 2nd house should be in Aries.	16°- 23'- 42"
Cusp of 3rd House in Taurus and so on.	16°- 23'- 42"

I have adduced very good astrological reasons for adopting this plan. The same were published in the form of an article in the Astrological Magazine published from Bangalore (See A.M. for March, 1954).

One thing very important to remember, is the basic difference between Western Astrology and Hindu Astrology, in the conception of the cusp of the house.

In Western Astrology the cusp of the house is the point of commencement of the house while in Hindu Astrology it is the Centre of the House.

So, the first house would commence 15 degrees before the cusp of the first house and would extend up to 15 degrees after the cusp and the jurisdiction of the first house would be from 1°-23'- 42" in Pisces to 1°-23'- 42" Aries.

of the second house :	1° 23' 42"	Aries to
	1° 23' 42"	Taurus
of the third house :	1° 23' 42"	Taurus to
	1° 23' 42"	Gemini
of the fourth house :	1° 23' 42"	Gemini to
	1° 23' 42"	Cancer and so on.

This is called the principle of equal division of houses. But as I have said, this is my view and the view of some important astrologers. This is, however, not the traditional view of house division. The traditional method of house division is now being explained.

We have shown before that the cusps of the first and tenth houses in the *tropical* Zodiac are as follows:

	Sign.	*Deg.*	*Min.*
Cusp of the 1st House:	0	9	5
Cusp of the 10th House:	9	5	46

We have also shown before that by deducting the precession of the equinox on the birth date, *i.e.* 22°-41'-18" we get the sidereal longitudes as follows:

	S.	*Deg.*	*Mts.*	*Sec.*
Cusp of the first house : (Sidereal longitude).	11	16	23	42
Cusp of the 10th house: (Sidereal longitude)	8	13	4	42

Having fixed these, we proceed to find the difference between the two thus:

	S.	Deg.	Mts.	Sec.
	11	16	23	42
−	8	13	4	42
	3	3	19	0

Thus, 3 Signs 3 degrees 19 minutes is the difference between the cusps of the 1st and 10th houses. This is divided by six.

S.	Deg.	Mts.	Sec.
3	3	19	0
0	15	33	10

So one-sixth division is equal to 0-15 Degrees 33 Minutes 10 Secs. Now we proceed as follows:

		S.	Deg.	Mts.	Sec.
Cusp of the X house :		8	13	4	42
	+	0	15	33	10
XI house ends XI begins :	=	8	28	37	52
	+	0	15	33	10
Cusp of the XI house :		9	14	11	2
	+	0	15	33	10
XI house ends XII begins :		9	29	44	12
		0	15	33	10
Cusp of the XII house :	=	10	15	17	22
	+	0	15	33	10
XII house ends I begins :		11	0	50	32
	+	0	15	33	10
Cusp of the I house :		11	16	23	42

After having calculated the cusps of 10th, 11th and 12th houses and the mid-points between these (mid-points are ends of the preceding houses and commencement of the succeeding houses) the calculation of the cusps of the other houses and their mid-points is comparatively easy:

		Sign.	*Deg.*	*Mts.*	*Sec.*	
(a) Thus, mid-point between		11	0	50	32	
XII and 1st. Add 1 sign:	+	1	0	0	0	
		12	0	50	32	or
Mid-point between 1st and 2nd	=	0	0	50	32	
(b) Add 2 signs to the Cusp of XII		10	15	17	22	
Add 2 signs.	+	2	0	0	0	
	=	12	15	17	22	or
Cusp of the II house		0	15	17	22	
(c) Mid-point between XI and XII :		9	29	44	12	
Add 3 signs:	+	3	0	0	0	
Mid-point between 2nd and 3rd	=	0	29	44	12	
(d) Cusp of the XI		9	14	11	2	
Add 4 signs :	+	4	0	0	0	
		13	14	11	2	or
Cusp of the 3rd house :		1	14	11	2	
(e) Mid-point between XI & X		8	28	37	52	
Add 5 signs :	+	5	0	0	0	
	=	13	28	37	52	or
Mid-point between 3rd and 4th houses :		1	28	37	52	
(f) Cusp of X house :		8	13	48	42	
Add six signs)	+	6	0	0	0	
	=	14	13	4	42	or
Say		2	13	4	42	

This is the cusp of the 4th house.

Calculation of the cusps of the other houses and their mid points is very simple:

(g) Add six signs to mid-point between X and XI, houses and you have the mid-point between 4th and 5th houses.

(h) Add six signs to the cusp of XI house and you have the cusp of the 5th house.

(i) Add six signs to the mid-point between XI and XII house cusps and you have the mid-point between V and VI houses.

(j) Add six signs to the cusp of XII house and you have the cusp of the VI house.

(k) Add six signs to the mid-point between XII and 1st house cusps and you have the mid-point between VI and VII house.

(l) Add six signs to the cusps of 1st house and you have the cusp of the VIIth house.

(m) Similarly, by adding six signs (6×30=180 degrees) or 180 degrees to the

(i) mid-point between 1st and 2 houses.
(ii) cusp of 2nd house.
(iii) mid-point between cusps of 2nd and 3rdhouses.
(iv) cusp of 3rd house.
(v) mid-point between cusps of 3rd and 4th houses.

You will obtain respectively:

(i) mid-point between 7th and 8th houses.
(ii) cusp of 8th house.
(iii) mid-point between cusps of 8th and 9th houses.
(iv) cusp of ninth house.
(v) mid-point between cusps of 9th and 10th houses.

In the beginning, this no doubt appears to be a tedious process, but once a few horoscopes are worked out, the procedure becomes very simple.

Those who possess Table of Houses by Dr. B.V. Raman or any other good Table of Houses on the basis of Hindu Astrology can take down the cusps of houses directly from such tables and thus save the trouble involved in the above calculations.

The advantage of working out the cusps of the houses and mid-points between the two houses is that a planet yields the greatest influence when it is on the cusp of the house. If it is distant from the cusp of the house its influence also decreases. If it is just on the mid-point between two houses its influence is almost zero. If it crosses the middle point and is so situated that it is not within the jurisdiction of the house, it gives the effect of the other house in which it is, according to the division of houses.

Sixth Step

Now the horoscope is complete. What remains to explain is the 'aspect' between planets. The principles governing aspects in Hindu Astrology are quite different from those in Western Astrology. In Hindu Astrology:

(i) The aspect between two benefics is always good.

(ii) The aspect of a malefic is always bad.

(iii) Jupiter and Venus, full Moon (or Moon having more than 8 digits) and Mercury associated with benefic planets, are deemed to be benefic planets.

(iv) Sun, Mars, Saturn, Rahu, Ketu, Moon (having less than 8 digits) and Mercury conjoined with a malefic are deemed malefics. Mars acts as a greater malefic than Sun. Rahu and Ketu are more malefic than Mars; Saturn is the greatest malefic.

(v) The lord of the first house, whichever planet it may be, is not considered a malefic.

(vi) In considering aspects, we do not take into consideration the actual degrees but confine our consideration to the sign only—a planet is in.

(vii) All planets aspect fully the sign—seventh from it.

Thus a planet in Aries will fully aspect a planet in Libra. A planet in Cancer would aspect a planet in Capricorn.

(viii) In addition to fully aspecting the seventh sign and the planet posited therein, Jupiter fully aspects the 5th and 9th signs also as counted from the sign it is posited in. Thus, Jupiter in Aries will fully aspect Leo or Sagittarius or a planet in Leo or Sagittarius.

Any other planet's (other than Jupiter's) aspect on 5th and 9th signs counted from the one it is placed in, would be only 50%.

(ix) In addition to fully aspecting the seventh sign, Mars fully aspects the 4th and 8th signs also as counted from the one it is posited in. The aspect of any other planet's (other than that of Mars) on a planet posited in 4th or 8th sign from it would be only 75%.

(x) In addition to full aspect on the 7th sign, from the one Saturn is placed in, it also fully aspects the 3rd and 10th signs counted from the one, it is posited in. Aspect of any planet (other than that of Saturn) on a sign 3rd or 10th from it would be only 25%.

(xi) Rahu and Ketu do not aspect (but are aspected). I, however, prefer to take into account their conjunctions only.

(xii) Two planets are deemed to be conjoined together or in conjunction if they are in the same sign irrespective of the distance between them.

Thus, Mars having 1° in Scorpio and Sun having 26° in Scorpio will be treated as being conjoined together.

(xiii) If a planet X is say in the sign owned by planet Y and the planet Y is in a sign owned by planet X, they yield the same effect as if fully aspecting each other.

(xiv) If a planet X is in a sign owned by planet Y and planet X fully aspects planet Y (though Y may not aspect X), this also will have the same effect as if X and Y were fully aspecting each other.

Example

I shall now illustrate how aspects are worked out, by reference to the example horoscope. In the example horoscope:

(a) Rahu and Moon are in conjunction both being in same sign (Rule XII above).

(b) Sun and Mercury are in the same sign, so they are in conjunction (Rule XII) above.

(c) Sun's aspect over Moon is 25% because Moon is in a sign which is third from that occupied by Sun (Rule X above).

(d) Sun's aspect over Jupiter is 75% because Jupiter is in a sign which is fourth from the sign occupied by Sun (Rule IX.)

(e) Mars is in the sign owned by Sun and fully aspects Sun. So the relationship between Sun and Mars is, as if they fully aspect each other. Also Sun is in a sign of Mars and Mars is in the sign of Sun (See rules IX and XIII, XIV).
Application of either rule XIII or XIV is sufficient. It is a matter of coincidence that both the rules XIII and XIV apply.

(f) Moon's aspect over Mars is 75% because Mars is in a sign which is 8th counted from the one occupied by Moon (see rule IX).

(g) Aspect of Mars over Mercury is full, because Mercury occupies a sign which is fourth as counted from Mars (See rule IX).

(h) Mars has full aspect over Jupiter, because Jupiter occupies a sign which is seventh counted from the one occupied by Mars (Rule VII).

(i) Mars has 50% aspect over Venus because the latter planet occupies a sign which is 5th counted from the one, occupied by the former (See rule VIII).

(j) Mercury's aspect over Moon is 25% because Moon occupies the third sign counted from Mercury (See rule X).

(k) Mercury's aspect over Jupiter is 75% because Jupiter occupies a sign which is fourth counted from Mercury (See rule IX).

(l) Mercury's aspect over Mars is 25% because the latter occupies a sign which is tenth from the former (See rule X).

(m) Jupiter's aspect over Saturn *is full* because Saturn occupies a sign which is fifth when counted from the sign occupied by Jupiter (See rule VIII) and Jupiter occupies a sign ruled by Saturn (See Rule XIV); so relationship between Jupiter and Saturn is *as if* they have changed places or fully aspect each other.

(n) Jupiter's aspect over Mars is full, because Mars is in 7th from Jupiter (See Rule VII).

(o) Jupiter's aspect over Mercury is 25% because Mercury is in a sign which is tenth from Jupiter; similarly Jupiter's aspect over Sun is 25%.

(p) Aspect of Venus over Jupiter is 25% because Jupiter occupies a sign which is third when counted from Venus (See Rule X).

(q) Aspect of Venus over Saturn is full, because Saturn occupies a sign which is 7th from the one occupied by Venus (Rule VII).

(r) Aspect of Venus over Mars is 50% because Mars occupies a sign which is ninth from the sign occupied by Venus (Rule VIII).

(s) Aspect of Saturn over Mars is full because Mars occupies a sign which is third from the one occupied by Saturn (Rule X).

(t) Aspect of Saturn over Venus is full because Venus is in a sign seventh from the one occupied by Saturn (Rule VII).

(u) Aspect of Saturn over Moon is 75% because Moon occupies a sign which is 8th counted from the one occupied by Saturn (Rule IX).

(v) Aspect of Saturn over Jupiter is only 50% but as discussed in clause (*m*) above, due to Jupiter's occupying a sign *owned* by Saturn and fully aspecting Saturn, the relationship between the two is as if they fully aspect each other mutually.

I could have explained the points, with greater brevity, but I want to impress the rules and the exceptions, on the minds of beginners. Those who already know astrology and are conversant with the rules governing aspects can safely skip over these pages.

If may also be mentioned that planets see or aspect the houses or cusps of houses but the cusps of houses do not aspect the planets.

Since the present book was composed and published in the name of "1000 Aphorisms on Love and Marriage", it had become necessary to bring about certain changes to make it more useful for the learned readers. Keeping this in view we have opted to give a common introduction for both parts viz., Part I 'Western Astrology' and Part II 'Hindu Astrology'. The purpose is to get as much as possible out of Astrology whether it is the Western method or the Hindu method. During the present time even medical practitioners of high caliber are turning to Ayurvedic and Unani medicines. The same is true of 'Vaidyas' who frequently use antibiotics and injections to give immediate relief to their patients.

Besides consolidating the introduction, we have given a new chapter by combining the general chapter in both parts together into one chapter 1. This chapter is the Key which will open up the 'Astrological Secrets of Friendship, Love and Marriage'. In the Western System, the chapters are combined because you cannot separate a part from the whole.

Chapter 2 has the Aphorisms, related to the Ascendant, Sun and Moon, In the third chapter aphorisms of Planets viz. Mars, Mercury, Jupiter, Venus, Saturn, Herschel (Uranus) and Neptune are dealt with. Rahu and Ketu are undertaken in chapter 8 where the influence of Sun, Moon, Mars etc. are depicted as per the Hindu system.

Chapter 4 takes up the mutual Harmony as per the Western Astrology. Chapter 5 is related to The Timing of Events. The calculation of the Directions in Western Astrology is explained in details in Appendix I. Chapter 5 deals with the Timing of events (W.A). The Hindu system of The Timing of Events is taken up in Chapter 12. Chapter 6 is devoted to the Directions of planets, Houses and their lords.

In Chapter 7 the effects of transits as per the Western System and in chapter 13 the results of the Transit as per the Hindu Astrology.

The remaining Chapters from 8 to 13 are all related to the Hindu Astrology.

Chapter 8 deals with the Aphorisms of Planets Sun, Moon, Mars etc, and these include Rahu and Ketu as the 8th and 9th planets respectively. In Chapter 9, we have discussed the Lords of the Houses. The Chapter 10 deals exclusively with the female nativity. In the Chapter 11 Mutual Harmony is discussed. The Chapter 12 is devoted to The Timing of Events and it is followed by Chapter 13 where Transits are taken into account.

Please notice that from Chapter 8 to 13 no mention is made of Herschel, Neptune and Pluto. It is so because in the traditional Hindu Astrology they were not taken into account as their light did not come to earth when Hindu or Vedic astrology came into being.

The Appendices are taken up at the end of the Chapters as per the convention. The subject matter of these Appendices could have been added in the main book itself but in order to preserve the rhythm of the subject matter theses are dealt with at the end. *The Glossary of Astrological and Technical Terms* follow at the end of this book. We have also added certain *Sanskrit Synonym* for English Terminology.

Readers will do well to refer to the Glossary at the end of the book for ready references. A cursory look even now in the beginning would be of great advantage and would make it easier to go through the book. We would like to mention that although we have explained how to calculate the planetary positions, Ascendants, Cusps of houses etc. yet so many correct programs of astrological software are available that the mathematical part will be done in the twinkle of an eye. This will not only save time but will be more precise and accurate.

The *Sudarshan Chakra* method of examining a house in Chapter 2, will make it easier for the readers to examine not only the love/marriage/friendship but all departments of life by using the *Sudarshan Chakra.* Conventionally only very learned pandits used it in the Hindu system but we have mentioned it in the Western section as it is useful in this system as well.

We would like to point out that with just three months study of this book, one will be able to unfold the subject and then with practice he will become perfect.

PART I

WESTERN ASTROLOGY

CHAPTER 1

PRINCIPLES TO OPEN THE ASTROLOGICAL SECRETS OF FRIENDSHIP, LOVE AND MARRIAGE

During the judgement of a horoscope, it is of prime importance to consider the racial background and the walk of life a person comes from. Planets may be in the same places and position but the reaction of an educated Indian from a conservative family will be different than that of a labour class Chinese or an Arab. Neglect of this factor in the interpretation of a nativity will lead to wrong conclusions.

It is unrecognized mystery that the lower in the scale of evolution one is, the more he responds to the planetary vibrations and the higher we ascend in the scale of attainment the more is our ability to meet the challenge of life and conquer the 'Stars'.

There are so many maxims, viz., "opposite attracts" or on the other hand "birds of the same feather gather together" We have seen that people passing through the Periodic Influence of the same planet automatically came in contact with one another like friends, employer, employee, classmates, lovers etc. This compact relationship lasts as long as they are in the similar periods and when the cycle changes in one case—separations or living apart or even a total break up takes place.

There is however another factor which causes attraction. One horoscope may have certain vibrations which match vibrations in the other chart or they are complementary to each other so much so that a relationship develops between them but no sooner a third party with more intense matching comes in the life of either party—a traumatic change occur in all thier lives.

At times under powerful transit a thirst is felt in a horoscope which creates a relationship but most times it is not a lasting relationship. For example,

(a) If it is due to a Mars factor then it lasts for two years and it is marred by discord and quarrels and then breaks with a tragic accident.

(b) If it is propelled into by Uranus then even married women leave thier husbands for an "Oasis" and by the time sanity returns to them (duration two years to three years), it is too late "the horse has already run away finding the stable doors wide open."

There are so many ways to climb to the top of the hill. In Astrology we have the Western methods, related to the Tropical Zodiac or the Hindu method which is based on the Sidereal System. We do not want to say which is better. However, there are some basic differences between the two viz., like aspects, like planets, like houses. For example, even a natural malefic will show good effect if it is the ruler of the 1st, 9th, or 5th, house in Hindu system: It will show much better effect if simultaneously it is the owner of an angle (1,4,7,10) and trine (5,9). It is then called a 'Yoga Karaka' and it is capable of conferring most things in life on its own.

We also consider 'Rahu' and 'Ketu' as planets in the Hindu System. Rahu if associated with the seventh house or with Venus, causes illicit relationship or living together without marriage. We do not consider Uranus. Neptune and Pluto as their light did not come to earth when Vedic (Hindu) Astrology came into being. We are of the opinion that now these too should be considered.

We now give some aphorisms which is applicable to all horoscopes:

Horoscopes

1. Two people may be good friends, their relationship as friends may be harmonious but they may not prove good

husband and wife due to astrological incompatibility of their 7th houses.

2. Love affairs are judged from the 5th, marriage from the 7th, friendship from 11th and secret attachments from the 12th.

3. If the lord of the ascendant is in Gemini, Sagittarius or Pisces, it inclines to more than one union.

4. Good planets in the third house aspect beneficially the 5th, 7th, 11th and 1st houses and as such must be considered in the Judgement of desires, marriage and friendship.

5. Evil planets in the 5th house or other planets therein in evil aspect with malefics impair happiness pertaining to desires of the heart. The 5th house should, therefore, also be judged in relation to marriage and love affairs.

6. The 5th house also indicates domestic circumstances and environment, and as such should receive due consideration in the Judgement of married life.

7. If the 5th house is weak,—its lord is afflicted or the house itself is afflicted, then there would be no peace in the house and conjugal happiness would be impaired.

8. If there be several planets in the 5th house particularly near the cusp and Sun and Moon in the nativity are not afflicted but beneficially aspected, there would be early marriage.

9. The 7th house is the principal house for Judgement of marriage.

10. Planets in the 7th house, particularly those near the cusp influence materially the prospects of marriage and married life. If a planet therein be the *Ruling Planet* (lord of the Ist house), special importance should be attached to it.

11. Besides the 7th house and planets therein, Sun, Moon, Mars and Venus are chief significators:

(a) Sun and Mars have to be given more weight as significators in female nativities.
(b) Moon and Venus have greater importance in male nativities.

12. Any planet conjoined with or aspected by planets mentioned in No. 10 above, is important in consideration of marriage or married life, but if the lord of the 7th house does so, special importance should be attached to it.

13. The position of the lord of the 7th house by sign and house is very important.

14. Whatever be the ascendant, Sun and Moon form the spiritual and mental—'psychic' basis of the native and as such should be attached due weight as significators in a horoscope.

15. Mars represents the latent 'male' element in a female and Venus represents the latent 'female' element in a male, and as such due weight should be attached to Mars and Venus—as they preside over emotions in relation to sex and the physical desires and gratification thereof.

16. Mercury presides over speech, nervous system and expression, and as such its position and aspect would affect mental approach to problems of love and marriage.

17. The lord of the 1st house, or any planet on or about the cusps of the 1st house and the lord of the 7th house would also determine and affect physical union or attachment.

18. If Moon and Venus are free from affliction and strong in a male nativity and Sun, Mars and Venus strong and unafflicted in a female nativity and there is no association with or aspect of Saturn, it is good for married happiness. If Saturn be the lord of 1st, it is not so bad.

19. If there be any planet in the 7th house the wife's/husband's appearance would conform to it, nearer the cusp more influence it would exert. If there be several planets each one would exert its influence—the stronger one more than the weaker and that nearer the cusp more than the one distant from it.

20. In 17 above, the sign on the cusp of the 7th house would modify the effects. For example, Sun in Aries in the 7th house would give effect different from Sun in Libra in the 7th house. If there be no planet in the 7th house, the sign therein and its lord as also the sign it is posited in and other aspecting planets would describe the wife/husband.

21. The dowry of wife/husband should be judged from the 8th house.

22. The brethren and relations of wife/husband should be judged from the 9th house.

23. (a) If the 9th house is tenanted by benefics and is well-aspected by benefics there is benefit from husband/wife's relations.
    (b) Malefics afflicted therein denote trouble from them.

24. Good planets in 9th being in trine to 5th and sextile to 7th strengthen them.

25. Good planets in 11th being in trine to 7th house strengthen it.

26. Judge of the mental affinity from the 11th house as conjugal affinity is to be judged from the seventh.

27. When the two ascendants or the luminaries in the two horoscopes are in trine or sextile or are so situated that one is over the place of another (in the case of lords of ascendants the two lords should have natural affinity also), there is compatibility and friendship between the two.

28. Eleventh being the house of friendship (as the husband/wife should be a true friend) the 11th house should also be judged.

29. Good aspects to marriage significators from eleventh house are much stronger than from other houses.

30. Planets (luminaries and chief significators) in 'barren' signs or 'cadent' houses and suffering from affliction, delay or deny marriage or hamper married happiness.

31. Cancer, Scorpio, and Pisces are 'Fruitful' signs.

32. Gemini, Leo and Virgo are 'Barren' signs.

33. Fruitful signs on the cusps of the 1st, 5th, and 7th houses are conducive to early marriage/fruition of love affairs.

34. Barren signs thereon retard accomplishment of marriage.

35. A planet is treated as afflicted when it is weak or is in square or opposition to other planets—or in conjunction or parallel with a malefic.

36. Planets in their own signs or in exaltation are strong,

particularly so, if angular and well-aspected by strong benefics.

37. Planets in their detriment and fall are deemed weak particularly when not angular or when they are afflicted by malefics.

Aspects

1. In Hindu Astrology unlike Western Astrology, aspects* by themselves are not good or bad.

Example. In Western Astrology, Sun opposition Jupiter would be considered bad but in Hindu Astrology, Sun opposition Jupiter may not be considered evil if both are lords of benefic houses.

2. Qualitative value of aspects is different according to the *nature of planets* aspecting and not according to the nature of the aspects.

Example. In Western Astrology, trine aspect between two planets is considered good, opposition is considered evil. But in Hindu Astrology even trine between two lords, if one owns a malefic house would be considered evil. Opposition between two planets may be considered good, *e.g.*, between Moon and Jupiter because both are benefics.

3. Quantitative value of aspects is as follows:

(i) All planets have full aspect on the sign or planet posited in seventh sign from the one occupied by it.

(ii) All planets have 75% aspect on the sign or planet posited in fourth or eighth sign from the one occupied by it. Exception—but Mars' aspect is full even in above case.

(iii) All planets have 50% aspect on the sign or planet posited in 5th or 9th sign from the one occupied by it. Exception—but Jupiter's aspect is full in the above case.

(iv) All planets have 25% aspect on the sign or planet in 3rd or 10th from the one occupied by it. Exception—but Saturn has full aspect in the above case also.

---

* In Western Astrology planets in the 1st, 3rd, 4th, 5th, 7th, 9th, 10th and 11th aspect each other.

4. The aspect is calculated from sign to sign irrespective of the number of degrees intervening between the two planets.

Note. For example, Venus in 1° of Aries will have no aspect on a planet in 29° of Virgo though they are 178° apart.

Venus in 1° Aries will have full aspect on a planet in 29° Libra though they would be 208° or 152° apart.

5. Two planets will be deemed to be conjoined together if they are in the same sign though they may be 29° apart. For example, Jupiter in 1° of Libra and Mercury in 30th degree of Libra.

6. But two planets will not be deemed to be conjoined together if they are in separate signs though they may be actually 2° apart, *i.e.* Mercury in 29° Virgo and Jupiter in 1° Libra. Here, there is no aspect between Jupiter and Mercury.

Benefics and Malefics

7. Sun, Mars, Saturn, Rahu and Ketu are deemed malefics. Of these Sun is deemed a 'Krura' or 'malefic' but not 'Papa' (inauspicious) while others are deemed malefics as well as inauspicious, *i.e.* Papas. Exalted Sun is not deemed a malefic.

8. Moon with less than 8 digits (bright portion), *i.e.* from 9th day of dark half to 7th day of bright half is deemed weak and therefore a malefic.

9. The following are malefics in increasing order weak Moon, Sun, Ketu, Mars, Rahu and Saturn.

10. Jupiter is benefic; so also Venus. Jupiter is the greater of the two.

11. Mercury if associated (by being conjoined in the same sign) with benefics acts as such. If associated with malefics it yields result of a malefic.

12. A planet shows good or evil effect according as it has strength or is devoid of it, on account of position, exaltation, debilitation, and aspects it receives. That gives a fairly good idea of strength. The mathematical 'strength' of a planet can be computed only by calculating 24 kinds of strength (which is a very elaborate procedure outside the scope of this book).

13. Wherever reference has been made to a planet as being

debilitated, the planet should not be treated as debilitated if the lord of sign it is in, or the planet owning debilitated planet's exaltation sign, is in a Kendra (Angle) from lagna or Moon.

14. If a planet is debilitated but in exalted ansha it should be treated as fairly good.

15. If a planet is exalted but in a debilitated ansha the planet does not do much good.

16. When a planet is exalted, in its own house or in a friend's house, it gives good results. If it is in an enemy's house or associated with a malefic or combust or defeated in a planetary warfare it gives bad results. (For friendship and enmity see Glossary).

17. Give great importance to the navamsha of the planet in delineation or when predicting the effect of its dasha/antardasha.

18. Planets in 'shirshodaya' signs show their effect in the beginning. These signs are deemed benefic.

19. Planets in the 'prishthodaya' signs show their effects towards the end. These rashis are not deemed benefic.

20. A malefic acts more malignantly if posited in a 'prishthodaya' sign.

21. A benefic, acts more beneficially if posited in 'shirshodaya' sign.

22. The the 3rd, 6th, 10th and 11th houses are deemed 'upchaya' houses. An upchaya house is really fully efficacious, if it is not aspected by enemies or malefics.

23. 'Trik' means the 6th, 8th and 12th houses in a horoscope. Of the three houses constituting 'trik' the eighth is the worst. So also of the three lords of trik, namely, lords of the 6th, 8th 12th, and lord of the 8th is the worst except when it is the lord of the first house also, (*i.e.* in nativities having 'Aries' or 'Libra' as the rising sign, *i.e.* lagna).

24. Planets in prishthodaya signs give their effect most in the last 1/3 portion of their dashas.

25. Planets in the Shirshodaya signs show their greatest effect in the first 1/3 portion of their dashas.

26. A planet in Pisces shows its marked effect in the middle 1/3 portion of the dasha.

27. Qualities of a planet are modified by the rashi* and vargas. The planet is also effected by aspect and association. For example, Saturn in rashi and navamsha of Sagittarius and aspected by Jupiter would show quite different result from Saturn in rashi and navamsha of Mars and with Rahu or Ketu or aspected by Mars.

28. Benefics posited in 'papa' vargas and aspected by malefics lose their goodness and give rise to badness.

29. Malefics in shubh (benefic) vargas and aspected by shubhas shed their evil nature and impart good results.

30. When the planets, good as well as bad, tenant a particular house or aspect it, mixed results should be predicted.

Note. In all the aphorisms of Hindu astrology, if Moon is stronger than the frist house, the lunar ascendant should be fixed as lagna and Judgement arrived at as if the lunar ascendant is the main lagna; lord of the 7th would then mean lord of the 7th from Moon.

31. Moon is deemed stronger than lagna when

(i) The dispositor of Moon is stronger than the lord of the 1st house.
(ii) Moon is increasing in digits and has more than 8 digits, and
(iii) Moon is conjoined with and aspected by Jupiter, Venus and Mercury and unaspected by and not conjoined with malefics.

32. Judge always lunar ascendant also as if it were the ascendant; but attach it less value. On the other hand, if it is more powerful than the ascendant itself due to Moon's being stronger than the ascendant, give it (1.a) greater importance than the ascendant.

Significators

33. All about the wife should be judged from the 7th house.

34. All about the complexion, appearance, virtues and vices about the husband/wife should be predicted from the 7th house as well as from the Navamsha horoscope.

---

* 'Rashi' means 'Sign'. For 'Vargas' see appendix IV.

35. Marriage, union between the native and a person of the opposite sex and everything pertaining to the erotic nature should be judged from the 7th house.

36. Not only look to the 7th house but give equal importance to Venus in judgement of matrimonial happiness.

37. The following are the significators of love and marriage:

(i) Venus—the house, sign and sub-division of signs, it is placed in, the planets it is conjoined with or aspecting it should be judged.

(ii) Seventh house—the sign on the cusp, planets in the house and in trine or square to it as well as those in 2nd, 6th, 8th and 12th to it alongwith those aspecting the house exert influence on it.

(iii) The lord of the 7th house —the sign and sub-division it is placed in and planets associated with or aspecting it modify the effects for better or worse.

38. All benefic planets figuring prominently in the above give good results while malefics do otherwise.

39. Even a malefic will promote the 7th house happiness if it be lord thereof and posited therein.

40. Even a malefic will promote the 7th house happiness if it be the lord of the 7th house and be exalted, strong and in its own navansha.

41. If a planet has both attributes of doing good and doing bad—(by ownership of two houses or otherwise) it gives good results if strong and bad results if weak.

42. (a) If a malefic is strong,

(b) in shubha vargas,

(c) and is aspected by benefics in benefic vargas, it would yield good results.

43. If a benefic is (a) weak (b) in 'papa' vargas (c) aspected by malefics in 'papa' vargas, it would give bad results.

44. Quality or attributes of husband or wife may be ascertained from the attributes of planets affecting the 7th house.

45. An equal amount of malefic influence in the marriage partners' horoscopes nullifies the malefic influence of each other. For example, if a malefic planet is situated in the 12th house of a girl, a similar malefic in the 8th or 12th houses in the boy's horoscope would set off the evil if the two are married. (For details see relevant chapter.)

46. In a male or female nativity mark the planet which causes sinful conduct or liaison. The native would carry on with person described by the planet which causes this looseness of morals. (For example, if Saturn does so, the native would carry on with a Saturnine person if Venus does so, the native would carry on with a person having attributes of Venus).

47. For a proper appraisal of the 7th house, the third and 11th houses should also be judged because they are in trine to it. The trinity completes the full picture.

48. Wife and Venus are presided over by 'agya chakra' (plexus) between eye-brows.

49. If planets in the 8th, 6th, 1st, 4th and 10th houses from the ascendant are benefics it is good for the 7th house. *Vice versa*. Judge from lunar ascendant also.

50. The lords of the 6th house, 8th and 12th house from lagna and enemies of the lord of the 7th are inimical to the prosperity of the 7th house.

CHAPTER 2

THE THREE CENTRES

The Rising Sign, the Moon and the Sun are the three Centres in a horoscope from which judgement of any house is done. Together they rule the body, the mind and the Soul respectively of a person. If any one of the three centre is weak then it affects the entire horoscope in a negative manner. On the other hand, if all the three are strong then the remaining planets will not be able to show much adverse effects.

Let us come to the present book which deals with the Secrets of Friendship, Love and Marriage. The eleventh house in a horoscope rules the friends and if we have to consider friendship in a horoscope then we should consider the following:

(a) The 11th house from the Rising Sign,
(b) The 11th house from the Moon and
(c) The 11th house from the Sun.

All these centres have been attributed with equal strength. We would like to mention here that in the Western system importance is attached to the Sun and the Rising sign whereas in the Hindu system more importance is given to the Moon and the Rising Sign.

We shall now illustrate how to consider the strength of any house from the three centres at a glance. For this a consolidated chart is erected with all the three viz., the Ascendant, the Moon and the Sun placed in the first house. This chart is called the *Sudarshan Chakra*.

We illustrate this with the chart of a native born on May

1st, 1979, at New Delhi at 06.15 a.m. (in the Morning). The horoscope is as follows:

BIRTH CHART

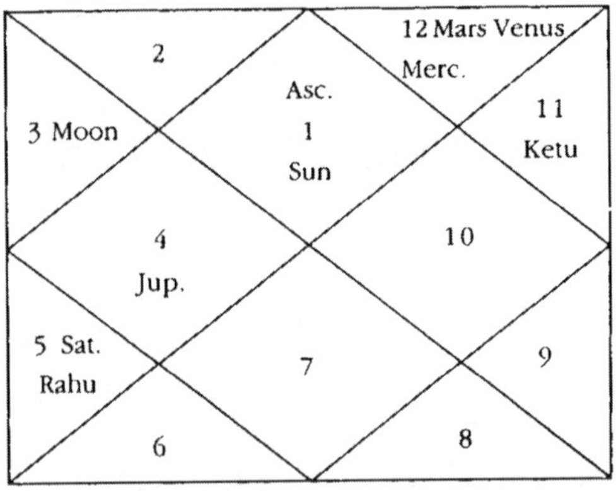

The position of planets in the above chart is as follows: The Ascendant is Aries, Moon is in Gemini in the 3rd house; Sun is in Aries in the first house; Jupiter is in Cancer in the 4th house; Saturn and Rahu is in Leo in the 5th house; Ketu is in Aquarius in the 11th house; Mars, Mercury, and Venus are in Pisces in the 12th house.

The above horoscope is now filled in the format of the chart called *Sudarshan Chakra*, given below. The three centres will be the Ascendant which is Aries in this case: the sign occupied by the Moon viz., Gemini; and the sign occupied by Sun which is Aries again in the above case.

Sudarshan Chakra

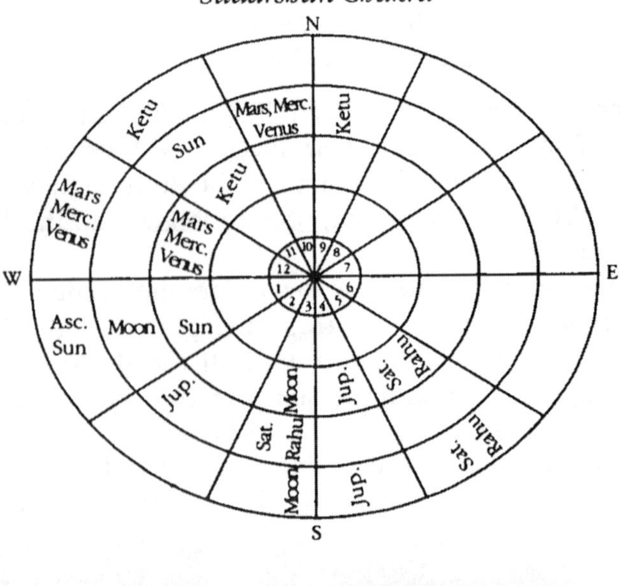

Construction and placement of Planets in the above chart;

We start by drawing five concurrent circles one inside the other as shown above. These circles are further divided into 12 equal parts consisting of 30 degrees each. These constitutes the twelve signs of the Zodiac viz., Aries, Taurus, Gemini etc.

We should now put the Meridian at the top where 'N' is written. Meridian is the highest point in a horoscope. It is in fact the tenth house.

We start with the outermost circle, we shall fill it by using the sign occupied by Sun which in this case is Aries, in the first house where 'W' is written. The Planets will be placed with Sun in the first house, Moon in the 3rd house, Jupiter in the 4th, Saturn and Rahu in the 5th, Ketu in the 11th, and Mars, Mercury, and Venus in the 12th house.

In the second circle as counted from the outer circle, we use the sign occupied by the Moon which is Gemini here, in the first house. Moon sign is also called Chandra Rashi or Rashi in short. The planets now will be Moon in the first, Jupiter in the second, Saturn and Rahu in the 3rd house, Ketu in the 9th house, Mars, Mercury, and Venus in the 10th house, and Sun in the 11th house.

Then we fill the Birth chart in the third circle as counted from the outer circle. The position of planets will be Sun in the first house, Moon in the 3rd, Jupiter in the 4th, Saturn and Rahu in the 5th house, Ketu in the 11th, Mars, Mercury, and Venus in the 12th house.

This composite figure is called Sudarshan Chakra.

If the eleventh house is strong by virtue of its lord being strong or is teneted by benefics from all the three centres than it will show excellent results. However, if it is strong only from one center and not from the other two than only partially good result will ensue.

Extreme good or bad results are experienced when in a nativity the Ascendant as well as Sun and Moon are together, which will be when Sun and Moon are in the first house.

Coming back to the eleventh house, the position of Mars in

the 11th house is the worst for friendly relationship when a so called friend proves to be a *Vampire.* On the other hand, the placement of Jupiter or Sun is the best for successful culmination of friendship.

In the example chart (Sudarshan Chakra) given above, the 11th house from the three centres is:

(a) From the Ascendant — Ketu
(b) From the Moon — Sun
(c) From the Sun — Ketu

Therefore with Ketu a natural malefic from the two centres, the 11th house is weak and so not much happiness from friends can be expected. 'Sun' will give a few high class friends who will be well to do and willing to help.

Let us also consider the 5th house, which indicates love affairs (without proper marriage) and the 7th house, which indicates marriage, in the above chart.

The best success and happy ending comes in love life and romance when the fifth house is strong from the three angles. In the present case we have ---in the fifth house: Saturn, Rahu: No planet; Saturn, Rahu from the Ascendant, Moon and the Sun respectively. With so many Malefics, romance and love life will not be happy. The good thing here is that the native has exalted Sun (ruler of 5th house) from the two centres and Venus is exalted which rules the 5th house from the Moon. So the horoscope would show mixed results.

Let us also examine the 7th house. Here the position is that there is no planet in the 7th house from the Ascendant, Moon or Sun. However, Venus is exalted and it rules the 7th house from the Ascendant and Sun, and Jupiter is exalted. It rules the 7th house from the Moon. Therefore, the married life will be happy and it will be in a comparatively better family.

There are controversial views about the 7th house. If the 7th house is strong than does it indicate a happy marriage or is it an indication of Plurality of Marriage. In our experience we have found that if the lord of the 7th is debilitated then it protects marriage from breaking up and the spouse will have long life although he/she may not keep perfect health.

We now give aphorisms of the different Rising Signs, and the placement of Sun and Moon in various positions.

The Aphorisms of Rising Sign

The Rising Sign or Ascendant not only rules the physical body, the constitution but also the face. As soon as we come across a person, we are attracted to repulsed by his appearance—face in particular. The maxim that "face is the index of the mind"—"the eyes are the mirror of the heart". It is true that when eyes meet, the lightening strikes. An old master one time said, "look into his eyes and smile and he will be your slave for life". Some women have this streak in abundance. And just with the look they draw the energy from the opposite sex. Planets according to their nature, impart their qualities. If there is no planet in the Rising Sign then it will became more dominant to show its qualities. We now states the results of different Rising Signs:

Rising Sign

1. If Aries be the ascendant, there is a strong element of the desire nature in the individual and much craving of the sex and since the individual is daring, unhesitating and aggressive, he/she* has ample apportunities of fulfilment of desires of heart and there may be a number of love-episodes, if the nativity so indicates.

2. If Taurus be the ascendant, the sense of discrimination is well developed and the native is inclined to pick and choose from the opportunities that come his/her way in the matter of love affairs/marriage. Also, the native may play comparatively passive role and wait for the initiative to come from the other side. The native is, however, quite capable of nursing a strong desire.

3. If Gemini be the sign rising, there may be much activity and correspondence in connection with love affairs/marriage. The native is of dual mind and may carry on love affairs with two individuals at a time if the nativity shows plurality of love affairs.

---

*In this book the 'male' lover/husband is referred to as 'he'; the female lover/wife is referred to as 'she'. Sometimes the general expression 'he' is used; 'he' therefore means 'she' also where the nativity is of a female, if the context admits of this meaning as well.

4. If Cancer be the ascendant, the native is outwardly mild and plans secret alliances with members of the opposite sex, particularly with those who are of lower status.

5. If Leo be the rising sign the '*ego*' stands between the native and the pleasures of life and the conjugal happiness is thereby much retarded.

6. When Virgo is the ascendant the native is 'shy' but makes efforts to capture the heart of person of the opposite sex and is more docile and passive than active in courtship.

7. If Libra be rising, the native's discriminating powers are much developed and he picks and chooses on whom to confer his love.

8. If Scorpio be rising the native is strongly sexed and bold in love affairs.

9. If Sagittarius is rising, the native may have two love affairs simultaneously.

10. If Capricorn be the ascendant the native is cautious and waits for pleasures of life, but is not inclined to spend much.

11. If Aquarius be rising, the native may have two love affairs simultaneously.

12. If Pisces be rising, the native is thoughtful and prudent and the pursuit of love affairs is fluctuating according to moods.

Note: The above general tendencies will be modified according to the planets tenanting 1st, 5th, 7th or 11th houses or aspecting them.

Aphorisms of Sun

The 'Puranas'* speak of the infinite solar systems which are connected to one another and this visible 'Sun' is not the only 'Sun'. It is in itself an emanation from the central sun which is the invisible source of all that 'EXISTS' in our solar system. When a 'Planet' becomes very highly evolved then it creates its own solar systems but it still adheres to the 'ORIGIN' which

* These are eighteen in numbers and is written by the immortal Sage 'Vyasa'.

is 'HE', the Supreme Power of Godhead. Sun is the 'ATMA', the soul, the inner strength and consciousness.

In a male chart, it represent the father, the spirit, his health and his qualities. In a women's chart it represent the husband, the father and the protector.

The appplication of Sun to a planet will give indication of the type of person she is most attracted to and ultimately end up marrying. If Sun simultaneously applies to many planets then many proposals of marriage or love relationship will take place. However, if Sun is weak or far advanced in degrees in a house and changes signs before applying to a planet then

(a) There may be no marriage, or
(b) Delayed marriage, or
(c) Not much conjugal bliss.

There are many methods to improve Sun in a horoscope. These are:

(i) Wearing a ruby.
(ii) Serving one's father and getting his blessings. After marriage husband should be taken care of.
(iii) Pouring water in the Morning to Sun (after facing towards the East.)
(iv) Eating food without salt on Sundays and that too before Evening.

We now indicate the effects of the Sun in different signs, house etc.

1. If Sun is in Aries, the love affairs would come up without pre-meditation; they may be a little capricious and not very lasting. There may be acquisition of property through marriage. There is also likelihood of monetary gain due to patronage of or liking by women. There would, however, not be happly flow of conjugal love; may be even quarrels which if the other stars so indicate may become problematic in relation to the emotions. The native would not be very constant in affairs of the heart. Marriage comparatively at an early age is indicated.

2. If Sun is in *Taurus,* the native would change over from one love affair to another. His jealousy would be easily aroused. There is danger of loss or frittering away of property due to

some complication connected with the spouse or due to marriage. There is also possibility of monetary gain through love/marriage. It is probable the native would have to experience deep heart sorrow (due to disappointment from or death of the beloved or non-consummation of marriage with the loved one).

3. If Sun is in *Gemini,* there would be some skeleton in the cupboard in regard to his private life. Disruption in family life is also indicated. There would be more than one love affair and they may cause serious sentimental repercussions and unexpected troubles leading to deep sorrow which the native would take very much to heart. There would be enmity by relations of the partner and also some conspiracy or complication due to certain episodes in the native's own life or that of his partner.

4. If Sun is in *Cancer,* the native is fond of females but there is a general disinclination in both the sexes for entering into wedlock. Marriage even when entered into is not very satisfactory. The native may inherit property through the partner but would probably have to go to court to defend or obtain it. The native will have a number of friends and patrons particularly of the opposite sex.

5. If Sun is in *Leo,* the native would staunchly love and exact absolute allegiance in matters of love. His own affection would be steady. If the native is a woman, she may probably marry twice or have twins. Despite steadfastness in love there would be family disharmony and disruption in married life.

6. If Sun is in *Virgo,* the native will have to undergo sorrows due to some skeleton in the family cupboard, love affairs or through separation or divorce. There would be serious handicaps in the affairs of the heart; native may have to go to a law court. There would be disharmony and discord between him and those to whom he is attached may prove an obstacle between the native and his sweetheart. There may be more than one marriage. If so the second union would entirely change his/her existing circumstances for the better or the worse as other indications in the nativity point to.

7. If Sun is in *Libra*, there may be a law suit between the native and partner, leading to bitter enmity. Matrimonial life would have intermittent jolts and jars, the native may have a second family perhaps an adopted one or may himself be adopted. The native may gain financially through marriage. There is also some probability of gaining a legacy or by insurance due to the death of the partner. The native's friends or patrons would be instrumental in bringing about a marriage which may be considered an achievement. Some enmity from religious people or elderly persons is indicated due to social or family relationship or similar circumstances.

8. If Sun is in *Scorpio*, the native would be strongly sexed, and would surely marry though married life may not turn out to be very happy. There may be death of partner and the native may have to marry a second time. Out of the two unions one would be particularly unfortunate. It is likely the native may have some bereavement by the premature death of some deeply loved one—a relation or sweetheart or friend of either sex. The native's partner would run the risk of being involved in an accident (not fatal). One friend or patron would be of great impediment in career or love affairs.

9. If Sun be in *Sagittarius*, the native would marry more than once or he may marry only once but have a long and lasting love affair, over and above marriage. There would be marked enmity between the native and some other people who would not hesitate to ruin his prospects and prosperity—financial as well as conjugal.

10. If Sun is in *Capricorn*, the native may not be steadfast in matters of love. Any unfaithfulness would more be the result of other people's influence than his own inclination or initiative. His family members may upset his matrimonial prospects and put in impediments in the fruition of his love desires, by imposing their own choice or selectivity rather than allow the native a free hand in matters of love and marriage.

11. If Sun be in *Aquarius*, the native would be inclined to marray someone of high family or who be gifted in the realms

of art (music, painting, embroidery or other fine art). Children born of the wedlock would be rather of delicate health.

12. If Sun is in *Pisces,* the native would be more than ordinarily ardent in matters of love and attraction to the opposite sex would be one of the main features in his life. It will have such pull over his/her mind that he may get entangled with a widow, and there may be some scandal on account of love affair with her. The scandal would become a little too well-known and cause loss of social prestige at some time or other in his life. If there is no love affair and consequent ill name as indicated above, the native may marry twice, and one of the marriages may prove most unfortunate.

Sun in the 12th Houses

13. If the Sun be in *Cancer, Scorpio,* later half of *Capricorn* or *Pisces* and at the same time occupy the rising sign the native would be lascivious and too much fond of the opposite sex, thereby causing loss to his health and money.

14. Sun in the *5th house* increases the desires of the heart and gives too strong a yearning for the company of the opposite sex and makes the native excessively fond of it.

(a) It the Sun has conjunction, sextile or trine aspect from Jupiter, the native's desires of the heart would be fulfilled and the love affair would result in peace, prosperity, happiness and enhancement of social prestige.

The same will be the result but to a lesser extent if Sun be parallel with Jupiter.

(b) If Sun is parallel with or in sextile aspect with Venus there would be much pleasure coming out of the love affairs and the result would be ardent love, compatibility and mutual adjustments.

(c) If Sun is afflicted by Neptune or Saturn it is very unfortunate; much trouble would come out of the love affairs; marriage may not fructify or if it does, there would be discontentment, discord and even divorce. This would primarily be due to a tendency to have too frequent and unfortunately ill-placed love/confidences.

(d) If Sun is conjoined with Mars or Herschel or is in square, opposition or some other unfortunate aspect with these two planets, it would lead to unfortunate love affairs and unhappiness. There would be sudden and impulsive action resulting in grief. This is particularly unfortunate in female nativities where some tragic termination may be the outcome of the whole episode, i.e., it may lead to frustration or loss of social prestige and lasting unhappiness.

Note: Much of the unfortunate results given above come out of the 'ego' nature of the native and he/she may modify the ill-effects in some measure by curtailing pride and jealousy and unfortunate attachments out of the wedlock.

15. If Sun be in the *7th house*, the native would have a husband/wife who would have 'ego' developed to the extent of making him/her a little too proud but he/she would be tactful enough to cater to the whims and caprices of the native and keep him pleased.

(a) The characteristics of the marriage partner would conform to the attributes of the sign, Sun is placed in.

(b) If Sun has square or opposition aspect of planets or is conjoined with malefics, there may be delay in marriage or there would be much conflict and impediments would be placed either in the way of marriage or matrimonial happiness would be curtailed by the opposing nature of the native's husband/wife. The evil—the nature and extent of trouble can be judged according as the afflicting planet be Mars, Saturn, Herschel or Neptune, and whether the same is in detriment or exalted or otherwise.

If the afflicting planet be Moon or Jupiter the evil effect would not be so great as in case of malefics.

(c) If Sun herein is afflicted by any planet judge the nature of the event by looking to the inherent qualities of the planet as well as the houses sun and the afflicted planet are lords of and also where the afflicting planet is—whether in the first, fourth, tenth or seventh house itself.

16. If Sun is in the *7th house* unafflicted and there be no influences to expedite marriage, it would take place when the first flush of youth is over. Judge of happiness in married state by the nature of aspects, which Sun receives and according to the inherent strength or weakness of this luminary. For example, Sun in Leo or Aries would be deemed to be strong and would, if well-aspected, confer matrimonial happiness. But if in Libra or Capricorn, judge otherwise—particularly if in square or opposition to other planets.

17. If Sun be in the *8th house*, the wife or the husband of the native would be a spendthrift and would not care to put by money. But if it be in Aquarius, there may be gain by legacy. Some such effect may be produced by Sun in Taurus also. If Sun be in Leo the marriage partner would not be extravagant.

18. If Sun be in the *12th house* :

(a) in Leo, the native may have clandestine love affairs and there may be trouble due to affairs with the opposite sex.
(b) if in Sagittarius, there may be sorrow from loved ones or bereavements.
(c) in Capricorn, the marriage would not be a fortunate one.
(d) if afflicted, *i.e.*, in conjunction, square or opposition or in parallel declination with Mars, Saturn or Herschel, there might be much sorrow due to affairs with the opposite sex and the native may have to live away from society due to ill health, or to avoid some scandal.

Sun's Aspects

19. If Sun be in sextile or trine to Moon it is indicative of happy marriage.

20. If Sun is in good aspect with the major planets particularly lord of the seventh, there would be conjugal happiness and concord but if in square or opposition with

major planets or in conjunction with malefics, there would be disharmony and disruption, particularly so in a female nativity, and if the afflicting planet be the lord of the 7th or posited therein.

21. If Sun and Moon are in conjunction and in good aspect to other planets, happiness would result and there would be harmony between the couple. But if these two planets are in conjunction along with another malefic or in ill-aspect to major planets judge otherwise. Particularly so, if the afflicting planet be in the 7th house.

22. If Sun be in square or opposition or in some other ill-aspect to Moon there would not be harmony. If either or both are afflicted, it would be worse.

23. Sun free from affliction—happy marriage—particularly so in a female nativity.

24. If Sun be very near to Moon or if Sun and Moon both are afflicted, marriage is delayed.

25. When there is no planet in the 7th house and Sun is the lord of the 7th house, wife would be of the Solar type and in case there is disharmony and discord between the couple, it would be better to iron out differences by reference to a senior man or arbitration instead of going to a court of law. In other words, going to a court of law would entail further trouble.

Note: Wherever reference has been made to Sun being in affliction, square or opposition with a malefic the result would be doubly worse if the malefic be elevated. For example, if Sun be in 26th degree Scorpio in the 4th house and Saturn in 27th degree in Taurus in the 10th house the result would be doubly worse, than if Sun were in 26th degree Scorpio in 10th and Saturn in 27th degree in Taurus in the 4th.

Sun in Female Nativities

26. Sun's position and aspects in a female nativity are of greater importance than in a male nativity, because Sun represents the male relations of a woman and the husband is the most important of them all. It should be seen whether Sun is conjoined with or in aspect to any planets. If this be so,

mark carefully whether Sun is applying to or separating from them. The husband would have to attributes of the planets which apply to Sun. This would of course be modified by the sign's the applying planets are in.

27. If Sun be in a double bodied sign, *i.e.*, in Gemini, Sagittarius, or Pisces, she may marry more than once, particularly so, if Sun applies to or is in conjunction with more than one planet*.

28. If Sun be between the cusps of the 10th and 7th or fourth and 1st, women marry early in life or are married to young persons.

29. If Sun be in a place other than those mentioned in 28 above, they marry late in life or rather to elderly persons.

30. In aphorism 26 above, it has been mentioned that the husband would have the attributes of the planet which applies to Sun in a female nativity.

(a) If Sun applies to Moon, he would be of noble disposition, imaginative and generous but would be rather meek and vacillating. If the Moon be in Cancer or Taurus, the husband would have the above qualities in greater measure and he would be cheerful and rather steady.

(b) If Sun applies to Mars, the husband would be a little aggresive and self-assertive with a tendency to get into temper on the slightest provocation or without provocation. He would be very dominant if Mars be in Aries or Scorpio but more dignified, if it be in Scorpio but more dignified, if it be in Capricorn. If it be in Cancer, his ill temper would be much worse.

If Sun is in trine or sextile or some other good aspect to Mars and Mars is strong by sign and house: good marriage. But if Sun be separating from parallel of Mars it is not a happy augury; the

* This should be applied to female nativities belonging to a society where widow marriages, divorces, separations, etc. are very much in vogue, and not to orthodox Hindu families.

full fruits of marriage may not be enjoyed. If there are other indications in the horoscope, there might be widowhood. Sun conjoined with Mars particularly within orbs has a hampering effect. There may be much unhappiness because unless Mars be strongly and favourably aspected by planets like Jupiter, there would be too much dominance by husband and there would be too frequent quarrels in the conjugal state. The same would be the result if Mars be in square or opposition to Sun.

Much depends upon the strength of Sun and Mars; if both are well- placed and strong and there is trine or sextile aspect, the husband would be high-minded and strong rather than quarrelsome or cruel. If Sun has absolutely no aspect with Mars but is afflicted by Saturn there would be much hindrance and delay in marriage.

(c) If Sun applies to Mercury, he would be of the Mercurian type, *i.e.*, clever, in speech, active and fond of talking. If Mercury be well-aspected, he would talk sense but if Mercury be weak or in ill-aspect to other planets, he would be garrulous. If Mercury be strong and be conjoined with or in good aspect with Jupiter, the husband would be well placed in life and learned. If Mercury be conjoined with Venus and be not afflicted by any malefics, the husband would be a neat, tidy and a good-looking person. In other words, Mercury applying to Sun in a female nativity would give a Mercurian type of person as husband but whether he would be a good type or a bad type depends upon the sign, house Mercury is in and the aspects it receives.

(d) If to Jupiter, the husband would be generous, prosperous, sober and inclined to be obliging. He would be fair and just in his dealings. If Sun be conjoined with or in sextile or trine aspect to Jupiter or be in parallel declination, there would be an honourable marriage, *i.e.*, marriage in a good family which would redound to the credit of the family. If Jupiter be applying as above and be the significator of the husband and it be strong and not conjoined with any malefic nor in square or opposition to any planet and similarly, Sun be also strong and unafflicted, the marriage would be a happy one. But if Jupiter be not strong but weak (say in a cadent house or debilitated or in Gemini or Virgo or afflicted by malefics) the husband would be a good-natured one, Jupiter an in qualities but would not be fortunate, *i.e.*, prosperity and other attributes conferred by a strong Jupiter would be denied.

If Sun applies to the conjunction of Jupiter and also apply to trine of Saturn, there is likelihood of more than one union.

(e) If Sun applies to Venus, the husband would have the qualities and attributes of Venus. He would have effeminate beauty, would be loving, amorous, and pleasant as a companion and a lover. He would be neat and tidy and fond of good dress and expect his wife also to come up to his standard. All the good qualities characteristic of a Venusian would, however, be found in the husband only if Venus is unafflicted for if that planet be weak and afflicted the husband may be sensuous and flirtatious and even fond of drinks.

(f) If Sun applies to Saturn, the husband would not be jolly but of a grave and serious type. He would not be generous but miserly—even stingy—if it does not receive aspects from Jupiter or other benefics. Sun in sextile or trine to a strong Saturn indicates marriage rather late in life or to a person having more than normal disparity in age (husband would be elder). If Saturn be exalted or in Capricorn or Aquarius or otherwise strong by being in an angle, the husband would be wealthy but one who believes more in accumulating money rather than in spending it, and the marriage may not be a very jolly or happy one. If Saturn is, however, forming a square or opposition or some other unfortunate aspect or Sun is so conjoined that it is within orbs of Saturn it denotes misfortune in marriage. There may be premature death of the husband if other testimonies so warrant or there may be great delay in marriage or marriage may not fructify at all. In such case, even if marriage takes place, the husband would be mean, miserly and of substance. If Saturn be afflicted in Cancer, Scorpio or Pisces and applying to Sun the husband would be a lazy person by nature and there would be no happiness out of the marriage. No prosperity either may be expected for a husband indicated by a weak, afflicting Saturn is rarely prosperous. Unless there are other markedly good features these marriages are rarely happy. The husband is egoistical and exacting. He is uncultivated and rather cruel.

If Sun as well as Moon both be afflicted it is worse. There may be premature widowhood. If the affliction by Saturn be very severe and serious and there are no other markedly strong features indicating conjugal happiness, there may be premature death of husband and more than one marriage.

(g) If Sun applies to Herschel there would be something out of the common in the matter of marriage or union. The husband would be bold and independent but rather of an eccentric type who would go off at a tangent according to his whims and caprices. The attachment is brought about under romantic circumstances and the development of love affair/courtship is on quick and unconventional lines. If Herschel in its turn may have an aspect of Mars, the husband would be very headstrong also. If Sun has the square or opposition aspect of Herschel it is worse but if it be in conjunction with or parallel even then, it affects adversely the morals of a girl. It leads to rather early cohabitation in life and unless there be benefic aspect of a strong Jupiter, there is likelihood of some dishonour or disgrace and the native should be cautioned against impending scandal. When Sun Herschel configuration is the prominent feature in a horoscope the marriages are rarely fortunate. If the affliction be severe (if the conjunction or square or opposition is almost exact and Sun be weak and there be no benefic aspect of other planets) the girl would be led astray; particularly so, if there be affliction from Mars and/or Saturn as well; or the outcome may be, that a girl married to her husband would leave her husband and carry on with someone other than her husband or there may be constant quarrels and bickerings leading to separation. If Sun be in Gemini, Virgo, Sagittarius, or Pisces, it is worse.

If Sun be in good aspect to Herschel there is sudden and strong attachment to a male and either this may turn into a marriage after a period of romance or may be limited just to an immoral and illicit connection. If there is a very close sextile or trine between Sun and Herschel, the women would succumb rather easily to the romantic overtures of a male and she would be seduced, particularly so if Cancer or Pisces be rising (be ascendant).

The keynote of Sun-Herschel configuration is romanticism and unconventional love, separation, and this should be judged against the general nature of the horoscope.

(h) If Sun be severely afflicted both by Saturn and Herschel and may not have benefic aspect of Jupiter there would be premature death of the husband.

(i) If the Sun applies by any aspect of Herschel or Saturn or both and these two planets aspect each other marriage would be very unfortunate and unhappy.

(j) If Sun applies to several planets particularly Mars, Saturn and Herschel by trine or sexile, several males would like to marry the girl or there may be more than one marriage. But if some aspects be square or opposition, unhappiness and frustration would result.

31. Sun-Neptune configurations are also unfavourable particularly square, opposition and conjunction leading to

disillusionment in the end. Sun and Neptune in good aspect lead to love of pleasure. If in bad aspect to excess and lax morals. The effect of above configuration is stronger if either planet is Ruler in a horoscope or angular. If the planets be in middle ground or background, except 5th house or without essential dignity, they do not exert so much influence, but the effect is rather marked in 5th and 7th houses.

Sun in 7th House in Female Nativities

32. If Sun be weak or debilitated by sign and may not have good aspect or conjunction of benefics and be in the seventh house there may be separation from husband.

33. Sun in 7th house if applying to a conjunction, sextile or trine of Jupiter indicates a happy marriage-magnitute of this depending upon the strength of Sun as well as of Jupiter.

34. Sun in 7th house conjoined with or in square or opposition or in parallel to malefics in unfavourable.

35. Sun in the 7th house if applying to Saturn, the husband would be Saturnine (grave and exacting, miserly, or elderly). The above description would be modified according as the aspects Saturn itself receives from other planets.

Sun in 8th House

36. (a) Sun much afflicted in the 8th house may lead to rather premature death of husband. For this it is necessary that the affliction be from more than one planet and it may be unmitigated by any benefic influence. The 7th house likewise should also be afflicted.

(b) Sun essentially strong and well-aspected in 8th house; there may be gain through husband or legacy.

Note: (i) Note the signs and houses Sun and the applying or afflicting planet are in.

(ii) Planets separating from Sun are not so important as applying.

Aphorisms of Moon

What Sun is for a women, Moon is for a man. Moon is the second half and represents his left portion of the body, his emotions, the satisfaction in the life with his counterparts. When Moon is strong in a Male horoscope it brings in his life a good looking woman as paramour. It also indicates a very understanding mother. It imparts to a man a maternal instincts, a motherly touch which attracts many females to him. Benefit from women and their associations. However, in many horoscopes we have seen, a young man gets attracted to an older woman (even if she is married).

When analysing female horoscopes, the health, the emotional nature, the relationship with the mother and her life after forty should be considered by Moon.

In Hindu Astrology, more importance is assigned to the Moon not because it is the satellite of Earth or because it is closer to us or it is cooling to the eyes but the reason is that it represents the 'Mana', the conscious emotions. It is born out of the heart or Mana of the 'VIRAT PURUSH', the Supreme Power of Godhead. What is good, satisfying, beautiful or otherwise is just a condition of the mind. In this World everything is Him so how can they be ugly or repulsive ? It is only how our thoughts have been conditioned by our upbringing that we feel happiness, repulsion or any other emotions. These desires are not static and they also under go a change with the age and times.

We now proceed to give its general effect and also its effect in a male and then in a women's horoscope:

1. Moon in Taurus makes one fond of females, particularly those slightly elder in age.
2. Moon in Scorpio *inclines to many evil actions particularly with the opposite sex.*
3. Moon in Capricorn disposes to mean actions and debauchery.
4. Moon in Pisces makes one much fond of the opposite sex.

Note: The evil nature of relations with the opposite sex increases if there is affliction by malefics whereas the nature becomes more refined, if there is a trine or sextile of benefics or Moon is conjoined with them.

5. If Moon be in Gemini, Sagittarius or Pisces plurality of wives is denoted, specially if Moon applies by conjunction or aspect to more than one planet, particularly so if Moon be oriental or angular.

Moon in Different Houses

6. Moon in the 1st house: the native is fond of the opposite sex and is liked by them.

7. Moon in the 5th house: very much inclines to indulging in pleasures; the native has a number of love affairs. While the native is given to much pleasure seeking, he lacks in constancy on account of a fickle disposition and may carry on with more than one member of the opposite sex. This applies particularly to male nativities.

8. Moon in the 5th house: if afflicted there is no fulfilment of the desires of the heart, or sorrow and trouble ensue as a result of love affairs. There would also be illicit connection if there is sextile or trine aspect with malefics. If, however, there is conjunction, square, or opposition with Herschel, Neptune, Mars or Saturn there is likely to be frustration and also scandal. But if Moon be strong and there be sextile or trine of benefics, particularly if Jupiter or Venus be conjoined with these and be free from affliction happiness and pleasure would be the outcome of love affairs.

9. Moon in the 7th house; the native may marry rather early. The marriage partner would be changeable and fickle like Moon—he/she would be fond of much travelling.

10. Moon in the 7th house; if conjoined with or in square or opposition to malefics, there would be trouble and sorrow resulting from marriage. If afflicted by more than one planet and other indications confirm, there may be premature death of the wife/husband.

11. Moon in the 7th house: Not conjoined with nor aspected by any planet: Judge the attributes of the sign Moon is in. Moon is very receptive and imbibes very easily the qualities

of the planets it is aspected by or if there be no aspect Moon takes in great measure the attributes of the sign it is in. Judge of the marriage partner in the above light.

12. Moon strong and well-aspected in the 7th house denotes good marriage and conjugal happiness. If Moon is in its own house or in the house of Venus or Jupiter or in Aquarius and in good aspect with Saturn it denotes a hard-working, careful and thrifty wife/husband.

13. Moon in the 8th house, if strong and well-aspected: money by marriage, legacy from a woman or insurance.

14. Moon in the 9th house, if strong and well-aspected: assistance from brethren or relations of husband/wife.

15. Moon in the 10th house: the native may be recipient of favours from ladies of high position and there may be gain from them.

16. Moon in the 11th House is good for family life; one mixes easily with masses and ladies.

17. Moon in the 11th house:

(a) If in Aries, may lead to romantic adventures.
(b) If in Taurus, intrigues and sensuous outlook.
(c) If in Gemini, there is a tendency to have two love affairs simultaneously or the native may be of dual mind in regard to love affairs.
(d) If in Virgo, attachment to a shy person who may be inferior in status.
(e) If in Libra, free love and marriage to one already known.
(f) If in Scorpio, secret attachments would turn out badly leading to sorrow.

18. Moon in the 12th house leads to romances and the native may live for some time secluded from others. If Venus be conjoined with Moon or be aspecting it, such living away cut off from society, may be due to some love affairs or with the beloved one. But if such Moon is afflicted by Mars, Saturn, Herschel or Neptune there would be trouble and unhappiness.

19. If Moon and many planets are between *1st* and *10th* or

7th and *4th* early marriage or men will marry rather young girls.

20. If Moon is in any position other than that mentioned above, men marry late or comparatively grown-up women.

Moon's Aspect

21. If Moon is occidental and afflicts Sun, delay in marriage.

22. Moon in evil aspect to Sun; loss through love affairs, marriage/women.

23. If Moon is conjoined with Sun or forms a sextile or trine with Sun :

(a) in male nativity, it shows marriage with a lady coming from a good family, dignified and self-willed and of good conduct.

(b) in a female nativity, this is indicative of good success in life. But if Sun and Moon both be in Cancer or Leo, there will be delicate constitution.

24. Strong Moon in conjunction or evil aspect to Mars: the native is too much given to the company of the opposite sex. There is some loss of wealth and health thereby. In a male nativity it shows much unhappiness in married life and frequent quarrels. The wife one gets is fond of drinking, sensuous, hot-tempered and worthless.

25. Moon in good aspect to Mars: sensuous, disposition and inclined to drink. In female nativity good health.

26. Moon weak and afflicted and in conjunction or evil aspect to Mars shows too much indulgence with opposite sex and loss of money and vitality thereby.

27. Moon in conjunction or good aspect to Jupiter: success in marriage and a good wife. In female nativity good for health and money.

28. Moon in conjunction or good aspect to Venus: the native is well-mannered with good tastes and is much liked by women. In a male nativity it denotes happy marriage and if Venus be not afflicted by other planets, the wife is good and pleasing.

29. Moon afflicted by Venus shows trouble in courtship in a male nativity. In a female nativity it shows the native to be frequently a 'slattern.'

30. Moon aspected by Saturn: marriage is delayed, particularly in male nativity.

31. If Moon is afflicted by conjunction, square or opposition of Saturn, trouble with or ill health to wife. If Moon and Saturn be in signs of Mercury or Jupiter and if affliction is serious and other confirmations present, death of wife and another marriage.

32. (a) If Moon in afflicted by Saturn and unaspected by other planets and other indication do not point to premature death of wife, the native gets a useless wife, not good-looking, low, mean-minded and slovenly.
   (b) In a female nativity this leads to intemperate habits of drinking and low conduct and may also result in disgrace.

33. Moon in conjunction with or in evil aspect to Herschel is of much significance for native's married life. The native will have many liaisons with other people's wives/young girls and there is likelihood of estrangement and separation from wife. In a female nativity it shows that the husband would be adulterous and would carry on with other people's wives.

34. Moon in good aspect to Herschel: The native has adulterous intercourses with other people's wives, even after his marriage. But there may/may not be separation from his own wife.

Judgement of Moon in Male Nativities Only

35. Moon's position and aspect in the case of a male horoscope are of chief importance, in Judgement of marriage. The nature and aspect of the planets to which Moon applies are significant.

36. The planets which apply to Moon and the sign which the former are in, would give a rough appraisement of the physical and mental attributes of the women, the native is likely to come in contact with (love affairs or resulting in marriage). Of all the planets applying that one is of the greatest importance, which is the first to apply.

For example, if Moon applies to Venus the lady one would meet with would be handsome and comely in appearance, voluptuous, with a full face and body; if Moon applies to Mercury she would be slim and slender. In the above example, if Venus be in Libra she would be more refined that if Venus were in any of the signs of Saturn; similarly, if Venus were conjoined with Jupiter the lady would be just and noble but if Venus be in the sign of Mars or conjoined with that planet the lady would be haughty and amorous. In this way, the description would vary according as the planet is one or the other, the sign it is in and the planet it is conjoined with or aspected by.

37. If Moon is in the third, sixth, ninth, or twelfth and afflicted by Saturn and without any benefic aspect and if it (Moon) be at the same time in Aries, Gemini, Virgo or Capricorn marriage would be delayed or hampered by unforeseen obstacles.

38. If there be Gemini, Sagittarius or Pisces on the cusp of the 7th house and Moon is simultaneously applying to several planets, more than one marriage or love affair with more than one woman at a time is indicated. There is greater possibility of the above if Moon or the planets it is in aspect with are in Cancer, Scorpio, or Pisces.

39. If Moon applies to Sun, the wife would be from a noble family, well-bred, firm, a little proud but not vacillating. Of course, the description should be modified accordingly as Sun is in Leo, or Capricorn or Aquarius, etc. The planet Sun is conjoined with or in aspect with will also modify the influence but the general characteristics of Sun, nobility of character, pride and firmness would be found.

40. If Moon is conjoined with or in evil aspect to Mars and does not apply to any other planet the native would be unhappy in married state because his wife would be quarrelsome and hot-tempered. If a society woman, she would be fond of drinks, would be too bold and arrogant—always liking to command. If Moon be in adverse aspect or in parallel to Mars there would be much discord and disharmony. Family

life may frequently be disrupted. This will particularly be so if either or both planets are in the 7th or 4th house and in Aries, Leo, or Sagittarius. The wife would be much worse—rather lewd and vulgar if Mars be in Cancer and having an aspect of Saturn.

41. If Moon applies to Mercury, the wife would be clever in speech but rather a little too garrulous. If Mercury is well-aspected, she would be intelligent and her speech would be full of wit and wisdom, but if Mercury be afflicted by other planets she would have a sharp and long tongue and would be a constant source of irritation to the native.

42. If Moon applies to Jupiter she would be well-bred, just, kind and bring in prosperity in her wake. The native's conjugal life would be happy and harmonious. The wife may not be so good-looking but she would be steady in character and virtuous and would not stir up strife.

43. If Moon applies to Venus she would be of a loving temperament and handsome in appearance (refer to Aph. 36 above).

44. If Moon applies to Saturn the wife may come from a poor family, unless Saturn is exalted or the lord of the 7th house is exalted. She would be careful and industrious. She would be grave and serious, and not jolly or mirthful but prudent. She would excel as a housewife and would be regular and attentive to her duties.

45. If Moon applies to Herschel the wife would have many peculiarities—she may be romantic, would have a period of unlicensed courtship and prepared to go off at a tangent at the slightest provocation. Her rashness and independent ways may be a constant headache to the husband. There will be little domestic peace or comfort. If Moon is in opposition or square to Herschel and if the 7th house is also afflicted there might be frequent quarrels or even separation. If Moon be conjoined with Herschel or be in square or opposition to that planet and the degrees of the two planets are close within orbs, the native will have love affairs with women who are married to other people. If Moon be in sextile or trine to

Herschel same as above, with the rider that the native may carry on with other married women even after his own marriage.

46. If Moon is applying to Herschel and the application is very close and without any benefic aspects the native may get trapped in a sudden romance and enter into wedlock which may not turn out to be as he had imagined. This would particularly be so, if the two planets Moon and Herschel are afflicted by Mars, Saturn, or Neptune; and there may be much disappointment and sorrow. But if a strong Jupiter aspects Moon and Herschel and there are benefics in the 7th house and no affliction, even a romantic marriage may turn out to be happy.

Note: (i) Trine and sextile aspects are deemed good while opposition and square are deemed evil. But much depends upon the inherent nature as well as strength or weakness of the aspecting planet. Square from an afflicted Mars in Cancer will be much more evil than a square from Jupiter in Pisces. Also, if the afflicting planet is elevated the evil will be more than if the same planet were not so.

(ii) Have regard to the sign in which the Moon and the applying planets are.

47. In the above aphorisms, describing effects of Moon's application to various planets, the effect would be much more marked, in case of native's being born with sign Capricorn rising in the eastern horizon.

48. Moon's application to planets in a male nativity should be judged along with the application of planets to Venus and the Ruling planet.

49. If there be a planet in the 7th house and Moon apply to a planet other than that in the 7th house, there may be more than one marriage, or love affair.

50. If Moon be occidental and be in a square or opposition to Sun or conjoined with, in square or opposition to Saturn, there is delay in men's marriage. In order to bring out this result Moon and the other planet (Sun or Saturn) should be within orbs.

51. Judgement about the wife, her appearance and temperament as given according to Moon's application to one planet or the other should also be synthesised with that of the 7th house in the male nativity. Planets near the cusp of the 7th house also influence greatly the type of women one would marry. She would have the attributes of the planet conjoined with the cusp of the 7th house, or strongly aspecting it. If no planet in the 7th house, the sign on the cusp of the 7th house is to be taken into consideration as a contributing factor.

52. Moon in the 8th house much afflicted and if the 7th is also afflicted: there may be premature death of wife (look for other indications also for confirmation). Judgement about death should be arrived at only when there is overwhelming corr-oboration.

53. If there be no planet in the 7th house and Moon is the Ruler in the horoscope:

(a) if Moon is afflicted, it would bring notoriety and ill repute.
(b) if well-aspected, there would be good name and fame but financial loss.

54. When Moon is the Ruling planet and forms an aspect with Neptune there is illusion about a lady's love; generally trouble ensues and association with ladies leads to all kinds of unfortunate happenings. There may be some deceptions or fraud or slander. This influence hinders marriage and obstructs married happiness.

55. If Moon be strong in 5th or 7th house and forming aspects to a number of planets— if these aspects are favourable there would be early marriage but if aspects are square or opposition with malefics, there would be frustration or the outcome of the romance would lead to unhappiness.

Female Nativities Only

56. If Moon be in conjunction or evil aspect to Herschel, the husband of the woman would be fond of adulterous intercourse with other married women.

57. If in a female nativity Moon is in conjunction or in any

other evil aspect with Saturn, it is an unfortunate influence. It may result in disgrace. The native would be fond of drinks and would be depraved.

This would be so if the lord of the 1st house and planets (near the cusp of the 1st house) are weak and afflicted and if the 9th house is also weak/afflicted.

58. If Moon is in 7th house, it is indicative of the native having some romances in married life and the affection of the partner would fluctuate.

59. Moon in 7th house, unless it is well-aspected by benefics is not a good influence because it acts as an unsteadying influence. But Moon has the quality of taking in the attributes of the planets it is in aspect with. As such, the goodness or badness of this position would depend upon the aspect this planet receives. If there be no planet forming aspect with the Moon, judge according to the sign it is in, and also take into consideration the lordship of the house. For example, lord of the 1st in 7th, if it be strong would have quite different influence from a weak lord of the 6th, in the 7th house.

Note: (i) Planets separating from Moon are not so important as applying.
(ii) Full Moon is good, weak Moon is bad.
(iii) Waxing Moon is good; waning Moon is bad.

CHAPTER 3

APHORISMS OF PLANETS

We have in the previous chapter discussed the effects of the Ascendant and the Luminaries. Sun and Moon are Luminaries but for the sake of easy references these are referred to as planets in Astrology. In the Western Astrology we have at present eight other planets excluding the Sun and the Moon. These planets are Mars, Mercury, Jupiter, Venus, Saturn, Uranus, Neptune and Pluto.

The present chapter deals with the effects of the seven planets viz., from Mars to Neptune. The effects of Pluto which was discovered in 1930 has not been touched upon as its authentic effects has not been verified so far. The only thing the scientist know about it is that it has the biggest magnetic force than any other known planet. If it conjoins with the cusp of the Rising Sign, Sun or Moon than it imparts to the native with a magnetic power to attract others. Such a person even with his look will charm others. In the case of a woman it will endow her with tremendous power over men.

Now we give the aphorisms of Planets:

Aphorisms of Mars

A good Mars in a horoscope endows one with courage, dash and drive and desires in abundance. The ability to take initiative and that too with confidence ensures success in most department of life particularly related to interaction with others. It ensures success in love for a man. In the case of women strong Mars in dignity ensures early marriage. If Mars in placed in the 11th house in a female chart then she becomes a victim of playboys and selfish friends. This effect start manifesting at an early age of seventeen years and continues on and off. She is taken advantage of physically, morally and financially and if she ends up marrying a friend who is exacting and demanding, cruel and arrogant then there is no escape for her.

If Mars is weak in a male chart then, he has no courage or is 'Chicken-hearted' so to say and as such unable to take initiative because of the fear that he may even lose the thread of friendship and so he is never successful in love. Even after marriage he is at the receiving end unless the weak effects of Mars are mitigated by another strong planet.

In the Hindu System when we match horoscopes, the placement of Mars in a chart is very important factor. It posited in the 8th, 7th, 12th, 4th, and 1st, (according to a different view in the 2nd house, it constitutes a 'Kuja Dosha' or 'Mangalik' dosha which unless counter balanced in the other chart, causes more than one marriage (due to death or separation).

Mars has control on 'Fire and Iron'. It is well-known that every living body is 'warm' and this is due to Mars. A weak Mars reduces "Iron" in the blood which exists in the form of hemoglobin and without which there would be no oxidation and consequently no heat. In order to strengthen Mars in horoscope one should wear a 'red coral' or he can also take *Praval Bhasam. This will strengthen Mars in a horoscope. When a person passes through the Mahadasha** of Mars or through a Direction of Mars then the body temperature shoots up by one degree to two degrees which baffles many persons who do not know this.

We now give below the effect of Mars in a horoscope on account of its placements or due to its association with other planets:

1. Position and aspects of Mars are very important, particularly in a female nativity.

2. Mars in a female nativity represents the desire of congress with a male.

3. If Mars is in the 1st house in watery signs, it inclines one to low company, wine and women.

---

* An Ayurvedic medicine made of Coral.

** Periodic influence of Mars (Major or minor periods of Mars.)

4. Mars in the 4th house seriously disturbs home life, giving rise to constant disputes.

5. Mars in the 5th house gives fondness for pleasures of life. A keen edge is imparted to the desire nature. One is inclined to have romances with the opposite sex and acts under great impulse of emotions in this direction. In a male nativity this should be interpreted as inclining to a number of love affairs, their success depending upon benefic influences, this planet may be receiving and the frustration, on the evil aspects that it may be forming. In a female nativity, if in evil aspect, it may lead to disgrace.

6. Mars in the 5th house gives, abundance of emotions and excess of feelings.

7. Mars in the 5th house if afflicted by—

(a) Sun—acts as adverse influence particularly in a female nativity.
(b) Moon—an adverse influence particularly in a male nativity.
(c) Mercury—there may be indiscretion in writing love letters.
(d) Jupiter—there may be waste of vital-force or squandering of money due to opposite sex.
(e) Venus—brings frustration and ruin through the opposite sex.
(f) Saturn—there may be frustration of desires, delay in marriage, sorrows in love.
(g) Herschel—As a result of impulsive desires, foolish infatuations are formed, resulting in frustration or disgrace.
(h) Neptune—same as affliction of Saturn. There may be some illusion in regard to one's beloved and consequent poignancy of grief.

8. If Mars is much afflicted in the 5th house particularly by the lord of the 7th and unmitigated by any benefic influence it acts as a very evil influence. There may be separation with the husband/wife and the parties may have to go to a court of law, for compensation/divorce.

9. Mars in the 5th house in a male nativity inclines to love affairs particularly if forming aspects with the lord of the 1st or 7th. In a female nativity if afflicted by the lord of the 10th, it may lead to disgrace.

In such a case the overall influence must be taken into consideration—whether the evil aspects are modified by benefic aspects or *vice versa.*

10. Mars in the 7th (not in its own sign): This is an evil influence. The marriage is unfortunate; there are constant quarrels with the marriage partner, and if other indication confirm, there might be premature death of the marriage partner (look for other indications for confirmation).

11. Mars in the 7th denotes a wife who is combative, aggressive and tries to dominate. In a male nativity, this shows that it is the wife who wears the trousers.

12. Mars in 7th: The partner is endowed with courage and boldness and much constructive energy. But he/she would be overbearing and assertive to a fault. If such Mars receives good aspects from strong planets, this may indicate in a female nativity that the husband may be employed in the Military or Police or follow some occupation falling under Mars (surgery, electric engineering, work connected with colours, copper, etc.) and this may not be taken as an adverse influence, if Mars is essentially strong. But weak or afflicted Mars would indicate that the marriage partner would be quarrelsome, unruly and cruel husband/wife. In a male nativity, this is rarely a good influence unless Mars is in Aries, Taurus, Libra, Scorpio or Capricorn.

13. Mars in the 7th house:

(a) If afflicted therein, indicates quarrels and unpleasantness in conjugal life. If more than one malefic afflicts and Venus be also afflicted without benefic aspect of Jupiter to the seventh house or marriage significators, home life may break up and there may be separation due to the uncontrollable temper or sexual craving.

(b) Even when well aspected, it is not a very good position, but if forming good aspect with Moon in a male nativity or with Sun in a female nativity it is not so bad. The marriage would continue, and not disrupt particularly if it has the sextile or trine of Jupiter.

(c) The evil influences emanating from this position of Mars must be modified according to the sign it is in, if in hot and fiery sign the partner may be fiery in temper, if in watery signs, inclined to drink or lewd; in Aries and Scorpio it is not so bad, but inclines to more than one marriage if other indications confirm. Mars in Capricorn in seventh: one marries well and the social position of the native is enhanced by such an alliance.

14. If Mars in the 7th house is much afflicted by Sun or Moon or is in conjunction with malefic planets or forms evil aspects with several planets, one's wife/husband is always causing a jarring note in the domestic life. There is much aggressiveness and uncontrollable temper on the part of the partner and the peace and serenity of home life is shattered. Also, there may be more than one marriage.

15. Mars in the 7th : The native is inclined to have love affairs.

16. Mars in 8th: A disastrous influence for the husband, in a female nativity.

17. Mars in 8th: There may be financial difficulties after marriage and it is possible wife/husband may be directly or indirectly connected with or be cause of such financial difficulties. One will have to face indebtedness.

18. Mars in the 9th: There may be losses through relatives of wife/husband. Also gives rise tc some friction with relations by marriage.

Aspects of Mars

19. If Mars is afflicted in a woman's horoscope marriage becomes a problematical affair. Also, unless there are other favourable features, marriage may be denied or delayed.

(a) This is particularly so if Mars is afflicted by a strong Saturn.

(b) If Herschel afflicts Mars, engagements made may be

broken. The female would be inclined to have romantic attachments and may have a number of affairs.

(c) If Neptune is the afflicting planet there may be homosexuality or some other sex perversion.

20. If Mars is afflicted by strong Venus there may be irregular unions. Unless the lord of the 1st house and those of 4th and 9th are strong there is unbridled licence and dissipation. This would be particularly so if these planets are conjoined in the 5th or one of them is in 5th.

21. Mars in conjunction with or in affliction by weak Venus; the native is too much addicted to wine, women, and wantonness. Self-indulgence leads to dissipation of vital energies. When Venus is very weak or debilitated in a male nativity, the native has congress with women of low status but in a female nativity this would be so, particularly if Mars be debilitated or otherwise weak.

22. When Mars is afflicted by Venus and the former is in elevation, it is a greater evil than if Venus be in elevation.

23. Mars in good aspect to Venus makes one inclined to pleasures of life and female company. In a female nativity it has similar effect. One may marry well.

24. If Mars is very weak and is afflicted by conjunction or malefic aspects of Neptune, Herschel and Saturn (if not by all the three at least by two) the path of love affairs is beset with difficulties and dangers before as well as after marriage and may lead to sorrows and a series of regrettable actions.

25. Mars in conjunction with or evil aspect to Herschel is bad (make sure that in case of aspect they are within orbs).

This would be particularly unfavourable if in 7th house (which is the house governing marriage, law suits and partnership).

26. If Mars be the Ruling planet in a horoscope and be in bad aspect with Neptune it leads to unbridled licence. Passions are strongly marked and there is much emotional disturbance. The native seeks sex gratification, if not outside by self-indulgence. Also, there may be some scandal and disrepute pertaining to some love affair.

27. Unless there are strong benefics in the 7th house or aspecting it, if Mars be the lord of the 7th house, it is unfavourable for disputes. And the person would not be well-advised to go to a court of law in connection with marriage suit or divorce.

28. (a) Mars (representing the sexual urge in female) if afflicted in a female nativity shows non-fulfilment of such craving.

(b) If Mars be very weak and be in conjunction square or opposition to an elevated Saturn or (Saturn in first or the 7th house) the female may remain a spinster. See also for confirmation, whether barren signs are on the cusps of 5th and 7th houses.

Aphorisms of Mercury

Just as Mars rules Courage, Mercury has jurisdiction over discrimination, intellectual abilities, logic and speech. If Mercury is the deciding factor in marriage or love life then it attracts one to an intellectual or wise person. At times it leads to attraction (in the case of women) to persons who are eighteen to thirty years older. In the case of a male, Mercury in the 7th house (alone) causes physical or psychological impotency after forty years of life.

Mercury being the Messenger of the Gods to other planets. It also takes colour from other planets. It is also a planet which is treated as a 'Eunch' in Hindu Astrology. When associated with Venus, it makes one desirous of 'Perfection' and this is what one seeks in a life partner or a girl of his dreams. When conjoined with Mars, it makes one irritable, spontaneous in decisions, daring and one is prepared to take big risks in life. The mind is strengthened. When in configuration with Jupiter, one seeks a kindhearted, charitable, generous spouse; if in association with Saturn then the life partner is tolerant, helpful but in the end gets tired of the native's clandestine and scheming methods of approach. Mercury-Sun or Mercury-Moon are good aspects which bring in life a spouse from a high-class family, who is magnanimous, popular and dignified.

We now give the effects of Mercury:

1. Mercury in the 5th house if afflicted by Mars or Herschel: there is some scandal or ill repute pertaining to love affairs.

2. Mercury in the 7th house denotes much wordy warfare in the married life, and a marriage partner who would be too talkative, critical and argumentative. If Mercury occupies a good sign and is well aspected the partner's talks would be full of wit and wisdom. But if occupying a bad sign or ill aspected, the wife/husband would be garrulous and would mostly talk nonsense.

Generally speaking, Mercury denotes a clever wife/husband who may not always be relied upon if Mercury is afflicted.

3. Mercury in the 7th house in conjunction with or in sextile aspect, to Venus: the native is very fond of persons of young age and the native may marry or fall in love with a person much younger than himself.

4. If there is no planet in the 7th and Mercury is the lord of the 1st or 7th and in conjunction or sextile aspect to Venus and unaspected by any other planet, the same effect as in No. 3 above.

5. Mercury in 7th in conjunction with or afflicted by Mars gives the husband/wife who is quick-witted but sarcastic in speech and hotly argumentative.

6. Mercury in 7th in good aspect to Moon or Jupiter is a favourable indication in a male nativity.

7. Mercury in 7th in company with Sun would be favourable if the latter planet is strong and lord of a good house.

8. Mercury in 7th when in conjunction with a planet takes the attributes of that planet and denotes a partner signified by that other planet. This would be particularly so if that other planet is near the cusp of the 7th house or if Mercury be within orb of influence of that planet. (Also look to aspects it is receiving).

9. Mercury in 7th house if unaspected by any planet gives a husband/wife who is lean and thin, young and very talkative.

10. Mercury in 7th house may denote much correspondence or travelling in connection with matrimony. This would be

particularly so if the lord of the 3rd house is in the 7th or the lord of the 7th is in third or there is some aspect between the lords of the 3rd and 7th houses. If the aspect is a favourable one travelling or correspondence would result in success. But if the aspect be an evil one, it would be otherwise.

11. If Mercury in 7th is not conjoined with any planet, note carefully the aspects it forms and the sign it is in.

(a) If well-aspected by Jupiter the wife/husband would be good, clever, active and progressive.
(b) If Mercury is afflicted in the 7th house the conjugal life of the native may be full of bickerings and wrangling.
(c) If much afflicted and the lord of the 7th house be not strong it may give rise to legal trouble in connection with marriage.

12. When there is no planet in the 7th house and Mercury is the Ruler of the horoscope the native would be well advised to avoid litigation because unless well aspected by Jupiter such litigation, may result unfavourably for the native.

13. Mercury in the 8th house signifies worries pertaining to the financial affairs of the partner. It also denotes some quarrels in relation to getting money from husband/wife or their relations. This would be particularly so if Mercury is afflicted.

14. Mercury in 11th if in Cancer; the native may be attached to inferiors.

15. Mercury is a very volatile planet and easily absorbs the good or bad qualities of other planets in conjunction or in aspect with it. Its position *vis-a-vis* other planets is, therefore, very important.

16. Mercury is considered a eunuch and if this planet be in a female nativity in the seventh house unfortified by any benefic and the lord of the seventh is not strong, the native's husband may not be very virile.

Aphorisms of Jupiter

Jupiter is of utmost importance as it rules conjugal bliss in a woman's chart. If it is powerful then the husband will be endowed with long life and will surmount difficulties in life. If it is in a bad configuration with the Sun in a nativity then she will have a very good husband but the husband will not be wealthy. In Hindu Astrology when selecting an auspicious date for marriage, we avoid it if

(a) Jupiter is combust.
(b) If Jupiter, in transit is passing through the 8th house from the natal Moon (Birth—Rashi) in a girl's chart.

The main reason is that it affects the life span of the husband.

In matters of love and marriage, it indicates help or interference from religious people in the surrounding. The amount of help and support depends upon its strength in the horoscope.

Another factor which should be kept in view is that the placement of Jupiter in the 5th house may give sudden gains, success in love but it destroys happiness from sons (male children). What is intriguing is that in Sagittarius, which is its own sign. It only gives only daughters.

We now give the effects of Jupiter vis-à-vis love and marriage:

1. Jupiter is a benefic, and if in 5th house exerts benefic influence in relation to success and happiness in love affairs. There may also be gain from the opposite sex.

2. Jupiter in the 5th: one would prefer to love a person having a religious bent of mind and the native is more likely to fall in love with or be attached to a Jupiterean wife/husband.

3. Jupiter in the 5th house in a female nativity: one may be attached to or married to a person who has had a previous engagement or marriage. (Take into consideration the community and society of the native.)

4. Jupiter in 5th: if afflicted is not favourable for fruition of desires.

5. Jupiter in 7th house: wife/husband is robust in health, generous, broad-minded, good-natured and fond of good living.

6. Jupiter in 7th well aspected: the husband/wife is good and faithful and there is conjugal happiness; also, there may

be gain from marriage or partnership; in any case, financial affairs would improve after wedlock.

7. Jupiter in 7th house well aspected. There is social advantage after marriage, also pecuniary gains, likely from marriage/partnership.

8. Jupiter in 7th if weak denotes probability of marriage to one who has been previously engaged to someone else or married.

9. Jupiter in 7th: if well aspected by luminaries and unafflicted by others: good indication for happy married life. The partner may be religiously inclined.

10. Jupiter in 7th in Virgo. Nullifies in great measure the good effects described before. If afflicted, may produce positively evil effects.*

11. Jupiter in 7th if conjoined with or afflicted by malefics: the wife/husband is extravagant, conceited, fond of pomp and show and of a boasting nature.

12. Jupiter in 7th if conjoined with, in square or opposition to Saturn. If the aspect be exact and latter planet strong and elevated, there is some impediment or delay in marriage.

13. Jupiter in 7th: if afflicted by Sun, Moon and Saturn, marriage may be denied.

14. Jupiter in 7th: gain by marriage or partnership, particularly so if Jupiter be strong and no other planet be there and Jupiter be the ruling planet.

15. Jupiter in 8th: indicates gain from husband/wife (in those communities where dowry is in vogue).

16. Jupiter strong and unafflicted in 8th is good for monetary gain through wife/husband. Financial affairs improve after marriage.

17. Jupiter in 9th house denotes financial benefit from relatives by marriage wife/husband's brother, etc.

18. Jupiter in 11th if unafflicted by other planets and forming a good aspect with Saturn may bring a lasting attachment, particularly so if Saturn be in the 1st or 7th house.

---

* This is the view of one of the old astrologers. I do not concur.

19. Jupiter in 12th house: the native may have dual love affairs simultaneously or one after the other.

20. If Jupiter be lord of 7th house and in parallel or good aspect with Saturn, there would be gain by marriage.

21. If there is no planet in the 7th house and Jupiter is the ruler of the horoscope, it indicates success through partnership, legal affairs and gain thereby.

Aphorisms of Venus

In this chapter the effect of Venus in various situations has been mentioned. What part Mars and Sun play in a female horoscope, similar is the function of Moon and Venus in a male chart. Venus confers charm of looks, expressions, harmony, an amiable temperament as well as an elegant wife, paramour and pleasures of bed. One who has an unafflicted Venus has affluence and ability to enjoy it.

In Hindu Astrology, Venus is called "Shukra" which is synonym with semen. A weak Venus causes weakness so a man is not able to have children. An afflicted or weak Venus in a female chart will make her not so Pleasing to the eyes due to her unkempt appearance and the habit of dressing shabbily. Venus also has jurisdiction over children. No marriages in India are performed when Venus is combust. It is also because a marriage undertaken at this time destroys the family life. A strong Venus in a male nativity gives popularity with the women and if Uranus is in good aspects then with young girls (age disparity exists). However, an afflicted Venus brings in life nuisances, loss of money due to lovers and children. At times it draws some people to excessive drinks and drugs.

We now give the effect of Venus:

1. Venus is the most important planet for Judgement of marriage and success or otherwise in love affairs.

2. The position by house and sign, strength of Venus as well as conjunction or aspect of other planets to it are very important both in male and female nativities. Particularly so, in male nativity.

3. Venus has the same importance in a male nativity as Mars in a female nativity.

Venus in Different Signs

4. Venus in Aries: The native has much lust and carnal desires. He is rather impulsive in matters of sex and may commit acts which may not be quite discreet.

5. Venus in Taurus makes the native fond of opposite sex and is much liked by them. Venus in Cancer inclines to wine and women.

6. Venus in Scorpio inclines to wine and women particularly of the lower rank.

7. Venus in Capricorn: one is too much inclined to the company of the opposite sex and thereby loses in health and spoils the changes of worldly success.

8. Venus in Gemini, Sagittarius and Pisces: there may be more than one marriage, in any case more than one love affair.

Venus in Different Houses

9. Venus in the 1st house is good particularly in Taurus, Gemini, Libra, Aquarius and Pisces.

10. Venus in the 1st house if in Aries, Scorpio or Capricorn is not good. Venus in the 1st house if in Scorpio makes one inclined to the company of women of low status or loose morals particularly so, if afflicted by Mars. One may be fond of drinks and there is no refinement in the matter of gratification of sex. There is greater emphasis on physical craving.

11. Venus in the 2nd house is good for money and gain from or through women but if weak and afflicted, the native would squander money on wine and women. He would be a pleasure-seeker seeking company of wanton women.

12. Venus in the 5th house: the native is too much given to female company. In any case, he has abundant desires of the heart; their fulfilment or otherwise depending upon the aspect Venus receives. There is too much desire for love affairs, amusements, gaiety and society. Excessive indulgence injures health.

13. Venus in the 5th house:

(a) If free from affliction of any planet and strong denotes successful termination of one's love affairs.
(b) If well aspected by Sun in a female nativity and by Moon in a male nativity love affairs would be successful. If, however, Venus is afflicted there may be much hindrance and obstacles in the path of love.
(c) If afflicted, by Mars, leads to excessive emotional development which remains ungratified.
(d) If in conjunction square or opposition to Saturn leads to disappointment in the affairs of the heart; if heavily afflicted there would be much sorrow and lasting unhappiness. To determine the depth of sorrow and unhappiness, make sure that evil influence is not mitigated by any benefic aspect. If Venus be in parallel to Saturn, then also, there is disappointment.
(e) If afflicted by Herschel, love affairs are sudden but there is ultimate frustration; but if Herschel be in trine or sextile there is fruition.
(f) If afflicted by Neptune leads to strange love affairs but there is generally disillusionment coming in their wake.

14. Venus in the 7th house: the native is inclined to marry early but if Venus be in Scorpio or Capricorn he may form improper connections at an early age.

15. Venus in 7th the house promises a happy marriage. The partner would be attractive, pleasing and fond of good living.

16. Venus in 7th house well aspected: success socially and financially comes after marriage. Particularly so, if well aspected by Jupiter from 11th house. If Jupiter be in the 9th, wife's relations may help; if in third there may be gain by one's own relations, travelling or short-writing, after marriage.

17. Venus in the 7th house if well aspected by Moon and Jupiter in a male nativity or by Sun and Jupiter in a female nativity, the benefic influence described in 16 above is augmented.

18. Venus strong in the 7th house and well-aspected by benefics, improves the whole career of the native due to the benefic influence of the partner and one's own favourable psychological improvement.

19. Venus in the 7th house strong and in a good sign: gives a partner who is refined and of good taste. She/he would be pleasing and presentable but may be fickle.

20. Venus in the 7th house if unafflicted by any malefic, gives a neat and artistic wife who adorns and beautifies the house; if afflicted by benefics she would be extravagant; if afflicted by malefics she may be fickle in the affairs of the heart. The native himself may be fickle in matters of the heart.

21. Venus in the 7th house even in sextile or trine with Mars, Saturn, Herschel or Neptune; good effects are spoiled.

22. Venus in the 7th house if seriously afflicted: there would be much unhappiness also delay and hindrance in marriage.

23. Venus in 7th house if afflicted by luminaries or malefics, denotes a husband/wife who has lapses in morals, is easy-going and inclined to self-indulgence and of weak character.

24. Venus in the 7th house if seriously afflicted by Mars particularly if Mars be elevated, gives a wife who would be licentious. This evil effect may be modified if there be conjunction, or trine aspect of Jupiter.

25. Venus in the 7th house if afflicted by Saturn particularly if the latter planet be elevated: a wife who is slovenly, weak and colourless in character. This would be particularly so if Venus be in Scorpio or in either of the signs owned by Saturn.

26. Venus in the 7th house if afflicted by Herschel particularly if Herschel be elevated: there will be sudden attraction and much romance coming to the fore in the life of the native, but the outcome would not be happy. There would be sudden breaks and the intimacy developed would not lead to the marriage altar. If there be affliction by Mars and Saturn also, such marriage brought about by an unexpected romantic affair may break up and leave a trail of sorrow behind.

27. If Venus in the 7th house be afflicted by Neptune particularly if the latter planet be elevated, the native would

have a tendency to have a secret marriage or elopement which may end in disillusionment and frustration.

28. Venus in 8th house, if strong brings about gain by marriage or partnership or after marriage.

29. Venus in 8th house, if well aspected: the native progresses well after marriage. There is considerable improvement in financial affairs. To what extent it would show good effect can be gauged by looking to the strength of Venus and the strength of the aspecting planet.

30. Venus in the 9th house: there may be benefit from relatives through marriage, particularly from female relations of husband/wife.

31. If Venus be in the 10th house—particularly near about the meridian cusp, the native would marry well in life, *i.e.*, his wife would come from a high/higher family. This would be particularly so, if the lord of the 7th house is also elevated and stronger than the lord of the 1st house.

32. If Venus is in the 10th house, the native is much esteemed and honoured, specially among females. Unless Venus be debilitated or in Scorpio wife comes from a higher family.

33. Venus in the 10th house, if strong and well aspected shows gain through wife or women.

34. Venus in the 10th house, if afflicted shows affections to be selfish.

35. Venus in the 11th house if in good aspect—

(a) With Sun brings gain and prosperity from women or through articles patronised by women—articles of fashion, silk, etc.

(b) With Moon the person is fond of good society and company of women who may not be very young. It leads to pleasure and amusement and the native is not wanting in a number of woman friends.

(c) If applying to Mars, the attraction to friends of the opposite sex is more sensuous that arising out of deep love. If good aspects are formed between the two planets there would, be generally speaking, fruition of desires, otherwise frustration.

(d) Applying to Jupiter there is much pleasure and even gain from women.

(e) If applying to Saturn causes fatalistic attachments and if afflicted would lead to sadness and sorrow.

(f) If applying to Herschel, love affairs and romances come with unexpected suddenness. There is inexplicable fascination—though this may not be lasting.

(g) If applying to Neptune there would be remarkable love affairs and attachment of "Free love" type, to one with whom there may be much disparity in age or dissimilarity in community or status. If the aspect is unfavourable, disillusionment would follow.

36. Venus in the 12th house leads to secret love affairs and romances. These will become known if Venus is afflicted by Mars. The native would also spend very heavily on women.

37. Venus in the 12th house leads to marriage or sex indulgence comparatively early in life but the native would have a number of love affairs after marriage also and would get entangled with the opposite sex. (As to age at which the native would marry, look to other indications also and to the Directions favouring matrimony.)

38. Venus in the 12th house if seriously afflicted by Saturn, particularly if Saturn be elevated, would lead to disagreement. If other indications confirm there may be divorce or separation from wife due to further love affair of the native.

39. Venus in the 12th house in Aries, Cancer, or Capricorn: there are several love affairs.

40. Venus in the 12th house well aspected, the native would do much for those he loves.

Aspects of Venus

41. Venus in conjunction or any aspect to Sun: the native is fond of company particularly those of females. If Venus be in

the 2nd, 5th, 7th or 12th house the native is likely to spend much in female company and pleasure, wasting his time and fortune.

42. Venus in conjunction or good aspect to Jupiter: gain by marriage, also inclines to chastity particularly in female nativity.

43. Venus afflicted by Jupiter: squandering of money over fineries, jewels, dress and females. This would particularly be so if both planets are weak and either of them in the 12th or the 2nd house.

44. Venus afflicted by Saturn: marriage would be full of problems. If there is severe affliction and other indications confirm, there may be no marriage or marriage may be delayed. This would be so if Moon in a male nativity or Sun in a female nativity is also afflicted and Saturn is strong and elevated. In the Judgement of the above, Venus and Moon are to be given importance in a male nativity and Sun and Mars in a female nativity.

45. If Venus is afflicted by a weak Saturn, there would be much trouble and unhappiness and sorrow coming out of marriage or love affair.

46. Strong Venus afflicted by weak Saturn: there would be trouble in courtship and the native may have a series of handicaps and hindrances or disappointment may result. Grief through female. But if Venus is fortified with the benefic aspect of strong Jupiter, ultimate triumph.

47. Weak Venus severly afflicted by weak Saturn shows depraved tastes. The native may be addicted to secret unnatural practices.

48. Venus in good aspect to Saturn: if both strong, shows sincerity of attachment. The family life would be characterised by a sense of security and service and there would be no unnecessary effervescence of calf-love.

49. Venus in good aspect to Saturn in a female horoscope shows that the native would be careful, sincere, chaste, thrifty and thoughtful.

50. All aspects between Venus and Herschel bring about

sudden attachments under romantic circumstances. There is a great inclination for illicit connection, particularly so in male nativities.

(a) If the aspects are good, such occasions would be more and no scandals or evil results may emanate.
(b) But if there is affliction between the two, it leads to unsuccessful romances—broken engagements. There is much disappointment ridicule or scandal.

51. Weak Venus in evil aspect to Herschel: much trouble and jealousy in courtship. In female nativities it is indicative of the female's dislike to be fastened up with bonds of matrimony yet secretly forming immoral attachments. In male nativities, it is indicative of the man wasting his substance over worthless women.

52. Venus in conjunction or parallel with Herschel: one is very fond of women and pleasure. The native is much given to the company of young females and often forms illicit connection with them even after his marriage.

53. Venus aspected or afflicted by Herschel:

(a) In a male nativity, the subject forms illicit connections with young and unmarried women.
(b) In a female nativity, the subject forms illicit connections with young unmarried men.
(c) If there is affliction by Mars or square or opposition of Saturn, the scandal would be known.
(d) If there be trine or sextile aspect of Saturn, there would be much prudence and care in carrying on the affair in a secret manner and there would be no scandal.
(e) If there is benefic aspect of Jupiter, the affair would not be known and there would be no scandal.

54. Strong Venus in good aspect to Herschel gives easy success in gaining over the ears of the opposite sex, by whom one is much liked.

55. Venus in good aspect 1o Neptune makes the native very susceptible to the admiration of the opposite sex.

56. Venus afflicted by Neptune leads to sex perversions or peculiar sex vices.

57. Strong Venus in good aspect to Neptune: the native falls easy prey to the beauty of the female sex and there may be several love affairs even after marriage.

58. Weak Venus severely afflicted by Neptune: there may be fickleness in the affairs of the heart and much indiscretion in love or marriage. There is liability that the marriage may prove unenduring and there may be even scandal. There may be some element of fraud or deception on the part of the marriage partner or on one's part, and there may be separation of disillusionment.

59. When there is no planet in the 7th house and Venus is the ruler in a horoscope, it is favourable for partnership. But if much afflicted, there would be disappointment.

Aphorisms of Saturn

Saturn is endowed with full directional strength of one out of one in the 7th house (of marriage). It brings in life a spouse who is hard working and faithful. However, in the 7th house it also causes—delays due to interference from elderly people or wrong advise of people who wants to create problems on account of jealousy. After marriage the in-laws cause troubles. In the 1st, 10th, and even in the 5th,—Saturn is not good as it creates delays and at times lead to disappointments in life and marriage. The passage of love is not smooth.

The position of the Saturn in the 8th, house is real bad. It also causes acute differences or break in marriage when the first child is eight years of age.

In fact Saturn is called the planet of sorrow and it does so to make one stronger or to draw one towards 'Divine love'. Saturn in any aspect with Venus draws one towards older people and when one is old then towards younger people (age disparity exists in love and marriage). Saturn is the planet of higher wisdom, of philosophy and when very strong in a horoscope then it denies marriage or permanent relationship.

We now give the various aphorisms of Saturn:

1. Aversion in marriage is caused when Saturn is *prominent or dominant* in a horoscope. Saturn engenders excessive caution and this undue restraint or lack of enterprise causes extreme diffidence in matters of marriage/love overtures.

2. Saturn if dominant would delay or deny marriage particularly if it afflicts, by square or opposition:

(a) Venus in a male horoscope.
(b) Mars in a female horoscope.

Saturn in Different Houses

3. Saturn in the 1st, 5th or 7th houses: the native whether male or female seldom leads a chaste life. If well aspected by Jupiter or there be benefics in the 4th or 9th house, judge otherwise.

4. Saturn in the 5th house: the native exercises checks over his desires. Due to this restraint over emotions, there is obstruction in love affair. It is indicative of delays and disappointments in the fruition of heart's desires.

5. Saturn in the 5th house: if forming any good aspects to Moon or Venus in a male nativity or Sun and Mars in a female nativity, one may be attached to persons older than oneself. But if Saturn be severely afflicted there may be sorrow or disappointment from the loved one. If other indications confirm, the sorrow may be the outcome of death of the loved one.

6. Saturn in the 5th house if seriously afflicted by Mars or Venus inclines to sensuousness. The native may be addicted to unnatural practices for the gratification of his lust.

7. Saturn in the 7th house: unless it be the lord of the 1st house, it confers little conjugal happiness. If well aspected and other indications in the horoscope point to conjugal happiness, the evil influence would be modified in great measure, but still minor troubles would continue.

8. Saturn in the 7th house: if the planet is afflicted and there are no relieving benefic aspects, marriage would be unfortunate and disastrous.

9. Saturn in the 7th house if well aspected, will give a partner who is thoughtful, methodical, industrious and of thribty disposition. The husband/wife of the native would, however, be a little too exacting and cold and frigid.

10. Saturn in the 7th house in a female nativity frequently indicates marriage to a widower/or person disproportionately elder in age. This would be particularly so, if Mars is in sextile or trine to it.

11. Saturn in the 7th house: if well-aspected by Moon in a male nativity or Sun in a female nativity indicates that despite any roughness or dissatisfaction in matrimonial state, there would be no divorce or separation.

12. Saturn in the 7th house if strong, shows a faithful partner (marriage to a comparatively) grown-up and sober person. The partner would not be demonstrative in affection but serious and thoughtful, hardworking and prudent. If Saturn is not strong and has no aspects of luminaries or of Venus or Jupiter, she/he would be cold and frigid but stable.

13. Saturn in the 7th house conjoined with Moon—if much afflicted: married happiness would be spoiled, particularly so in a male nativity.

14. Saturn in the 7th house conjoined with Sun if much afflicted married happiness would be spoiled, particularly so in a female nativity.

15. Saturn in the 7th house: if strong and in good aspect to Moon in a male nativity: the marriage will continue and not disrupt.

16. Saturn in the 7th house: if strong and in good aspect to Sun in a female nativity: the marriage will continue and not disrupt.

17. Saturn in the 7th house strong and well aspected shows a partner who is prudent, and persevering.

18. Saturn in the 7th house if strong and well-aspected (particularly by Jupiter), husband or wife will possess money or property and marriage may be to a widow (where custom allows it) or to a widower.

19. Saturn in the 7th house if badly aspected or afflicted by

luminaries shows a partner who is cold, reserved, cruel, avaricious and mean-minded. This will be particularly so if there is evil aspect of other planets and no benefic aspect to improve Saturn's influence.

20. Saturn in the 7th house strong and in good aspect to Jupiter. Marriage or partnership may be a source of gain/ accumulation of money: or there may be accumulation of money after marriage.

21. Saturn in the 7th house much afflicted indicates sorrow and grief in married life. Marriage may be delayed or the benefits of marriage may be spoiled by death, divorce or separation. If none of these happens, the married life becomes a shell of thorns either due to illness, loose morals or ill temper of wife.

22. Saturn in the 7th house weak and unaspected by any benefic gives a wife who is cold and melancholy. It is seldom that the marriage turns out to be happy. If Saturn be in a common sign, there may be more than one marriage. Look for other indications also.

23. Saturn in the 7th house in conjunction with or bad aspect to Herschel is very unfortunate for married happiness.

24. Saturn in the 7th house is an unfortunate position for chastity. This would be particularly so if there be no benefic aspect of Jupiter.

25. Saturn in the 8th house is not a good position for gain by marriage partner or through wife. There is little accumulation of money till after 36th year of life.

26. Saturn in the 9th house : there may be trouble or losses through, relations by marriage. Relations—wife/husband's brothers and sisters would not be congenial.

27. Saturn in the 11th house is not a good influence for conjugal happiness. But, if well aspected, one may have in one's intimate circle of friends—persons older than oneself.

28. Saturn in the 12th house if afflicted by Sun or Moon leads to sorrow due to the death of a beloved one. One lives separated, isolated and generally cut off for some period or other in one's life.

29. If Saturn be the Ruler or lord of the rising sign and benefics form good aspect with Saturn, there may be gain by marriage.

30. If Saturn be the Ruler (or lord of the rising sign) and in bad aspect with Neptune, it may lead to scandal or ill repute.

Aphorisms of Herschel

The influence of Herschel (or Uranus) is very strong. In the Western Astrology, it is supposed to rule the sign 'Aquarius' which so far has been ascribed to Saturn. It is so because, Uranus is a planet which indicates one who is a genius, unrestricted, sort of eccentric and whose mind suddenly goes to a tangent. An 'Iconoclast' is what a Uranian person is. He chooses his own path, his own way to express. In the matters of love, Uranus brings a changeable disposition. In the 7th house it gives an eccentric spouse or one who passes through nervous disorders. Overall speaking, Herschel is a benefic planet except that it causes various changes in emotional set-ups, particularly when afflicted. The result of Uranus is given below:

1. Herschel in the 1st, 5th or 7th house makes one very impetuous in matters of sex relations and the native is inclined to have clandestine affairs in the most unexpected fashion. If aspected by strong benefics or benefics be in the 4th or 9th house, the inclinations would be modified, otherwise there is a liability to have many affairs.
2. Herschel in the 5th house: there is much romanticism, in one's make-up. Love affairs are sudden and of the unconventional type.
3. Herschel in the 5th house, if in very close aspect to Venus gives homosexual tendencies.
4. Herschel in the 5th house, if in trine or sextile to luminaries gives secret love affairs. It inclines to idealism rather than inconstancy.
5. Herschel in the 5th house trine or sextile to Mercury may lead to much correspondence with the beloved, particularly during courtship.

6. Herschel in the 5th house, if afflicted, brings domestic troubles; the native has a markedly flirtatious tendency. There is inconstancy and there would be several irregular unions or desire for such affairs, The cumulative effect of all this is that there is trouble and the domestic atmosphere is full of unhappiness.

7. Herschel in the 5th house if well aspected, inclines the native to have a number of irregular unions and his efforts are crowned with success. There is a tendency in him to be a pleasure-seeker.

8. Herschel in the 5th house, due to the characteristics of this planet described above, is an unfortunate position in a female nativity. There may be irregular unions or other indiscretions leading to disgrace and ill repute particularly:

(a) If Cancer or Pisces be the rising sign.
(b) Herschel be afflicted and there be no benefic aspects of good planets.

Herschel in the 7th House

9. Herschel in the 7th house threatens a most unhappy marriage. The wife/husband would be eccentric and not inclined to be faithful in the married state. There may even be separation.

10. Herschel in the 7th house confers little married happiness; if well aspected by strong benefics, the evil effect may be modified to some extent. But minor troubles would still continue.

11. If Herschel is in 7th house and if there is affliction by weak malefics and no benefic aspects, marriage would be unhappy and unfortunate and only evil would come of it.

12. Herschel in the 7th house if in good aspect with Moon in a male nativity, the marriage would not break up, though serene married happiness would be denied.

13. Herschel in the 7th house forming good aspect with Sun, in a female nativity: the same effect as described above.

14. Herschel in the 7th house if in bad aspect with Sun and Moon denotes an insubordinate and independent spirit. The

native would be headstrong, unruly, and one who may fall in love in the most unexpected quarters and without thought. The native may not prove reliable as husband/wife.

15. Herschel in the 7th house, if in good aspect to Moon in a male nativity and to Sun in a female nativity is not so bad (vide 12 and 13 above). The evil may be modified further if Herschel has benefic aspect from benefic planets or if Jupiter is angular.

16. Herschel in the 7th house denotes flirtatious tendencies, hasty, impulsive nature and romantic attachments, particularly so, if in close aspect to Mars or Venus.

17. Herschel in the 7th house if in close conjunction, square, or opposition to luminaries; there are unexpected developments in the matrimonial sphere. If the aspect be with the Sun the native himself takes the initiative. If the aspect be with the Moon it is the other party which takes the initiative and the native falls in line with the wishes of the other party.

18. Herschel in the 7th house if very well aspected by strong benefics: one may marry a person whose eccentricity may well amount to genius. The partner may be quite original in ideas and peculiar in tastes. She/he may not be of loose morals.

19. Herschel in the 7th house: a very romantic marriage, particularly if Venus, Mars or luminaries be in the 5th.

20. Herschel in the 7th house much afflicted: the marriage partner may be instrumental in causing loss of reputation or money. There may be much unhappiness in matrimonial life leading to separation.

Herschel in others' Houses

21. Herschel in 8th : not a benefic influence for gain or wealth through marriage but if beneficially aspected, particularly by a strong Jupiter there may be sudden gain to or through marriage partner.

22. Herschel in 9th: not a happy influence for harmonious relationship with relations by marriage.

23. Herschel in 11th: brings about sudden friendships in most unexpected quarters. If in aspect to a planet in the 7th or

with the lord of the 7th house, this friendship may well lead to marriage.

24. When there is no planet in the 7th house and Herschel is the Ruler in a horoscope: not a very happy influence for marriage or partnership and trouble through opponents and strangers is indicated. If there is matrimonial trouble, the native is advised not to go to a court of law. He is generally advised not to enter into any partnership agreement.

Aphorisms of Neptune

Neptune is a planet which endows one with dreams-something vague, something undefined. According to Western Astrology most drug addicts come under it. It leads to living together without binding one into bonds.In the 7th house Neptune gives vague—undefined relationships. In the 5th house children are born out of wedlock or a person becomes a foster father (or mother). It does give many children. If it is afflicted in the 5th house then a person loses its children due to theft at an early age. When very strong it leads one to Divine love and renunciation.

When Neptune in transit passes over a planet then it creates unlimited dreams of realization but ultimately there is no concrete gains. This is very much true when Neptune is transiting over Venus in a chart and the native will fall in love with the girl next door due to fancied reciprocation.

We now give below the effects of Neptune:

1. Neptune in the 5th house gives strange propensities in matters of sex behaviour. There is a tendency to indulge in 'free' and platonic relationships, not frequently free from evils pertaining to such matters.

2. Neptune in the 5th house well aspected: the native is inlined to have illicit connections and has extraordinary experiences. His desires are nebulous, yet there is fruition in concrete shape.

3. Neptune in the 5th house afflicted therein: there is much sensuousness and animal tendencies preponderate.

4. Neptune in the 7th house is not a very happy position for love or a marriage.

5. Neptune in the 7th house inclines to romantic, out of the wedlock alliances with the opposite sex which do not prove very stable.

6. Neptune in the 7th house if afflicted by Sun or Mars in a female nativity and Moon or Venus in a male nativity: there are love affairs which may not lead to marriage. There is a tendency to secret love deals and the native may be betrayed by the beloved or a hoax may be played upon the native in matters of love. The native may elope and his/her prestige would be lowered. The effect would be worse if Neptune is afflicted by Herschel or Saturn as well.

7. Neptune in the 7th house leads to magnetic attraction to persons of the opposite sex but if Neptune is afflicted, the attraction terminates in disillusionment and disappointment. If Neptune is well aspected, the disillusionment proves a blessing in disguise to the native.

8. Neptune in the 7th house if much afflicted and other indications also do not point to married happiness, the native would be well advised not to marry.

9. When there is no planet in the 7th house and Neptune is the Ruling planet, it may lead to strange relationships in the married state. There may be clandestine attachments, seduction or platonic unions. If afflicted, many handicaps would have to be faced. There may be delay in marriage or other complications may arise.

10. Neptune in the 8th house is not a happy influence for gain by matrimony.

11. Neptune in the 11th house if afflicted by planets by square or opposition or in conjunction with malefics, and the planet afflicting is a significator, there may be some trick or deception played upon the native by seeming friends or loved ones.

CHAPTER 4

MUTUAL HARMONY

When we match horoscopes for love and marriage, we find that in one case the configuration is excellent whereas in the second case, it is not so. Besides, what is true of the type of person who will come in life due to an indication in a horoscope and so one will link with such a person but in spite of this they may not have a harmonious relationship. This is because, in the second chart, the type of person indicated may not be the first person. This is the reason why so many marriages or love relationships break. There are other factors as well, which may cause breakups in the modern societies:

(a) Economic independence of women which make the male ego suffer.
(b) Both parties are so busy in their professional lives that the time for mutual relationship is curtailed.
(c) Working women has always to meet the challenges of amorous disposition of thier colleagues and it is easier to fall in love or feel affinity towards the one you spend more time with.
(d) Two people have harmonious love life but a third party enters whose horoscope indicates better harmony with either party.
(e) Due to day to day stress in life, the relationship between a couple becomes more like a brother-sister relationships.

We should keep in mind that separations, breakups etc.

depend upon the background, the culture and the society to which we belong.

We now proceed to give some principles of mutual harmony between two horoscopes:

1. So far, in this part have been given aphorisms which are to be applied to any one nativity (male's or female's) alone. Here are being given those astrological aphorisms which deal with mutual harmony between couples or lovers, *i.e.*, relative positions in the *two* horoscopes (positions of planets in one horoscope *vis-a-vis* the other) which determine mutual attraction, harmony and adaptability between two persons of the opposite sex. It is by Judgement of these that one can determine whether there would be attraction between two persons (of opposite sex) and if they are married, whether they would be happy and if the union would be fruitful.

For example, milk may mix well with honey but would curdle at once if mixed with lemon juice, or say milk and water would mix well but not water and oil.

2. If the ascending signs of husband and wife be in the same triplicity* it is good and conducive to harmony.

3. If the signs ascending are in square or 6th or 8th from each other, there is no harmony.

4. If partner's ascending sign is one which is on the cusp of the eleventh house in the other horoscope, it contributes to harmony.

5. If the ascendant of one is on the 10th house cusp or (M.C.) of another, the former tries to dominate and rule the other.

6. The Ruling planets in two horoscopes, if in good aspect: bring harmony; if the planets are benefics in both the horoscopes and if they are in conjunction, it is good, but if they are malefics and in conjunction it is bad. (Two planets in two horoscopes

* Aries, Leo and Sagittarius are in one triplicity. Taurus, Virgo, and Capricorn in another. Gemini, Libra and Aquarius are in one triplicity. Remaining Signs are in yet another triplicity.

are said to be in conjunction when their longitudes are the same). Some allowance may be made for "orbs".

7. Ascendant in one horoscope over the position of Saturn, Herschel or Neptune in the other horoscope shows disagreement. The two will not pull together well.

8. The lord of rising sign in one horoscope if located in the eleventh in the other horoscope, it is good for harmony.

9. Lord of the 7th house in one horoscope in good aspect to lords of ascendant and seventh houses in the other horoscope—is conducive to harmony. If these be benefics their conjunction is also good. If these be malefics or either be malefic, the conjunction is evil.

10. If the lord of the 7th house in one is in square or opposition to the lords of the ascendant or the 7th house in the other, it is not conducive to harmony.

11. If Sun in one horoscope has the same longitude as Moon or the rising sign in the other horoscope, it is conducive to mutual attraction and harmony.

12. If Sun in the male's nativity has the same longitude as Moon in the female nativity it is an indication of mutual attraction and congeniality.

13. If Sun in a female nativity has the same longitude as the Mars in a male nativity there will be strong attraction between the male and the female.

14. If Moon in one horoscope has the same longitude (same sign, same degree or near about) as the rising sign or Sun in the other horoscope, it is conducive to harmony.

15. Luminaries in the two horoscopes constitute strong points of sympathy, so Sun in one, attracts Moon in the other.

16. Either of the luminaries in or over the ascendant in the other is conducive to harmony:

(a) Sun in one, in good aspect to ascendant or Moon in the other is a good feature.

(b) Moon in one, in good aspect or conjunction with ascendant or Sun in the other exercises similar influence.

17. The following are also good:

(a) Sun in one in good aspect to Sun in another.
(b) Moon in one in good aspect to Moon in another.

18. Sun in one nativity in square or opposition to Sun in another shows that parties will not pull together well.

19. Sun in one nativity in square or opposition to Moon in another shows want of harmony.

20. Moon in one nativity in square or quadrature to Moon in the other shows that there would be mental conflict or different ways of thinking.

21. Sun in one horoscope over any of the following planets in the other is not good:

Saturn, or Herschel, or Neptune.

If Sun's longitude in one nativity coincides with the longitudes of any of the three planets in the other nativity there would be trouble, disharmony and the consequences would not be happy.

22. Moon in one nativity having the same longitude as Saturn, Herschel or Neptune in the other shows quarrel and trouble in married life.

23. If in a male nativity Moon forms an adverse aspect with any planet, it is not advisable to marry a woman having the attributes of such planet.

For example, (i) Moon in the male nativity applies to a quadrature of Saturn then it would not be advisable to marry a Saturnine woman, and (ii) If Moon applies to opposition of Venus in a male nativity the male should not marry a Venusian woman.

24. If in a female nativity Sun applies to an adverse aspect of any planet, she should not marry a male described by such planet.

Example. Suppose in a female nativity Sun is in 12° Pisces and Mars is in 15° Gemini, here Sun is applying to a square aspect of Mars. The female should, therefore, not marry a male described by Mars *i.e.,* a man in the army or military service or even if not in military service, one who may be martial in appearance and attributes.

25. Sun in one horoscope having the same longitude as Venus in the other shows that the male and the female would be able to afford each other much pleasure and enjoyment by their company.

26. If Sun in one horoscope is in square conjunction or opposition to malefics in the other (except Mars) there would be dispute and discord.

27. If the longitude of Sun in one horoscope is the same as the longitude of Saturn in the other, it would be a disharmonising factor. But the person who has such Saturn would benefit from the other person.

28. Luminaries in the two horoscopes, if in parallel, are conducive to harmony.

29. Moon in one nativity having the same longitude as Venus in the other shows mutual pleasure and sympathy.

30. Moon in one nativity having the same longitude as Mercury in the other shows mental affinity.

31. If Moon's longitude in one nativity is the same or '85° to 95°' or '175° to 185°' from any of the malefics in the other, this would lead to dispute and disagreement.

32. If the longitudes of Mars in one nativity is the same as the longitude of Venus in the other, it would lead to mutual attraction, though this may not endure. The attraction would be stronger if the longitude of Mars in the female nativity coincides with the longitude of Venus in the male nativity.

33. If the lords of the 1st or 7th house are seriously afflicted by any malefics in a nativity such a person should not marry a person having the appearance or attributes of the afflicting planet. (See examples under 23 and 24 above).

34. If Mars in a female nativity has the same longitude as the ascendant in a male nativity there would be attraction. There would be similar effect though in lesser measure if longitude of the Mars in the female nativity is about 60° or 120° from the rising degree—ascendant) in the male nativity.

35. If Mars in the female nativity has the same degree of declination as Venus in the male nativity there would be attraction.

36. Mars in one nativity having the same degree (longitude) as Saturn in the other is a sure indication of much quarrelling in married life.

37. Mars in one attracts Venus in the other—a martial man may be attracted to a Venusian lady and *vice versa*.

38. If the longitude of Mars in one horoscope is the same or near about the longitude of Neptune in other horoscope there would be attachment in the beginning but this would lead to separation after much disillusionment, if there are malefic aspects of other planets to such Mars and Neptune.

39. Mars and Venus represent in the female and the male strong points of sex attraction:

(a) If Mars in the female nativity is in conjunction or good aspect to Venus in another, there would be harmony and pleasure; similar result would follow it Mars in the male nativity is in similar aspect with Venus in the female nativity, but in lesser measure.

(b) If they be in square or opposition (Mars in one to Venus in another) there would not be much harmony.

40. Jupiter in one nativity having the same longitude as Saturn in the other leads to better understanding sympathy and appreciation of the other.

41. Jupiter in one attracts the Saturn in the other. Example: a Jupiterian male may be attracted to a Saturnine female or a Saturnine male may be attracted to a Jupiterian female.

42. Jupiter in one having the same longitude as Venus in the other is good for social company.

43. If the Venus in a male nativity has the same longitude as the rising degree (ascendant) in a female nativity there would be mutual attraction. Judge similarly though in a lesser measure if the Venus in the male nativity forms a sextile or trine aspect with ascendant in the female nativity.

44. Venus in one having the same longitude as Saturn in the other would strike a sympathetic chord in each other's heart. The two may share some sorrow together. (Saturn is the planet of sorrow, privation, poverty and suffering) and

therefore brings bond of sympathy by striking the chord of such emotions.

45. If the Venus in one horoscope has the same longitude as Herschel in the other, there would be spontaneous attachment at first sight but such violent attachments seldom last unless there are other helpful configurations in the two horoscopes.

46. If the longitude of Saturn in one horoscope is the same or near about the longitude on the meridian cusp in the other, such a marriage would lead to trouble, fall in position and prestige. This would be particularly so, if the female's Saturn is over the M.C. of the male.

If the M.C. degree is one falling in Capricorn or Aquarius the result would not be so bad.

47. Saturn in one horoscope over or in square opposition, or parallel to luminaries in the other is unfavourable.

48. Herschel in one horoscope over M.C. in another brings sudden estrangement which may lead to much bitterness.

49. Neptune in one horoscope having the same longitude as M.C. in the other shows trouble and complications in married life particularly in the social sphere.

50. Benefics in one horoscope over the ascendant or luminaries in the other horoscope are favourable.

51. Conjunctions or good aspects between benefics in the two horoscopes lead to lasting sympathy and friendship.

52. Squares and oppositions between planets in the two horoscopes lead to disharmony and discord. This would be particularly so if the affliction is between malefics in one with the malefics in the other.

53. There would be mental affinity and era of friendship when the Ruler of one transits the ascendant of the other or the planets described as being harmonious would transit vulnerable points) (longitudes of Venus, Mars, ascendant or luminaries) in the other.

54. Periods of discord are those when the afflicting planets or those described as bringing about disharmony transit vulnerable points in the other. For example, Mars in one, if Ruler, transiting the Saturn in the other horoscope.

55. Results of 53 and 54 above should be predicted only when such inferences can be drawn from the two nativities.

For 'Timing of Events' please refer to subsequent Chapter 5.

CHAPTER 5

TIMING OF EVENTS

The timing of events is most important. Seeds planted during the season at a favourable time will grow into beautiful trees and bear flowers and fruits. The same is true of associations and marriage. We come across a person in a party or at the airport or it may be a chance meeting due to certain directions or Transit of Planets. It may also be due to the radical position of the Planets. The Planets exert an influence on us and so we are forced to take some actions. The success or otherwise of these actions will depend upon the basic strength of a horoscope as well as to the strength and nature of a Planet which is giving these thrusts.

> "Coming events cast their shadows before but the shadow varies in length according to the exaltation of the sphere of the life whence it is cast".

In the matters of love and romance, Moon and Venus in the case of men and Sun and Mars in the case of women, play the most important role in culminating an event. How long they will last and what changes will occur subsequently, differs from planet to planet. For example Sun Progressed Venus results in a new romance and duration of this is generally three years. At the end of this either the romance is turned into legal marriage or it breaks as one party moves over to a far off city.

We give some aphorisms related to the Timing of Events:

General Principles

1. There is fruition or frustration of efforts or prospects in

respect of love/marriage only when there is indication of it, in the nativity.

2. Results are produced by directions when there is basic tendency towards a particular result in the nativity. Otherwise, directions would show little result.

3. If the nativity is strong and favourable for love/marriage even ordinary good directions would bring fulfilment of desires, and there would not be serious frustrations even under adverse directions.

4. If the nativity is weak and planets are unfavourably placed by house and sign and the mutual configuration is unhappy and disastrous, even favourable directions would achieve little, while adverse ones would totally ruin the prospects.

5. Benefic directions of planets which are in benefic positions by sign and house, and configuration are positively benefic.

6. Malefic directions of planets which are ill placed by sign/house, and mutual configuration or which are afflicted otherwise, show positively evil results when in conjunction, square, opposition, or in parallel.

7. A planet essentially good and strong shows good results by directions, while one very weak and evil shows extremely bad results under evil directions.

8. If a planet is well placed by house and sign and strong and unafflicted, even bad directions to it would not bring markedly bad effects.

9. If a planet is ill placed by house and sign and seriously afflicted, even good directions to it would be of little avail in producing good result.

10. Two planets which are good and mutually configurated beneficially would show very good results by directions also.

11. Two planets which are evil and afflicting each other would always give trouble when in evil directions.

12. A benefic planet, if weak and afflicted in nativity, does not do any good even when it forms good directions with another planet or with ascendant or M.C.

13. Similarly, a malefic planet exalted or dignified and strong by house and sign does not do much ill, even when it forms an adverse aspect with ascendant or M.C. or with another planet.

14. A planet strong and unafflicted would produce maximum good effect if it be a benefic and form a good direction, *vice versa*.

15. It is very important to see what aspect the planets (now forming mutual aspect) were forming in the nativity. A planet forming trine or other good aspects would not be so bad when forming a square aspect by direction, similarly, a planet forming a square aspect radically would not prove so beneficial when forming a trine or favourable aspect.

16. While judging directions, due note should be taken of the houses, directing planets in the nativity, and also of the houses they own.

17. Do not fail to attach sufficient importance to the ownership of houses by the planet, because a planet gives effect pertaining to the house it is posited in or is lord of. As such, lords of 1st, and 7th have greater importance than say of 2nd and 3rd to determine incidents pertaining to love/ marriage.

18. (a) Good or bad directions show the result when there is accompanying lunar direction also.

(b) Aspects between slow-moving planets remain in force for a long time. Sometimes, the period stretches over 3 or 4 years. Effects come to be felt only when there is a lunar direction also. Fullest effect would, however, be felt when a solar direction of the same nature synchronises.

19. Directions between a progressed planet and a radical one are stronger than those between two progressed planets.

20. Greater importance should be attached to the rulers of natal houses then of the progressed horoscope.

21. Good generally happens when a train of several good directions are in operation, similarly, evil results follow a train of evil directions.

22. Good directions show their full effect only when a number of them are in operation more or less simultaneously and are powerfully and beneficially excited by actual transits.

23. Evil directions show their full effect generally when a train of them operates simultaneously or in quick succession and are evilly excited by malefics who may be actually transiting and aspecting the radical and progressed positions of planets forming directions.

24. If solar and lunar directions are also in operation and of similar nature (vide 21 above) results are sure to follow.

25. Good directions show the result only when there is strong and favourable excitement from benefic planets at that time of life when the directions operate.

26. Evil directions show evil results generally when there is strong and unfavourable excitement by transit from malefics at that time of life when the directions operate.

27. Sometimes, when there is no excitement from a benefic or a malefic, the directions do not give any result at all. It is therefore imperative to have an excitement (by a benefic planet to a benefic direction and by a malefic planet to a malefic direction). This is a condition concomitant for achieving results.

28. The point of excitement cannot be overemphasised. If the particular degrees and sign tenanted by the progressed and the radical planets are aspected in the year (when directions would show result) by a strong benefic, it would modify the effects beneficially. *Vice versa.*

Example

Suppose, in a female nativity the direction Sun progressed, radical Venus conjunction occurs on the 18th day after her birth corresponding to 18th year of her life, in 10th degree of Pisces and when she is actually running her 18th year, Jupiter by transit from 8th degree in Cancer, aspects this 10th degree of Pisces by strong favourable aspect, the benefic effect of the direction would be much enhanced and it would bring about marriage.

29. When an afflicting direction is formed and the degrees occupied by the progressed and the radical planet are excited by a malefic planet, the evil is much worse.

Example

Suppose, a lady has Saturn in 20th degree in Aries in 7th house and Mars is in 29th degree in Pisces. Now, if on 30th day after birth the direction Mars progressed conjunction Saturn radical is formed, this will correspond to her 30th year of life. Now, when she is actually running her 30th year if Saturn by transit comes to 20th degree in Aries and thus evilly excites the degree of the radical and progressed planet, the effect would be much worse.

30. If a benefic direction has evil excitement, the benefic result doesn't show itself. Similarly, if a malefic direction has benefic excitement the evil does not come to pass. The two kinds of different effects are set off.

Example

Suppose, the direction Moon progressed conjunction Venus radical is formed on 20th day of a lady's birth corresponding to 20th year of her life. If this position is transited by Saturn when the native is actually running her 20th year, the possibility of marriage may not be predicted, due to evil excitement. It would be delayed or hindrances would come in or negotiation would fail.

Example

Suppose, the direction of Venus progressed square Saturn radical occurs on 20th day corresponding to 20th year in life. Now, when the native is actually running his 20th year, if Saturn's radical position is strongly aspected by an exalted Jupiter, no evil results may ensue from the above unfavourable direction, due to Jupiter's benefic excitement.

31. The rules about directions apply to all the three kinds of progressions (i) 1° of M.C. equal to one year of life, (ii) 1 day after birth equal to one year of life, and (iii) 1 day prior to birth equal to one year of life. The principle remains the same. (See Appendix II).

32. When judging directions, the inherent nature of planets should not be forgotten, *e.g.* Jupiter is warm, peaceful, harmonising, Venus is conducive to attachment and emotional upsurge, Saturn is limiting, cold and calculating, Mercury is full of agility, speech, giving speed in expression and writing, Mars is sensuous, full of energy, exciting cravings of the flesh, etc. Those tendencies must be combined with the ownership and positions of planets, to arrive at correct appraisal of the resultant effect.

Example

If Leo be rising, lord of 1st (Sun) in square or opposition to lord of 7th (Saturn) would show quite different results from say if Gemini be rising lord of 1st (Mercury) would show, if in square or in opposition to the lord of seventh (Jupiter).

33. Look to the other directions also when a particular one pertaining to love/marriage is operating. If the accompanying direction is say, Jupiter trine M.C. it would enhance prestige by marriage, while, on the other hand, if Saturn conjunction square or opposition M.C. is operating simultaneously with a direction of love/marriage, it would bring about lowering of position.

34. When making predictions, one cannot attach too much importance to the background (age of the native, social customs, family, traditions, religious customs, etc.). For example, if a direction favourable to 7th house is formed or even if a strong Venus conjoins another benefic in the 7th house, one would not predict marriage if the age of the native is 10 years. Similarly, marriage or love affair should not be predicted in the horoscopes of widows belonging to orthodox families, where widow marriage is prohibited.

35. In societies, where flirtation or illicit connections between the sexes are frequent, slightest directions would incline the native to such acts but in families following an orthodox code of conduct, there might be slight emotional disturbance, but no overt act.

36. Another important point which cannot be too strongly emphasised is the scope for a particular activity in the nativity itself. He who is destined to marry late would not have a matrimonial alliance even when a good direction is formed in the progressed horoscope in earlier years.

37. Mutual aspects, *i.e.* aspects between two planets denote events connected with the houses two planets are posited in/ or the houses they are lords of. They also bring about events according to their inherent nature, *e.g.* Saturn brings about limitation, Jupiter expansion, Venus affection, etc.

38. Directions to the ascendant are more important for health than for love affairs or marriage. But they may be considered, particularly, in case of ladies who leave their parents' home and shift to their husbands' after marriage.

39. Directions to the ascendant sometimes create mental perturbation and they may have a bearing on matrimonial side if the affliction is from a planet in 5th/7th house or Venus or lord of the 5th/7th house.

40. Directions to the radical planets as well as to the angles are important. Directions to the cusp of the 1st house relate to health, to 4th domestic environment, to 7th partnership, to 10th position. Where marriage affects life in more than one department, look to all of these.

41. In Judgement, the order of the importance should be as follows:

(i) Radical position of planets.
(ii) Directions.
(iii) Transits.

42. A good planet inherently strong by house and sign and forming benefic aspects in the nativity would bestow/show very good result under favourable *transits*. *Vice versa*.

43. Directions between two planets (including luminaries) have been arranged in the order Sun, Moon, Mars, Mercury, Jupiter, Venus, Saturn, Herschel, Neptune, 1st house, 2nd house, 3rd house, 4th house and so on.

44. If the distance in a direction between the two planets forming direction is the same, it will have the same interpretation whether the first named planet progressed is in direction to the second named planet's radical position or *vice versa*.

For example, (i) Sun parallel Venus or Venus parallel Sun both should be treated alike and (ii) Sun trine moon, *i.e.* Sun progressed trine radical moon will have the same interpretation as Moon trine Sun, *i.e.* Moon progressed trine Sun radical.

45. Since, there are 12 houses and 9 planets and each house covers a number of departments, of life and each planet is significator of a large number of interests in human life—the directions in subsequent chapters would be found to have effect on the plane of love and marriage only when those circumstances are expected to be in operation.

For example, Venus in seventh in good direction to Jupiter in eleventh may mean love affair/marriage and gain thereby. It can also mean partnership in silk/silver business and gain thereby. Do not fail to look to the circumstances of the individual, his/her background, age and expectations.

CHAPTER 6

DIRECTIONS OF PLANETS, HOUSES AND THEIR LORDS

Another important system to judge the timing of the events is the directions*. Of these the Solar directions are most important and generally the effect lasts for three years. One year before the progressed Sun forms an aspect, second year when the aspect is the exact and the third year is one year after the aspect is complete. For example let us say Sun (Progressed) Trine Venus (Radical) in the 39th year. Then the effect of this direction would be felt during the 38th, 39th and 40th year (running years). Generally the Solar Directions ushers in the new era in the life.

The lunar directions with the radical planets (Planets at birth) is next in importance. They show very strong effects if simultaneously Sun is also in the direction with the same planet or with a planet of similar nature. The effect of lunar direction lasts for two months to three months.* For example Moon (Progressed) Square Mars exactly at 28 years and three months—then the effect will be felt during 28 year 2 months, 3 months and 4 months. Whereas Solar Directions indicates years when event will take place. The lunar directions indicate the months when they occur.

In the same manner the direction of other planets viz., Mars, Mercury, Juipter, Venus and Saturn are important. When these planets form a direction with Sun, Moon, Ascendant or the

---

* Calculation of directions (western system) in Appendix I.

M.C. (meridian cusp), the directions became as strong and important as the Solar or lunar directions. As Jupiter and Saturn, (Uranus, Neptune also) are slow—very slow in motion. The directions of these planets lasts for many-many years (Please see the daily motion to work out how many days they will last).

These two or three months depends upon the motion of the Moon. If it is faster then the effect is reduced to two months. If it is average say 12 degree to 13 degrees per day then it would be for three months.

In Western Astrology if we follow method of one day=one year then the number of days will indicate the number of years, these directions would lasts.

The learned readers should also note that the effects of directions become more intensified when planets are in Transit over sensitive points simultaneously in a horoscope.

Next in importance is the directions to houses or directions between the lords of houses. We give below the effects of the directions:

Solar Directions

1. Solar directions if good, are particularly beneficial in the nativity of women; if bad, are particularly harmful in female nativities (in Judgement of love and marriage).

2. Solar aspects of the same nature as other directions prevailing, greatly augment the force of directions. If there are no solar aspects, the year may be uneventful and other directions, even powerful, act as less potent.

3. Sun's directions to Moon are important inasmuch as if Sun is strong both in the radical and the progressed horoscopes Moon acquires added strength and consequently gives stimulus to other directions.

4. Sun in parallel to Moon may bring in the influence of someone of the opposite sex into the native's life. In a female nativity, this may not have a very fortunate reaction.

5. Sun conjunction Moon; there is likely to be some change and the native may form new unions or attachments.

6. Sun semi-sextile Moon; a favourable time to pursue affairs pertaining to love/marriage; generally good.

7. Sun sextile Moon; it is a good period and there may be success in love affairs which may result in marriage, if the aspects are formed from the 5th house and the 7th house or from the 7th house and the 9th house.

8. Sun semi-square Moon; not a favourable direction; domestic affairs may go wrong and there may be some ruffled feelings in love matters. All the more unfavourable for ladies.

9. Sun square Moon; an unfavourable direction which coupled with others of similar nature may give rise to some split or separation between the native and his beloved, and there may be some depression or disappointment due to mental attitude or physical separation. This may be a period of difficulty and if any negotiations for marriage are going on, there are likely to be hindrances and setbacks.

10. Sun trine Moon; it is a favourable direction for love/marriage and if there are benefic directions prevailing, they acquire added force resulting in fruition of efforts pertaining to love/marriage. The native may have some new attachments and gain through friends.

11. Sun opposition Moon; if either significator be lord of the 7th house or the direction fall in 1st or the 7th house, there may be some disappointment or sorrow adversely affecting the love emotions. In a female nativity, where there is some evil configuration with Herschel, Neptune or Saturn, this threatens disgrace.

12. Sun sesquiquadrate Moon; not a favourable period.

13. Sun sextile Mars; new friendship and attachment may form with emphasis on physical union more pronounced.

14. Sun square Mars; there is likely to be some trouble or bickering on the domestic front; an unfavourable indication.

15. Sun trine Mars; great warmth of feelings and enhanced desires makes itself felt. There may be some new attachments, if the nativity so indicates.

16. Sun conjunction Jupiter; human emotions are more platonic than sensuous and new contacts made in this direction

would enhance the prestige of the native and with a person of the opposite sex would prove materially beneficial also.

17. Sun semi-square Jupiter; if occurring at appropriate age may lead to some setback, and disappointment in affairs of the heart. There may be temporary separation from the loved one, but is not so evil.

18. Sun sextile Jupiter; favourable for marriage resulting in increase of honour and beneficial to the native. Marriage occurs generally to a high-minded and noble person, if Sun or Jupiter be in the 7th house in the nativity.

19. Sun square Jupiter; there is some setback in domestic peace and happiness, particularly so, if either of the planets be afflicted radically. There is likely to be much expenditure.

20. Sun trine Jupiter; a very favourable aspect resulting in enhancement of prestige and addition to the purse. New unions or attachments, if occurring under this direction are lasting and beneficial.

21. Sun sesquiquadrate Jupiter with accompanying unfavourable lunar directions; it may lead to some disappointment in affairs of the heart due to misunderstanding over monetary affairs or separation.

22. Sun opposition Jupiter leads to much disappointment and if either planet be in the 12th house in the nativity, the native may find that he has unnecessarily wasted money over the affairs of heart, which may terminate in disillusionment.

23. Good directions of Sun to Venus emulate the passionate nature and may bring about marriage if occurring at suitable age in a female nativity.

24. Sun parallel Venus shows its effect only when Moon also forms a favourable aspect conducive to happiness, union, attachments, and generally affairs of the heart particularly in female nativities.

25. Sun conjunction Venus, if occurring at suitable age or stage of life, may result in marriage. Particularly so in female nativities. If marriage is eliminated as being unlikely due to the person having been already married, or due to other considerations and circumstances, great emotional attachments

to a person of opposite sex is indicated resulting in pleasurable emotions and fruition of desire.

26. Sun square Venus. This is an unfavourable direction and during the stage of courtship may indicate some setback in progress and act as an hindrance.

27. Sun sextile Venus. Good for love and affairs of the heart generally. There may be new unions or attachments if the nativity so indicates.

28. Sun-Saturn favourable directions will give steadiness.

29. Sun square Saturn; there will be domestic trouble and occasions of ill health. If occurring from the 4th and the 7th houses there may be breaking up of home; if from the 7th and the 10th house, loss of prestige, due to some unfortunate alliance; if in 1st and the 10th house may result in some compromising position, resulting in disgrace, if the nativity so indicates. All this is so in relation to or due to a person of the opposite sex or partner if either of the significators be in the 7th house or lord thereof.

30. Sun sesquiquadrate Saturn is an unfavourable direction and may result in sorrow or disappointment.

31. Sun opposition Saturn may result in sorrow and separation with the loved one, if either significator may have a bearing on love or married life.

32. All unfavourable directions between Sun and Saturn result in limitation, freezing of human emotions, disappointment, ill health, and demise and are particularly bad, if Saturn be elevated above the Sun.

33. Sun conjunction Herschel; there are sudden developments resulting in eccentric love/courtship if occurring in the 1st , 5th, 7th or 12th houses. The passionate nature is inflamed and unless the nativity is strong, it shows bohemian type of love and also elopement, if the nativity so indicates. Attachments may be formed to which senior family members may be opposed.

34. Sun square Herschel leads to estrangement, disagreement and brings about unfavourable turn in events. Changes are for the worse. If there be accompanying directions

of Venus also, the native may make a change due to some love affair or marriage, which may turn out to be unfortunate.

35. Sun trine Herschel; favourable for romantic attachments and fruition of the affairs of the heart. Particularly so, if occurring from the 5th or 7th house or there be accompanying favourable direction from Venus or lord of the 7th house.

36. Sun sesquiquadrate Herschel may lead to sorrow and separation, if accompanied by unfavourable lunar directions.

37. Sun opposition Herschel; if either of the planets be afflicted at birth, particularly by Saturn there may be disgrace or some scandal if occurring in angles. In female nativities, there may be separation from husband or great opposition if the 7th house in the nativity shows dispute, and discord.

38. Sun conjunction Neptune; the native would make many castles in the air in relation to his desired object of love, but it may result in disillusionment or ultimate separation.

39. Sun square Neptune; if either planet be aspecting at birth or be in the 1st or 7th house there may be troubles and even elopements in female nativities resulting in disillusionment and disgrace due to over impetuosity; particularly so, if either planet be conjoined with or be in opposition to Venus.

40. Sun sesquiquadrate Neptune: the native's affairs drag on and circumstances more hampering and hindering than helping occur.

41. Ascendant trine Sun may result in marriage in case of females; in male nativity, it may bring some honour or enhance the prestige.

42. All good aspects between ascendant and Sun are similar to 41 above.

Lunar Directions

1. Lunar directions show their effect when there are accompanying solar aspects to planets and also mutual aspect between two planets. The year becomes eventful only if lunar, solar and mutual aspects of similar nature synchronise and are not set off by directions of contrary nature.

2. When there are lunar directions and no solar or mutual directions, nothing may turn out as a tangible result and the whole prospect for good or bad may remain vague, uncrystallised and nebulous.

3. In directions of progressed Moon to the radical or progressed position of a planet the interpretation should be modified due to ownership, association and position of the aspected planet in the progressed horoscope. Suppose, there is Moon progressed trine Venus progressed and the progressed ascendant becomes Taurus and Venus comes in 6th house; the interpretation would be Moon trine Venus lord of 1st and 6th in 6th.

4. When lunar directions are unfavourable they cause relaxation of mental control and the native is too easily swayed by feelings, emotions and sentiments. This easy excitement takes the form of awakening of sex desires, if there is an acompanying ray of Mars and Venus or if, the lunar aspect is to a planet in 7th or 5th or lords thereof.

5. Moon in favourable direction with its own radical position: these are good and would give strength to favourable directions of Venus or lord of the 5th or 7th house, if the same synchronises.

6. Moon in unfavourable adversely if any direction having a bearing on matrimonial affairs or affairs of the heart is unfavourable and in operation at the time this lunar direction is formed.

7. Moon progressed parallel Moon radical; if the progressed Moon is beneficially excited, the result would be good; on the other hand, if malefics excite the progressed Moon the result would be unfavourable.

8. Moon conjunction Moon radical; if the Moon at birth is beneficially aspected and well-placed, this direction would bring in good luck and happy time. On the other hand, if the Moon was afflicted at birth unfavourable results would ensue. As lunar directions bring into action the result of other directions, it is important to note whether Moon is well-placed in the nativity.

9. Directions of progressed Moon to radical positions of other planets in the nativity would have the same interpretation as directions of progressed planets to radical Moon.

10. *Example.* Progressed Moon trine to radical Venus has the same effect as progressed Venus trine to radical Moon.

11. If in lunar directions the Moon be in Aries under favourable progressed aspects of other planets, the mind would be joyful, impulsive and easily inclined to have physical attachments.

12. If Moon be in Gemini at the time of a favourable direction and if the nativity so indicates, the person may have dual love affairs simultaneously.

13. If Moon be in Leo when forming favourable directions with another planet, emotions of love or pleasure would be dominant.

14. If Moon be in Virgo when forming favourable directions with Mars, or Venus, the native would lay great emphasis on purity of love and would desire ample reciprocation.

15. If Moon be in Libra and form good aspect, the emotions would be more refined than sensuous.

16. If Moon be in Scorpio, the native may have secret attachments under favourable directions and there may be tendency towards depravement.

17. When Moon passes through the radical the 1st house, the 5th house, and the 7th houses, it is important in regard to love and marriage. When passing through 11th, it may bring in some friendship. Lunar directions are very important not so much by themselves as bringing into fruition, and crystallising the effect of other directions between two planets.

18. In directions of progressed Moon, to a radical planet, Moon's aspect to the planet should be judged and interpreted according to the ownership, association and position of the planet concerned in the nativity. Suppose, progressed Moon is in trine to radical Venus in the 5th house in a nativity with sign Aries rising at birth. The interpretation should be Moon trine Venus lord of the the 7th house in the 5th house.

19. The influence exerted by Moon's passage* through a particular house in the nativity should be borne in mind while

* The Moon's passage means Passage of Progressed Moon for which refer to Appendix I.

interpreting other directions. This would help the astrologer to determine in some measure the significance of other directions and the manner in which they would show their results:

(i) Moon's passage in the 1st house involves some change, particularly when it is in the progressed horoscope, exactly passing over the cusp of the 1st house.

(ii) Moon's passage through the 2nd house if forming good directions: these may lead to acquisition of wealth or gain by matrimony if other directions are strong and favouring, a union at that time. *Vice versa*.

(iii) There would be much activity in correspondence and if Moon is the lord of the 7th house in the nativity or forms directions with the lord of the 7th from 3rd, there may be much correspondence in regard to love and matrimony; particularly so, if conjoined with or aspected by Venus or if there be Mercury in the 7th house.

(iv) Moon's passage through the fourth house will bring domestic matters to the fore and if well-aspected there, peace and happiness would prevail. The native may more settle down than go about.

(v) The Moon's passage through the fifth house is likely to stimulate interest in the opposite sex; if favourably aspected there may be fruition of desire; on the other hand, if Moon forms adverse configurations, particularly with malefics, there may be frustration.

(vi) Moon's passage through the 6th house may cause come friction or setback in health.

(vii) (a) Moon's passage through the 7th house will bring into prominence matters connected with wife/husband or some kind of union, if this passage synchronises through a period in life when such attachment is likely. Those who are unmarried may have matrimonial alliances while those who are already married may have a good time particularly so, if Moon forms good aspect. *Vice versa*.

(b) Moon's passage through the 7th house in the progressed horoscope is particularly marked in those nativities, in which the sign Libra is heavily tenanted.

(viii) Moon's passage through the 8th house is not generally good and may be harbinger of only evil tidings—particularly, if ill aspected.

(ix) Moon's passage through the 9th house is not much of interest except in the possibility that the native may form a union abroad, if he/she undertakes a voyage at this time. This will be so, if Moon is beneficially configurated with lord of the 7th or Venus.

(x) Moon's passage through the 10th house will be important from the matrimonial point of view only if the directions for marriage/union synchronise, in which case the marriage may raise the status and prestige of the native.

(xi) Moon's passage through the 11th house if well aspected may bring gains from friends; *vice versa*. Since this house is trine to 7th house there may be some love affair or union if there be a strong benefic in the 7th house. If there is Jupiter in the 7th house Moon's passage through the 11th is bound to bring some gain, or an happy event.

(xii) Moon's passage through the 12th house is not good, particularly so, if Moon therein is in square, opposition, or conjunction with a malefic and if that malefic be the lord of the 7th house, and if other similar directions synchronise, the native may find his/her partner is playing some game of treachery.

20. Directions of Moon and Mars increase sensual craving—happy or unhappy results depending upon nature of directions.

21. Moon parallel Mars: there may be some impulsive activities. It may have a bearing on love affairs if occurring from 5th or 7th.

22. Moon conjunction Mars; similar to above but likely to be more marked in its effect.

23. Moon semi-sextile Mars: this is not a strong aspect but favourable. The native would show a little boldness and if any love affair is in progress he/she may be successful by shaking of some of his/her inhibitions.

24. Moon semi-square Mars: this is not a good aspect and the native is advised to exercise caution for impudence would rather spoil than help matters.

25. Moon sextile Mars; good for activity and new enterprises.

26. Moon square Mars; this is an unfavourable aspect and the native should try not to succumb to the influence of the opposite sex which may prove rather unfavourable and detrimental. If the native is having any strong urges of the heart they should rather be kept suppressed than allowed an outlet.

27. Moon trine Mars; this is a favourable aspect and is likely to have a bearing on the affairs of the heart if occurring from the 1st house and the 5th house, the 3rd house and the 7th house, the 5th house and the 9th house, or the 7th house and the 11th house. A little boldness during this time would achieve the objective.

28. Moon sesquiquadrate Mars; this is a weak aspect but unfavourable.

29. Moon inconjunct Mars: this is not favourable and there is likely to be some trouble or annoyance if the native indulges in extra-marital relations.

30. Moon opposition Mars; this is an unfavourable aspect and there may be trouble or discredit due to hasty action on the part of the native. No fresh adventures are likely, to prove helpful; rather the outcome may be unfavourable.

31. Moon Mercury directions accelerate the pace, of thinking and give additional momentum to expression.

32. Moon parallel Mercury: a good direction, particularly for making new friendships, attachments and entering into correspondence.

33. Moon semisextile Mercury: a weak but good direction.

34. Moon semi-square Mercury: not a favourable direction for correspondence.

35. Moon sextile Mercury: good direction. There may be correspondence with the loved one if the directions formed are from the 3rd, and 5th, or 5th, 7th and 9th house.

36. Moon square Mercury: an evil direction and if the native wants accomplishment of matrimonial negotiations or some gain from or through his/her loved one, correspondence should not be initiated while this direction continues, otherwise, there is likely to be no outcome favourable to the native. This may primarily be due to the native's being over critical in his/her approach and use of phraseology.

37. Moon trine Mercury and other favourable directions would quicken the mind and speech. They will tend to enhance the interest of the native if he/she enteres into correspondence with his/her beloved one.

38. Adverse directions between Moon and Mercury are not favourable for entering into correspondence or arguments. There may be quarrel with the loved one, if other directions of a similar nature are in operation.

39. Moon Jupiter directions are of elevating nature and tend to bring harmony and peace in native's life, particularly when in conjunction, parallel, or trine.

40. Moon parallel Jupiter: this is a good direction and will continue for some time. If any marriage is performed when this direction is in operation, there is likely to be gain of money.

41. Moon conjunction Jupiter; similar to above; it is a favourable direction and may bring marriage, if occurring in 7th house.

42. Moon semi-sextile Jupiter: this is rather a weak aspect and may have no bearing on affairs of the heart*.

43. Moon semi-square Jupiter: this is an unfavourable aspect and may have no bearing on marriage or love affairs.

---

* Wherever it is written that the directions would have no bearing, it should be presumed that there is no connection with the 5th and 7th houses or lords thereof.

44. Direction between Moon and Jupiter are likely to have little hearing on marriage or love affairs, because Jupiter imparts peace, philosophy, and puritanism. The native would therefore under directions of Jupiter be inclined to lead rather a pure life than otherwise.

45. Moon Jupiter directions may have some bearing on the affairs of the heart or may help in union/marriage if occurring from 5th or 7th house and may bring about favourable or unfavourable trends in monetary matters incidental to marriage.

46. Moon sextile Jupiter is a good direction for wealth and will have a bearing on the affairs of the heart if occurring from 5th and 7th or 7th and 9th houses.

47. Moon square Jupiter; an unfavourable direction for social or monetary matters.

48. Moon trine Jupiter: it is a very good direction and as it enhances the social prestige and is favourable for monetary matters, may synchronise with marriage, particularly in the case of girls, if occurring at appropriate age and if good directions between Sun and Venus or others favourable to marriage occur simultaneously.

49. Moon sesquiquadrate Jupiter: this is a weak and unfavourable aspect.

50. Moon inconjunct Jupiter: similar to above.

51. Moon opposition Jupiter: this is not a favourable direction. There may be some trouble or temporary separation, if other, directions so indicate.

52. Moon Venus directions increase the pleasure instinct and give mirth, cheerfulness and gay society, good clothes and ornaments.

53. Moon parallel Venus: this is a favourable direction for the pursuit of love and pleasure. The native is likely to have a pleasant time.

54. Moon conjunction Venus: likely to stimulate interest in the opposite sex and some new attachments or unions may be formed. It may bring about marriage if occurring in the 7th house.

55. Moon semi-sextile Venus; it is a favourable period for making friends and love affairs. But this is a weak direction.

56. Moon semi-square Venus; this is an unfavourable aspect but weak. There may be some delay or obstruction in the affairs of the heart.

57. Moon sextile Venus; this is a good aspect and here may be fruition of desires. Love affairs may have a successful conclusion, particularly so, if the direction is formed from 5th and the 7th or 7th and 9th house. If forming from the 3rd and 5th house there may be love letters exchanged.

58. Moon square Venus not a very favourable aspect and there may be some annoyance or hindrance in attachments or unions if occurring at appropriate age.

59. Moon trine Venus; this is a good and favourable aspect likely to stimulate interest in the opposite sex and if any negotiations or efforts are going on in regard to some love affair there may be successful conclusion of the same. If accompanied by good directions of Jupiter there may be gain also and a marriage/union, may come about if occurring from the 7th house.

60. Moon sesquiquadrate Venus; it is a weak aspect and not favourable. There may be some trouble or annoyance in zrelation to the opposite sex and the native would do well to weigh the pros and cons before hazarding.

61. Moon inconjunct Venus; the native is likely to have new attachments or the older one might be strengthened. This is not a very strong aspect but helpful for affairs of the heart.

62. Moon opposition Venus; this is not a favourable direction and may act adversely on the affairs of the heart. There may be disappointment or sorrow in relation to some loved one. The feelings suffer. If there are other good directions the disappointment or trouble may only be temporary.

But if there are simultaneous evil directions of Herschel, Neptune, or Saturn and if the nativity so indicates, there may be some love affair or union if the afflicting planet squares or opposes from the 7th house.

63. Moon-Saturn directions are limiting and the emotions are held under check; if trine or sextile, this would lead to good results; if in conjunction square or opposition the direction would lead to frustration and depression.

64. Moon parallel Saturn; this will cause trouble; the mind would be depressed; affairs would go wrong.

65. Moon conjunction Saturn; very bad direction likely to be troublesome, there may be some grief.

66. Moon semi-sextile saturn; a weak but unfavourable aspect.

67. Moon semi-square Saturn; similar to above.

68. Moon sextile Saturn; this is a good direction and if the native had been indulging in extra-marital relations he/she would rather become thoughtful and steady realising that puritanism is better than philandering.

69. Moon square Saturn; this is a bad direction causing trouble and sorrow. There may be domestic unhappiness and conjugal happiness would be much impaired if Saturn is elevated, and if the direction operates from the 4th house, the 7th house, or the 10th houses.

70. Moon trine Saturn; this is similar to 68 above.

71. Moon sesquiquadrate Saturn; likely to be unhelpful in any matter; rather it would bring disappointment and grief.

72. Moon inconjunct Saturn; a weak aspect and not good, causing worry and annoyance.

73. Moon opposition Saturn; this is a very evil direction bringing much worry, disappointment and sometimes synchronises with break or death in the family. Not at all good.

74. Moon parallel Herschel; the native is likely to form new attachments or union more on a sudden impulse than by process of reasoning. As a result of new affairs of the heart, there may be domestic trouble and bickering in home life.

75. Moon conjunction Herschel; similar to above. The native becomes more bohemian in his outlook and may form illicit connection with much disparity in age, caste, and social standing. He/she will be inclined to be more romantic than orthodox. This will be particularly so and leading to very erratic trend in life if occurring in the 7th house or the 5th house.

76. Moon semi-sextile Herschel; interest in opposite sex is likely to be much aroused.

77. Moon semi-square Herschel; any sudden alliances with the opposite sex would prove rather unhelpful and may bring trouble and annoyance in its wake.

78. Moon sextile Herschel; it is a good direction likely to stimulate sexual impulse if occurring from the 5th and 7th or 7th and 9th house.

79. Moon square Herschel; there is likely to be trouble and the outcome may be rather evil if the native forms any extra-marital relations for under the magnetic influence of this direction, the native is likely to succumb to sexual temptations.

80. Moon trine Herschel; this brings about some unexpected turn, and it may have some bearing on affairs of heart. There may be some attachment which may be a source of pleasure.

81. Moon sequiquadrate Herschel; this is an unfavourable aspect.

82. Moon inconjunct Herschel; it has not very marked effect unless accompanied by other train of directions.

83. Moon opposition Herschel; there might be some change and it may relate to native's matrimonial life or disturb home conditions if Herschel be in the 1st, 4th or 7th house. If the planet is afflicted at birth there might be change for the worse, resulting in temporary separation or misunderstanding.

84. Moon parallel Neptune; the native would more live in the world of his/her imagination than one of reality and would have vague and nebulous desires, difficult of realisation.

85. Moon conjunction Neptune; similar to 84 above.

86. Moon semi-sextile Neptune; this is a weak aspect developing more his intuition than bringing about any objective.

87. Moon semi-square Neptune; the native is likely to get entangled in some dealings with the other sex and caution and circumspection are advised.

88. Moon sextile Neptune; has not much bearing on matrimonial life unless Neptune be in the 5th house when it would give rise to vague hankering for love affair. If Neptune be in the the 7th house the native would become more sex conscious and receptive emotionally.

89. Moon square Neptune; this is an unfavourable aspect but does not have much effect on matrimonial life unless Neptune be in the 5th or 7th house, in which case it might prove troublesome.

90. Moon trine Neptune; the native would have day dreams about his enjoyments and will desire fulfilment of his vague hankering which may not be realised.

91. Moon sesquiquadrate Neptune; unfavourable. There may be worries.

92. Moon inconjunct Neptune; not a powerful aspect. The native would become more sex-conscious.

93. Moon opposition Neptune; this is an unfavourable aspect and the native may get entangled in some undesirable affair if simultaneous directions of Venus or lord of the 7th house are in operation, or if Neptune is in the 7th house. The native will have only disillusionment and the ultimate outcome would rather be unhappy than otherwise.

Mars

1. Mars parallel Jupiter may prove unfavourable if the native is involved in some case pertaining to matrimonial affairs. If both the planets are afflicted, it brings about loss of credit and good name.

2. Mars sextile Jupiter: this is an expanding influence making wider the social circle of the native and if either planet is associated with the 7th house, this social expansion may be due to or through his wife/partner.

3. Mars square Jupiter: may give rise to waste of money or bad health through matrimonial affairs if either planet be owner of the 7th or 12th house or be posited therein.

4. Mars trine Jupiter: this shows its effect and comes into fruition only when a good lunar direction synchronises; there may be gain of money or wealth through wife if either planet be owner of the 7th and if the aspect be from 7th and 11th houses.

5. Mars sesquiquadrate Jupiter: it is an unfavourable direction and may bring in adverse condition into play.

6. Mars inconjunct Jupiter: if there are other unfavourable trains of directions, particularly those of Saturn, this direction may bring about loss of some loved one.

7. If Mars be the lord of the 1st house and form good directions with Venus, the native pursues his love affairs or courtship with great enthusiasm and vigour, and may even show signs of pleasant aggressiveness.

8. If Mars be the lord of the 1st house or posited in the 1st and be in evil directions to Venus, the native may do something of an aggressive nature or due to his hot headedness, which may give an unfortunate turn to love affairs or result in disharmony.

9. Mars trine Venus: generally good for sensuous gratification bringing about opportunities for new contacts or revival of old ones, particularly so, if either planet be associated with the 1st house, the 5th of 7th house.

10. Mars sesquiquadrate Venus: generally unfortunate bringing out some kind of emotional frustration or troubles in connection with love affairs or in married life. If other solar or lunar directions supporting the above evil configuration are not present, the annoyance may only be a passing one.

11. All Mars-Venus directions excite the passionate nature and give stimulus to sexual craving which may be gratified or frustrated according to the directions being of benefic or evil nature. If the planets are essentially strong and well-aspected at the time of birth their good directions do not fail to bring some joy in life; if they be afflicted radically, evil directions bring much trouble.

12. Mars opposition Venus: there will be trouble and disappointment in love affairs or in married life and if (i) there is simultaneous application to Sun in the case of a female nativity and to Moon in the case of a male nativity and (ii) most of the planet afflict the luminaries in double-bodied sign, the trouble will have its roots in the other love affair which is developing simultaneously, *i.e.*, two love affairs, or one outside love affair other than in married life.

13. When Mars afflicts Saturn there is curb on sensuous desires resulting in frustration or in some other act in which animal nature in man leaves the path of harmony and deviates into that of brutality, such as sadism.

14. Mars conjunction Saturn: this is an unfortunate direction and there may be coming to the fore of latent cruel tendencies. Crude passions come into play and if either planet is in 7th, there would be matrimonial trouble. If both planets are afflicted and Saturn be in the 10th house there may even be disgrace due to violent passions coming into play. If the direction be in the 1st house, it will be bad for bodily health and if in the 4th house it will lead to domestic unhappiness.

15. Mars parallel Saturn: unfavourable, particularly if either planet is associated with 7th house.

16. Mars inconjunct Saturn: unfavourable, there would be bickering and critical faculties would come too much into play.

17. Mars opposition Saturn: very evil, particularly if occurring from the 1st and 7th houses; may lead to some tragedy if the nativity so indicates.

18. Mars parallel Herschel: there may be sudden flaring up of trouble; not a favourable time for quarrels as the same may terminate against the native. He/she is also liable to succumb to sex temptations and the same may turn out to be detrimental, particularly so, if in the 5th or 7th house.

19. Mars semi-square Herschel: likely to involve in disputes with husband/wife's relations if occurring from the 7th and 9th house. If from the 7th and 6th house may give rise to much quarrels with wife/husband. If occurring from the 3rd and 5th house there may be annoyances in regard to loved one, due to unfavourable correspondence or intervention of one's own relations. The native is inclined to be rather hasty in his Judgement and any tendency to be unduly authoritative when the direction is in force would prove harmful.

20. Mars opposition Herschel: this is a very evil direction and there may be sudden upheaval in domestic circumstances bringing about even loss of position, if these occur from 4th and 7th and if Mars be the lord of 5th house this may be due to some unfortunate love affair, while for those having Taurus or Libra as signs ascending at birth these adverse circumstances may be connected with their matrimonial affairs. The native may find himself frustrated in the pursued love affair and if he/she has been

recently married he/she may find herself extremely unhappy and disillusioned deeming marriage more a curse than a blessing. He/she may have much unhappy time suffering much mental grief, giving rise to crude passions of violent nature, all plunging him/her into trouble and unhappiness.

21. Mars semi-square Neptune: if occurring from the 7th or 5th house it may bring native into disrepute due to some unfortunate love affair or partnership. The period is not happy and disagreeable conditions prevail; if from the 6th making the native easily excited to wrath fulness.

22. Mars sextile Neptune: the native may be inclined to be more free and uncontrolled in forming attachments and associations which are generally not approved by society. They may bring in some pleasure if occurring from 5th and 7th; the native may also marry as a result of such a love affair.

23. When the above (no:21) is in operation if the lord of 10th be in square or opposition to Mars such marriage or love affair may lower native's prestige.

24. Mars square Neptune: the native is very susceptible to outside influence and may form some attachments in regard to which he/she may be subsequently disillusioned.

25. Mars sesquiquadrate Neptune: the native will have rather an unhappy time and for those born with Taurus or Libra as ascending signs this period may bring in fits of jealousy connected with matrimony or wife/husband. If this direction occurs in nativities with Sagittarius or Cancer as ascendant in the nativity, the native may find himself/herself loving someone who is the object of love of somebody else also, *i.e.* he/she may be a co-suitor and find himself faring rather unfavourably as compared to his/her rival.

26. Mars inconjunct Neptune: this exercises sex instincts and the result may not be happier or favourable. If the nativity indicates several love affairs, one of these may be formed under the influence of this adverse direction. The native is likely to get involved in some unworthy pursuit.

27. Mars opposition Neptune: this is an evil direction particularly so in the female nativities; and if the radical planets

so indicate a female may become the object of criminal as ault, or there is violent disturbance in the sex outlook and emotions.

28. Mars sextile to ascendant may lead to forming of attachments or unions or at least there may be impulse for such acts in a female nativity.

29. Mars trine ascendant acts similar to 27 above.

30. Radical Mars conjoined with 7th house cusp in progressed horoscope, may mean strife and quarrels with husband/wife or ill health.

Mercury

1. Mercury if in the 7th house and if in good directions with Jupiter may bring in money from wife/husband.

2. Mercury in good direction with Venus brings good and pleasant time in speech/correspondence with loved one. *Vice versa.*

3. When Mercury is afflicted by Saturn if the former planet be in the 5th or 7th conjoined with Venus, the native may enter into an agreement pertaining to marriage or write love letters which may turn out to be unfortunate. Apprehension about Children or wife.

4. Mercury in trine to Saturn: if the former be in the 5th or 7th house conjoined with Venus or if Mercury be lord of the the 5th or 7th house the native may enter into much correspondence with his beloved.

5. Mercury's evil directions with Herschel or Neptune would be evil. Good directions would bring good results.

6. Mercury's directions will have bearing on love affairs or conjugal life only if Mercury is in the 5th or 7th house or lord thereof.

Jupiter

1. Jupiter conjunction Venus is good for social success.

2. Jupiter semi-square Venus: rather unimportant but not propitious for engagements for those who have an eye on monetary gain by matrimonial alliance.

3. Jupiter sextile Venus: good for unions and marriage. There is financial gain also if either planet be lord of the 1st

house, the 2nd house, the 11th or 7th house. If resulting in marriage, the native's prestige would be enhanced thereby.

4. Jupiter square Venus: not good for love affairs or financial stability in married life; there is likely to be some separation from family. If Jupiter be in the 10th, the native may gain in honour and that may make up for domestic separation.

5. Jupiter trine Venus if occurring at appropriate time in life may result in marriage. Otherwise good for love/married life.

6. Jupiter sesquiquadrate Venus: not good for love/married happiness; there may be petty annoyances arising out of some dispute or disagreement over monetary affairs.

7. Jupiter opposition Venus: not a helpful time for suitors; they may be jilted; it may bring in opposition to marriage or financial troubles. If occurring when the couple is already estranged, it may bring about further legal trouble and waste of money.

8. When Jupiter is afflicted by Saturn there is limitation or restriction of that side which brings peace, happiness, harmony, power, prestige, social position and advantage. Therefore, a general setback in the above is felt and if the directions be connected with the 7th house or lord thereof or if there be a co-direction of a similar unfortunate nature by Venus, the above circumstances may result from unfortunate affairs of heart/marriage.

9. Jupiter in good aspect to ascendant may favour acquisition of wealth and if directions favouring union/marriage synchronise they may bring gain by marriage.

Venus

1. (i) When Venus is to the fore in directions there would be greater experience of emotion and the affectionate nature would come prominently into play.
   (ii) Venus progressed in good aspect to Venus radical; a good period for social contacts. This can occur only late in life yet it brings about joyful period.

2. Venus progressed in bad aspect to Venus radical (semi-square), normally this can occur only about 45th year. As this is an adverse direction, there would be setback in domestic affairs and the period will be marked by some frustration of feelings.

3. Venus afflicted by Saturn by direction may bring about frustration of love affair, disharmony in married life or delays and disappointments.

4. Venus parallel Saturn: this is a long-term direction and shows itself prominently only when similar directions from luminaries are in operation. It may protract love affairs or delay maturing of marriage despite some love affair being in progress or matrimonial alliance under contemplation or negotiation.

5. Venus conjunction Saturn: this is an unfavourable direction. Unless accompanying directions are very good and these planets are well-placed in the nativity, this influence leads to disappointment and even disgrace. The native may get involved with some one below his rank, with a widow/widower or with an elderly person. If the planets be strong and be excited by trine of Jupiter this may turn out to be favourable through union with a sober person of means.

6. Venus semi-sextile Saturn; this is rather a weak direction but not bad. It may bring in some new acquaintance with some person elder in age or below in rank.

7. Venus Semi-square Saturn; it is an adverse influence; affections would be chilled, and there would be obstruction in one's emotions being reciprocated.

8. Venus sextile Saturn: this is favourable for love affairs and even marriage. If at appropriate age, may lead to some permanent union and the native may benefit thereby.

9. Venus square Saturn: this is a very unfavourable direction for matters of the heart. There may be some serious disappointment in matters of affection or, if the native is already married, there may be some grief or sorrow in the married life. Domestic conditions turn out to be far from being happy. The native may indulge in some indiscreet acts and if Saturn is in 10th or

elevated and either planet connected with 10th, there may be some scandal.

10. Venus trine Saturn: it is similar to the sextile direction between these planets. The effects are more pronounced. The native may form some permanent attachments and there may be steady fulfilment of emotional aspirations.

11. Venus sesquiquadrate Saturn: this is an unfavourable direction, particularly so if accompanied by adverse lunar direction. It may lead to some disappointment, if the native is in the stage of courtship. If accompanied by other unfavourable directions may lead to some libel or scandal.

12. Venus inconjunct Saturn: this is an adverse direction and very weak also. It shows evil effect only if similar lunar direction (*i.e.*, unfavourable) be in operation.

13. Venus opposition Saturn: this is an evil direction and the native would have much disappointment and sorrow in relation to the beloved one. If already married and the nativity does not show matrimonial jars and jolts, this direction may bring about separation between the couple, due to exigencies of circumstances and affairs of the heart may thus suffer.

14. Venus parallel Herschel: the native is likely to form unorthodox attachments, romances, love affairs and may have out-of-the-way experiences in affairs of the heart; secret alliances with foreigners or new persons or those having wide disparity in age, caste, or status.

15. Venus conjunction Herschel: during this period, the native is very susceptible to form out of the way attachments. There may be sudden and impulsive attractions which the native may find difficult to resist and he is likely to form some illicit connections in a bohemian way, if the nativity so indicates.

16. Venus semi-sextile Herschel; the feelings and emotions have much sway. Care and discretion are required in forming new attachments.

17. Venus semi-square Herschel; the native is likely to get involved with persons of shady character and care is necessary in thoroughly screening new acquaintances.

18. Venus sextile Herschel; Venus-Herschel aspects bring about romantic attachments and bohemian experiences. During this sextile direction there would be much emotional upsurge. The native may form new connections if nativity so indicates. There will be much impulsive activity and the native may have unions quite in an unexpected manner brought about by peculiar circumstances.

19. Venus trine Herschel; it is good for pleasures and if the radical planet so indicates, the native may sow wild oats. He will have generally friendship or affections of a romantic character.

20. Venus sesquiquadrate Herschel; this is an unfavourable period and the native should avoid new entanglements, if other unfavourable directions are in operation, sudden troubles are threatened.

21. Venus inconjunct Herschel; this is a weak aspect and unfavourable. Only lunar directions would release energy stored, under this direction. The native may come in contact with persons of opposite sex to whose influence he/she would be very susceptible.

22. Venus opposition Herschel; this is rather an evil direction and there may be sudden trouble due to some misunderstanding, jealousy, or unfavourable intervention by a third party. There may be separation due to above causes and if the native goes to a court of law or indulges in some action involving money he/she would lose thereby. The native should exercise control over his/her emotions and not make any sudden change, or he may find this to be unfavourable. Women in whose nativity there is indication of secret love affairs will succumb under this direction and it may bring sorrow or disappointment in the end.

23. Venus semi-sextile Neptune: if these be afflicted at birth such a direction brings about disillusionment in relation to affairs of the heart, and resultant sorrow follows. The native may indulge in some act in the hope of building on steady foundations of affection but would find that he has been basing his hopes on sands of fleeting emotions.

24. Venus semi-square Neptune: there is likely to be some trouble or worry in relation to the affairs of the heart, if this direction operates at appropriate stage in life. If excited by Mars or Saturn by square or opposition or conjunction there may be some scandal also.

25. Venus sextile Neptune; there may be some new attachments bringing joyful experiences and some secret experiences. Particularly so if excited by Venus or similar lunar directions.

26. Venus square Neptune: this is an unfavourable direction and if the planets are afflicted at birth they would show similar but stronger result as described above under semi-square aspect between the two planets.

27. Venus trine Neptune: is a good period for romantic attachments and would bring pleasant experiences to the fore. If unaccompanied by untoward direction it may bring gain also, apart from emotional gratification, if there is excitement by trine or conjunction of strong Jupiter.

28. Venus inconjunct Neptune: this is an unfavourable direction having some qualities of melancholy and pathos.

29. Venus opposition Neptune; there may be disappointment and disillusionment in regard to loved one. The affairs of the heart would suffer particularly if they operate from the 1st and the 7th houses and there may be some breaking up of domestic peace if operating from the 4th and the 10th house.

30. When Venus forms a square aspect with the ascendant, sex temptations abound and there may be some trouble connected with women or love affair.

31. When Venus opposes ascendant by progressed directions, there is generally some indulgence bringing about extravagance and loss of money and bodily substance.

32. Venus trine Ascendant: is good for pleasure, pursuit of love affair, matrimonial alliance or some union.

33. All good aspects between ascendant and Venus have the same effect as 32 above.

34. Venus in good direction with the lord of the 5th house is fortunate for progress of love affairs and the passionate nature finds its fulfilment.

35. Venus in square of opposition to lord or the 7th house, brings about disharmony and irritation in conjugal life. If there be affliction of any kind pertaining to Venus or the 7th house in the nativity such unfavourable directions result in discord or temporary disruption but if the radical positions be fortunate, there may be only temporary separation with the loved one.

36. Venus in square or opposition to lord of the 5th house result in frustration in love affairs and if thereby similar unfortunate direction to Neptune also occurs, much disillusionment may come to the native.

37. Venus in good direction with lord of the 7th house is fortunate for bringing about marriage or harmony in married life.

38. Venus trine M.C. good for attachments, love affairs, increase of prestige by marriage/union.

39. All good aspects between Venus and M.C. are similar in nature to 38 above.

40. Venus square M.C., if configurated adversely with the malefics may bring about some loss of reputation in connection with some love affair. If favourably configurated with benefics, not so bad.

41. Venus opposition M.C. similar to 40 above.

42. Good directions of Venus generally bring about new friendships, or renewal of older attachments bringing in much pleasure and gaiety. Evil directions do otherwise.

Saturn

1. When Saturn is the afflicting planet by direction it brings limitation or check in the turn of events so that either the efforts or negotiations remain incomplete or there is permanent limitation, *i.e.*, frustration. If no permanent damage is done there is temporary check, *i.e.*, causing delay and therefore disappointment.

2. Saturn afflicting lord of the 7th house by direction denotes frustration, disappointment, and sorrow in marriage or married life.

3. Saturn afflicting lord of the 5th house or a planet in the 5th: disappointment in love affair or causing much delay in fruition of desire.

4. Saturn in trine to lord of the 7th or a planet in the 7th by direction brings steadiness in married life and if the other planet be a benefic, there may be gain of money by partnership.

5. Saturn in trine to lord of the 5th house; steady progress in affairs of the heart.

Herschel and Neptune

1. Herschel or Neptune square M.C.: the native may suffer due to fraud and treachery by/through women if the direction is from Herschel or Neptune in the 7th house.

Houses or by Lords Thereof

General

1. The reference to 'houses' in this part is primarily to the radical houses.

2. How lords of various houses, when in square or opposition to the lord of the 7th house, adversely affect the 7th house prospects has been mentioned. Similarly, when the lord of the particular house forms a favourable aspect by direction with the 7th house lord good results follow. *Vice versa.*

Note: Result of directions has to be arrived at by looking to the background and circumstances. Second house is the house of wealth; from the 5th house we judge children, speculation, love affairs. Evil directions between lords of the 2nd and 5th house may bring expenditure due to children in the case of an old man, loss in speculation to a businessman and waste of money in the case of a young suitor. Those who ignore basic possibilities likely to commit serious errors in prediction.

Between Lords of Houses

First House

1. Note the decanate and 1/12th division of the sign in which the progressed ascendant is. The native will exhibit traits and tendencies pertaining to the lord of the sign and the lord of the decanate and 1/12th division in which progressed ascendant is situated.

2. When Aries is the sign and Leo the decanate of the

progressed ascendant the native is likely to have a love affair and if already married there would be greater emotional upsurge and sensuous craving.

3. When Gemini is the sign and Libra the decanate of the progressed horoscope the native is likely to contact some new person and have attachment (union) with him/her.

4. When Leo is the sign and also the decanate the native is likely to have increased sex desires and form attachments.

5. When Libra is the sign and also the decanate of the progressed ascendant, the native's life would be marked by attachments to someone and that someone's influence may be prominent in his life and activities.

6. When Libra is the sign and Aquarius, the decanate of progressed ascendant, there is likely to be some firm attachment resulting in benefit to the native.

7. When Scorpio is the sign and Cancer the progressed decanate the native may have some romantic episodes, if the nativity so indicates.

8. When Sagittarius is the sign and Leo the decanate of the progressed ascendant, the native may fall headlong in love with someone, if there is an accompanying direction of similar nature to Venus or lord of the 7th house.

9. When Aquarius is the sign and Libra the decanate of the progressed ascendant, the native may have love for some one of the opposite sex and this would last for some appreciable time.

10. When Pisces is the rising and Cancer is the decanate of the progressed ascendant the native may fall in love with someone other than one's wife/husband or have two episodes simultaneously, if the nativity so indicates.

11. Good aspects to the cusp of the 1st house from the 1st or 5th house, *i.e.* conjunction or trine by Venus or lord of the the 7th house may be productive of beneficial change.

12. Lord of the 1st house in good aspect by direction with lord of the 5th house or planets forming a trine from the 1st and 5th houses may bring about fruition of love/marriage but if they be in square or opposition and operate say from the 3rd and 12th houses or the 6th and 12th houses they would show evil results.

13. Lord of the 1st house in good aspect with lord of the 7th house would lead to good harmony, love and pleasure from wife/husband.

14. Lord of the 1st house in trine to lord of the 7th house or if both be benefics in conjunction would show happy results but lord of 1st in square or opposition to lord of the 7th house (by direction) would show evil result.

15. Lord of the 1st house in favourable aspect with lords of the 4th and 7th houses would lead to settling up of a good a peaceful home and domestic happiness when the above direction is formed. If the two lords form adverse aspects contrary would be the effect.

16. Conjunction of the lords of the 1st and 7th houses by direction (if the two planets be of harmonious nature) in the 3rd house may lead to forming of matrimonial alliance by correspondence or while the two are away on a short journey.

17. Conjunction of lord of the 1st and 7th house by direction (if the two planets be of harmonious nature) in the 9th or 12th house may point to matrimonial alliance due to the parties being away on journey and meeting abroad or due to coming into contact together in some secluded or confined place like a hospital or meeting in some place of religious significance.

18. Lord of the 1st house in evil directions with lord of the the 7th house would bring quarrels and annoyances in conjugal life.

Second House

19. Lord of the second house due to ownership of second affects family, wealth and finances.

20. Lord of the 2nd house in square or opposition with lord of the 5th house both being malefics and operating say, from the 2nd and 5th houses or the 2nd and 11th houses or the 5th and 11th houses may bring about loss of money due to love affairs.

21. Lord of the 2nd forming square or opposition with the lord of the 7th house and conjunction of the two planets if they be of inharmonious nature would lead to squandering of money, breaking up of family unity, and may have repercussions on domestic life.

22. Lord of the 2nd house in good aspect with lord of the 7th house may lead to gain of money through partnership and generally to the acquisition of wealth.

23. Lord of the 2nd house in good aspect with lord of the 5th house may lead to sudden gain of money by love affair or speculation and if the two planets are of harmonious nature and their conjunction occurs in the 7th house the gain may be due to matrimonial alliance directions to the third house or lord thereof.

Third House

24. Lord of the 3rd house in good aspect with lord of the 7th house may lead to much correspondence with the loved one and cementing of family tie due to junior members of the family.

25. Lord of the 3rd house in evil aspect to lord of the 7th: house there may be quarrels in the conjugal stage, due to junior members (such as younger brothers or sisters) of the family or neighbours.

26. Lord of the 3rd house forming an evil direction with the lord of the 7th house may bring about bitterness in correspondence with the partner or temporary separation due to some short journey.

Fourth House

27. Lord of the 4th house forming good directions with the lord of the 7th house: there may be gain of conveyance or landed property through marriage. *Vice versa*.

Fifth House

28. Lord of the 5th house in good aspect with lord of the 7th house: the love affair may ultimately have a successful conclusion and marriage may be brought about. Also there may be good relations with the children due to benefic influence of husband/wife. But if the two lords are opposed or form square aspect there may be much trouble and opposition from children due to wife/husband when such direction is formed.

29. Similarly, an evil direction between two inimical planets if they be lords of the 5th and 10th houses may bring about loss of position due to an unfortunate love affair..

30. Lord of the 5th house in opposition to lord of the 12th house: the native indulges in waste of money due to love affairs and pleasure seeking.

31. Lord of the 5th forming evil directions with lord of the 7th from 2nd or 12th houses: expenditure of money due to wife/husband's illness or quarrels in conjugal state.

Seventh House

32. Aspects between two planets when either or both happen to be in the 7th house radical or progressed has a bearing on the 7th house affairs. The same is the result when either planet is lord or the 7th house.

33. Evil directions between lord of the 7th and 8th houses are particularly evil.

34. Lord of the 7th house forming good direction with lord of the 9th house may lead to acquisition of religious merit and pilgrimage or rise in fortune and prosperity with or due to wife or may benefit from wife's husband's relation.

35. Lord of the 7th house when opposing or forming a square aspect with the lord of the 10th house or if the two planets be of inharmonious nature and may form a conjunction, may lead to loss of prestige or service due to matrimony or some causes connected with husband/wife.

36. When lord of the 7th and 10th house form favourable aspect, it leads to greater activity of work and enhancement of honour and prestige or gain of some work due to co-operation of wife/husband.

37. If the lord of the 7th and 10th houses are of harmonious nature and form a conjunction, the results are similar to 36 above.

38. An evil direction between the lords of the 7th and 10th houses if between two inharmonious planets would bring about great opposition to marriage or if the nativity so portends, loss of position and prestige due to marriage.

39. If good directions by (conjunction or aspect) to the

meridian cusp synchronise with good directions bringing about love and marriage, the astrologer should predict that the marriage or union would be socially advantageous to the native. *Vice versa*.

40. In 39 above, it would be particularly so if the trine or conjunction of a benefic is from a planet in the 7th house or the lord thereof. This would particularly be so if lords of the the 7th and 10th houses are strong and radically in good aspect with each other.

41. If evil directions by conjunction or aspect to the meridian cusp synchronise with evil directions from the 7th house or lord thereof, there may be elopement, frustration and disaster in married life; the astrologer should conclude that such an event would also bring loss of prestige and would be specially disadvantageous.

42. In 41 above, this would be particularly so, if in the nativity, the lords of the 7th and 10th houses are inharmonious planets and afflict each other and are weak and debilitated.

43. Lord of the 7th house forming evil directions with lord of the 11th house: obstruction and impediment in acquiring of wealth or obstacle in married life due to some friend.

44. Lord of the 7th house forming good directions with lord of the 11th may lead to gain of money through wife/husband. This is particularly so if the directions are formed from the 7th and 11th houses or the 5th and 9th houses or from the 9th and 11th houses or from the 1st and 5th houses, or from the Ist and 11th houses or from the 5th and 7th houses, or the 1st and 9th houses.

45. Lord of the 7th in good aspect with the lord of the 12th house there may be saving of money and the native may be able to put away by some money due to the co-operation of the partner.

46. Lord of the 7th house forming evil directions with lord of the 12th house. There is much expenditure and waste of money due to marriage partner.

47. If in an evil direction between two planets lord of the 12th house also joins and if it be a malefic and if these directions

operate say from the 12th and 6th houses, the native may have to live in seclusion or under restriction if lord of the 1st house is also involved adversely.

CHAPTER 7

TRANSITS

Progressed planets are the principal significators of when an event will fructify. However, Transit of Planets on sensitive points and particularly related to the planets whose directions are in operation at that time, will bring more accuracy in the timing of events. The transits can actually strengthen the events or may even reduce its intensity, for example, progressed Moon trine Venus will show adverse results if at the same time Saturn in transit has an adverse aspect with either Moon or Venus. If on the other hand a good transit is simultaneous taking place then the results will be many times stronger.

Another factor which should be considered in Transit is when a lunation (or New Moon) occurs. If the New Moon or Full Moon is conjunct a radical planet then the effect of that will be felt for a few weeks to a few years. For example, a New Moon occurs on the longitude of Venus then Venus becomes excited and new chapter starts—related to the love life or to a child.*

The effect of eclipses falling on the sensitive points in a horoscope is many times stronger. If the New Moon, Full Moon or Eclipses takes place at the time of the Solar Return then the effect will last for the full year.

Sometime Transit do not show any effect due to the obstructions caused by other planet in transit.†

---

* Venus also rules children, many women conceive children at this time due to this configuration.

† For obstruction (viz., 'Vedh') see Astrolgy and You.

The Transit can be seen in the Ephemeris of the actual year of events.

We now give below the effects of Transits in General followed by the Transits of Sun, Moon, Mars etc.:

How They Influence Married Happiness, Love Affairs

General

1. For judging timing of events, transits must also be considered. Some important ones are being dealt with below:

2. As directions yield results only if there is scope for the fruition of particular events in the nativity (if radical planets so ordain) so transits are looked into for determination of specific influence to narrow down the margin of time in directions. For example, if Sun square Saturn is in operation the evil transits of Saturn or Mars may expedite producing tangible effect.

3. Transits are more important when they transit signs which are in angles. Even among the four angles the Ist and 10th houses are more important than the 4th and 7th house. For matrimonial purposes, 7th is more important.

4. In houses other than the Ist house, the 10th house, the 4th and 7th houses transits become important if the house transited by a planet is tenanted by a planet in the nativity. For example, transit of Saturn through the sixth house would have added importance if Sun is in the 6th house in the nativity.

5. A malefic planet weak by house and sign and afflicted in a nativity would show very evil results under unfavourable transit.

6. When Sun transits a house it stimulates the activities pertaining to the house.

7. When Sun by transit passes over the radical position of a planet it brings into activity the influence of the planet transited.

8. When Sun by transit passes the (180°) one hundred eightieth degree from the radical position of a planet, its influence is similar to 7 above.

9. Sun's transit over a malefic or over an afflicted planet or in opposition to these two is unfavourable.

10. When Sun and Moon simultaneously transit a particular house they stimulate the activity of that particular house, particularly when both of them form a conjunction on the cusp of that house.

11. The effect of conjunction of Sun and Moon by transit, particularly in angles is more pronounced and effective throughout the month.

12. New Moon in the 1st house is favourable for personal matters. Similarly, for matrimony or friendship its passage through the 5th house, the 7th and 11th houses is more important.

13. If the luminaries be in the 7th house, passage of Mars over them may rather prove a disturbing influence to conjugal happiness.

14. Mars precipitates events; its effects are sudden and unexpected.

15. Transit of Mars is generally unfavourable, unless the planet is transiting its own house.

16. Effect of transit of Mars is particularly pronounced when passing over angles or over radical Sun and Moon. Effects pertaining to love affairs may be felt if either Sun or Moon is in the 5th house, and the native may find it difficult to keep under control expression of his/her desires.

17. Mars while transiting the 1st house gives impetus to personal efforts and boldness. This may have significance pertaining to the subject under discussion, if Mars be the lord of the 5th or 7th house.

18. Transit of Mars through the 4th house if either or both of the luminaries be there, would produce domestic discord.

19. Passage of Mars through the 11th house if either or both luminaries be there, would stimulate friendships.

20. When Mercury passes through a house it brings into prominence the activity pertaining to that house.

21. When Mercury passes through the 1st house it gives stimulus to thought and the native is more prone to enter into correspondence.

22. When Mercury passes through the 4th house, the 7th or

10th houses similar results to those described in 21 above. The correspondence would be pertaining to love affair or matrimony if there are similar directions in operation and if Mercury is conjoined with Venus.

23. Transit of Jupiter is generally favourable, bringing luck pertaining to the house through which it transits.

24. Jupiter transiting through the 1st house would bring benefic influence to bear upon personal efforts.

25. Jupiter's passage through the 2nd house is productive of monetary gain and if Jupiter be the lord of the 7th house or posited there (in 7th) in the nativity or Jupiter's passage through the 2nd synchronises with directions of marriage, there may be gain from the alliance.

26. Jupiter's transit through the 3rd is good for correspondence.

27. When Jupiter passes through the 4th house, it produces harmony in domestic sphere.

28. Jupiter passing through the 5th house favours attachments, love affairs and pleasure-seeking in general.

29. Jupiter's passage through the 7th house should be judged *mutatis mutandis* as in 5 above.

30. Jupiter's transit through the 7th house is particularly good for matrimony, fixing up the alliance, etc.

31. Jupiter through 8th house may bring some gain through the partner.

32. Jupiter's passage through the 11th house is good for friendships.

33. Jupiter if lord of the 7th house or posited there, in the nativity when passing through the 12th house may bring in some secret attachments or extravagance connected with the partner.

34. Jupiter's passage over Sun or Moon is auspicious and brings some favourable opportunity. Particularly so, if the luminary be in an angle and if these two luminaries be in the 7th house Jupiter's transit which may bring in marriage, if a similar direction be in operation.

35. When Venus transits a house it brings some harmony or aesthetics into play in relation to that house. For example,

Venus through the fifth may give stimulus to love affair, through the 7th house to matrimonial affairs, through the 11th house to friendship or companionship particularly of the fairer sex.

36. When Venus is on the cusp of the 1st house, the 10th house, the 4th or 7th houses, it inclines to pleasure and gay society.

37. Saturn's transit through the 1st house generally exerts a restricting influence unless it be the lord of the 4th and 5th houses or the 9th and 10th* houses. It would, therefore, hamper affairs pertaining to love and marriage but for those born with Cancer or Leo as ascendant it may bring about marriage or give prominence to the 7th house affairs.

38. Saturn's passing through the second house disturbs the family equilibrium.

39. Saturn's passage through the third house is generally good. But if the house itself is afflicted or if the 9th house be afflicted one may have trouble through/due to relations.

40. Saturn's passage through the fourth house is generally unfortunate and if there be a planet in the 7th house it would particularly be so; it brings about quarrels, upsets domestic circumstances and there may be even bereavements.

41. Saturn's passage through the fifth house may break up some standing attachment or hamper some love affair if the same be in progress or in process of achievement.

42. Saturn's passage through the sixth house will have a depressing influence on health.

43. Saturn's passage through the 7th house may bring about quarrels with the loved one or wife/husband. There may be some sad affairs, if the prevailing directions are also unfavourable, but if Saturn be lord of the 7th house, this would not be evil. It may bring about marriage if the current directions so indicate.

44. Saturn passing through the 8th house would particularly

---

* Unless any sign is intercepted this is possible only in nativities having sign Taurus or sign Libra rising. When Libra rises Saturn is the lord of 4th and 5th. When Taurus rises Saturn is the lord of 9th and 10th.

upset the finances pertaining to wife/husband or to be received through her/him.

45. Saturn's transit through the 9th house may bring about misunderstandings or quarrels with wife/husband's relations, if this house is radically afflicted.

46. Saturn's passage through the 10th house adversely affects honour and prestige and if Saturn is the owner of the 7th house or afflicts the lord of the 5th/7th house radically, this loss of honour and prestige may be connected with marriage or love affair.

47. Saturn's passage through the 11th house disillusions one with regard to some friendship, or intimacy one had been banking upon.

48. Saturn's transit through the twelfth house would adversely affect health and would bring about enmity, sorrows and wasteful expenditure. This may be due to love affair or marriage or an offshoot of it, if Saturn radically afflicts lord of the 5th or 7th houses.

49. Saturn's transit over the place of Sun or in square or opposition to it is unfortunate and if either of the planet is connected with the 7th house or afflicts the same adversely or the lord thereof the trouble may pertain to that department of life.

50. Saturn's transit over the place of Moon or in square or opposition to it has the same effect as described in relation to Saturn's transit over or in adverse position to the radical Sun.

51. Saturn's transit is particularly evil through the angles, *i.e.*, when Saturn is passing over the exact degree on the cusp of the 1st house, the 4th house, the 7th and 10th houses. The 4th and 7th house cusps are more connected with the domestic and married life.

52. Transits of Herschel and Neptune are unfavourable, particularly over luminaries, angles or over radical or progressed position of planets or in opposition to them.

Transits of Sun over other Planets

1. Sun's transit over its own radical place is very important. All other transits have also greater significance on or about the Solar date of birth , *i.e.* when Sun has the same sign, degree,

minute and second as it had at the time of birth. This should be calculated in the sidereal or fixed zodiac.

2. Sun in good aspect to good planets confers good opportunities and they may pertain to love/marriage if Sun or the aspecting planet is the ruler of the horoscope (nativity) or lord of the 7th house or if either of the two (Sun and the aspecting planet) is located in the 7th house of the annual horoscope (Solar return horoscope) or in the nativity (birth chart).

3. Sun's transit over malefics or in square or opposition to malefics will have adverse influence and this may be pertaining to the domestic sphere or love/marriage, if either Sun or the aspecting planet is connected with the 1st house the 4th house the 5th or 7th house by ownership or association.

Transits of Moon over other Planets

4. Transits or Moon are very frequent as this luminary completes its circle round Zodiac in about 27days. Moon's transit over benefics is good. This luminary's transit over malefics or in opposition to them is evil. When over the cusp of the 5th or 7th house or over Venus, it may give a pleasant time.

5. When the transiting planet is itself afflicted it cannot confer good. Similarly, when the transiting planet is at the time of transit well aspected, particularly by a trine of Jupiter, it would not do much harm.

This principle should be kept in mind all through; particularly in Judgement of Moon's transit.

Transits of the Movers

Transits of the Mars

6. Mars in transit over radical Sun would endow the native with much energy. If the two planets were strong at the time of birth and if either of these be connected with 5th or 7th house, this may have a good effect on love affairs and matrimony. The native would become bold enough to achieve his object, but if either of the planets were afflicted in the nativity, such boldness would become impudence and there would be frustration.

7. Transit of Mars over radical Moon is unfavourable but if either planet is connected with 5th or 7th house and Mars is well aspected at the time of birth, the native would feel maritally inclined.

8. Transits of Mars over its own place would be good if this planet were strong and well aspected at the time of birth; *vice versa*.

9. Transit of Mars over radical Mercury. If either planet is connected with 7th house of or with Venus, the native would become critical of his partner's/beloved's behaviour. He/She may yield a strong pen of indulge in rash speech and thus evince his/her critical attitude.

10. Transit of Mars over Jupiter will be good but connected with some expenditure. If in 7th house or Mars or Jupiter owns the cusp of the 7th house in the birthchart, this may be connected with wife/beloved.

11. Mars transiting over Venus would lead to pleasure and enjoyment.

12. Transit of Mars over Saturn is unfavourable.

13. Mars transiting over Herschel brings about sudden actions; if in the 5th or 7th house they may involve the native in something he/she may regret in sober moments.

14. Mars transiting over radical Neptune inclines to wine and women if the chart of the native shows such inclination.

Transits of Mercury over other Planets

15. Mercury by transit passing over the radical position of Sun is good for writing letters or entering into correspondence. If the radical Sun forms good aspects with Venus or lord of the 7th house and is unafflicted otherwise, this would be a suitable and favourable time to enter into correspondence with a view to matrimony or with the beloved.

16. Mercury by transit passing over the radical position of Moon is good for entering into correspondence or making a proposal. (But if the Moon has square of any malefic avoid this time for misunderstanding may result. It would particularly be so, if afflicted by Neptune).

17. Mercury in transit passing over the radical position of Mars is likely to cause worries, fretting and fuming. If either planet is connected with 7th house or if the radical position of Mars is in square or opposition to some planet posited in the 7th the dispute may be with wife/beloved.

18. Mercury by transit passing over its own radical position would be good or bad, according to whether the radical Mercury is good or bad.

19. Mercury passing over the radical Jupiter is good for gains and success, in general. This may pertain to some love affair or marriage if either planet is in 7th house or if current directions so indicate.

20. Mercury by transit over radical Venus is favourable for pleasant time, making new friends or indulging in enjoyments. The native may receive a sweet and pleasant communication.

21. Mercury's transit over radical Saturn causes worries and anxieties. It would particularly be so if Saturn is weak and afflicted and Mercury while actually transiting is also afflicted.

22. Mercury passing over radical Herschel makes the native mentally alert. He thinks of new plans. This may pertain to matrimony, if either planet is conjoined with Venus or the transit itself is through the 7th house. If the radical Herschel is afflicted, this transit would be unfavourable.

23. Mercury in transit over radical Neptune would incline the native to enter into corresponddence, more based on one's own utopian ideas than on reality. If the radical Neptune is afflicted this correspondence, would result in frustration.

Transits of Jupiter

24. Transits of Jupiter over other planets (radical positions in the nativity) have generally benefic reaction.

25. Jupiter's transit over radical Sun brings gain from husband (in female nativity). In male nativities, the effect pertaining to love/marriage would be felt, if Sun is in the 7th house or the sign rising is Gemini or Virgo or Aquarius.

26. Jupiter in transit over Moon is particularly good if the rising sign is Capricorn or Gemini or Virgo. In a male nativity this may indicate gain from/through wife.

27. Jupiter's transit over Mars may involve some overt act pertaining to love/marriage if either planet is connected with 7th house. Goodness or badness of effect would depend upon strength or weakness of Mars in the nativity.

28. Jupiter's transit over radical Mercury would be good and yield some result pertaining to love/marriage if the rising sign is Gemini, Virgo, Sagittarius, or Pisces or if Mercury is in the 7th house in the nativity.

29. Jupiter's transit over radical Venus is good for love/marriage and the native would be well received in female society.

30. Jupiter's transit over its own place is good; particularly so, if Jupiter be connected by ownership or association with the 7th house.

31. Jupiter's transit over radical Saturn would be conducive to love and harmony or marriage only if Saturn is essentially strong in the nativity and if Cancer or Leo is the rising sign.

32. Jupiter's transit over Herschel would have something to do with love or marriage only if Herschel is in 5th or 7th house in the nativity or Jupiter is the lord of 5th or 7th house.

33. Jupiter's transit over Neptune would incline the native to pleasure through poetry, drama, art, etc. But it would have something to do with love affairs or marriage if Neptune is in the 7th house, or Gemini or Virgo is the rising sign.

Transits of Venus

34. Transits of Venus are very frequent, and as such it would show only a minor effect in the sense that it may not bring out any action or event, but only accelerate it if the current directions so ordain.

(a) Transit of Venus over radical Sun is good for love/marriage and enjoyment in general.
(b) Transit of Venus over radical Moon is good for enjoyment.
(c) Transit of Venus over radical Mars spurs sexual emotions into activity.

(d) Transit of Venus over radical Mercury is good for making friendships, renewing old ties, correspondence, etc.

(e) Transit of Venus over radical Jupiter favours gain.

(f) Transit of Venus over its own place is favourable for love making.

(g) Transit of Venus over Saturn would have any bearing only if Capricorn, Aquarius, Cancer, or Leo is the rising sign in the nativity.

(h) Venus transiting radical Herschel may spur into activity, sexual emotions in a sudden and impulsive manner.

(i) Transit of Venus over radical Neptune may be good for love affairs, if Neptune is strong and well aspected in the nativity. If Neptune be afflicted, there would be frustration.

Transits of Saturn

35. Saturn is a restricting planet and as such not much good may be expected out of his transits. Its transits over the various planets would bring about only handicaps, worries, and disappointments. But if Saturn is strong in the nativity, it may by transit bring about an alliance or affair with an elderly person and such association may result in gain.

But if Saturn is particularly afflicted, its transit over planets connected with the 7th house or transit over any sensitive point would bring out some trouble or other.

Transits of Herschel

36. Transit of Herschel over Sun in female nativities may produce some trouble pertaining to husband/beloved.

37. Transit of Herschel over Moon in male nativities may bring about some trouble pertaining to wife/sweetheart.

38. Transit of Herschel over radical Mars is particularly unfavourable if Taurus or Libra is the rising sign or if Mars is located in the 7th house. If as above, it would have something to do with quarrels or estrangements pertaining to husband/

wife. Transit of Herschel over radical Mars in 5th house would also bring about frustration of desires.

39. Transit of Herschel over radical Mercury would be good or bad according to whether Mercury is strong or weak in the nativity. It would have significance pertaining to correspondence with the beloved or any love affair or marriage only if Mercury is in the 5th or 7th house or any of the signs owned by Mercury are on the cusps of these two houses.

40. Transit of Herschel over radical Jupiter would be beneficial, if Jupiter be strong and well-aspected at birth. *Vice versa.*

41. Transit of Herschel over radical Venus would bring some trouble through love/marriage, if Venus is afflicted in the nativity. It may plunge the native headlong into some affair which he may regret later.

42. Transit of Herschel over Saturn is unfavourable. It may affect the domestic sphere if Saturn has connection with the 4th house, the 5th or 7th house.

43. Transit of Herschel over its own place can occur only if the native lives beyond 84 years, *i.e.,* at an age where affairs pertaining to love or marriage have no consequence.

44. Transit of Herschel over radical Neptune will involve the native into more than one affair, if the latter planet is in the 5th or 7th house in the nativity.

Transits of Neptune

45. Neptune's transit over radical Sun is unfavourable and may affect domestic affairs. It would be particularly so, in female nativities.

46. Neptune's transit over radical Moon is unfavourable and may affect domestic affairs particularly, so in male nativities.

47. Neptune's transit over Mars may lead to quarrels with the beloved/wife if Mars is associated with the 5th or 7th house by ownership or association.

48. Neptune's transit over radical Mercury may adversely affect the domestic circumstances, if Mercury is in the 5th or 7th houses or Aquarius, Taurus, Sagittarius or Pisces is the rising sign.

49. Neptune's transit over radical Jupiter would bring gain through husband or wife if Jupiter is strong and connected with the 5th or 7th houses. *Vice versa.*

50. Neptune's transit over radical Venus inclines to love affairs, goodness or badness of which would depend upon the strength or weakness of the radical Venus.

51. Neptune's transit over radical Saturn would bring about difficulties and troubles, particularly so if in the 5th or 7th house.

52. Neptune's transit over Uranus (Herschel) would have something to do with domestic affairs if the latter planet is in the 5th or 7th house. It is unfavourable.

53. Neptune's transit over its own place cannot occur in one's life.

Part II
HINDU ASTROLOGY

CHAPTER 8

APHORISMS OF PLANETS

We now undertake the interpretation of Friendship, Love and Marriage *According to the Traditional Hindu Astrological System.* Many details have already been mentioned in the Introduction and at various other places. Some Important facts has also been given in the appendices. In the present chapter we will give the Aphorisms of Planets.

Aphorisms of Sun

Sun is the centre around which all planets rotate. It is not only the giver of energy but also shows the inner strength of a person. The characteristics or traits of the Zodiac Sign in which Sun is posited at birth becomes very dominant in an individual. His nature, his behaviour, his courage indicates the amount of success in love that he will receive. For example, Sun in Virgo indicates shyness as well as an analytical and critical mind and so when it comes to interaction with a second party, the native is either lost in finding perfection or takes so much time due to shyness (or fear of rejection) that the opportunity slips out of hand. These people need someone to give them the push so they take faster action in most department of life.

We now give below the effect of Sun in signs, houses or when in association with other planets:

1. Sun in Aries if aspected by Moon; the native is of good appearance and is liked by ladies. If aspected by Venus, he has a bad wife.

2. Sun in Taurus makes one fond of women. But he has quarrels with them and enmity may arise with some loved

ones. If aspected by Moon the native has alliances with a number of women and is fond of dancing girls also. If aspected by Venus he gets money by association with women; if aspected by Saturn the native has association with an elderly woman.

3. Sun in Gemini: if aspected by Mars the native is shy of women; if aspected by Venus has a good wife; if aspected by Saturn has an ill-looking wife.

4. Sun in Cancer aspected by Venus makes one serve a woman and get money from ladies.

5. Sun in Leo: has a good wife of high family if aspected by Mars, attached to other people's wives.

6. Sun in Virgo; the native has effeminate body and is shy. If aspected by Venus, has a good wife; if aspected by Saturn has an ill-looking wife.

7. Sun in Libra; fond of other people's wives; if aspected by Moon, has alliances with a number of women and is fond of dancing girls also, if aspected by Venus, gets money by association with women; if aspected by Saturn association with an elder woman.

8. Sun in Scorpio; the native has a wicked wife, who may also predecease. If aspected by Moon the native's wife would be of good appearance and he would be liked by ladies; if aspected by Venus the native would have a bad wife and would also suffer from loath-some diseases.

9. Sun in Sagittarius: if aspected by Venus has a very good wife, if aspected by Saturn fond of low women.

10. Sun in Capricorn: the native is attached to a bad woman, if aspected by Moon, loses his money and happiness due to association with women; if aspected by Venus, gets money through women and has liaisons with them.

11. Sun in Aquarius: the native is attached to other people's wives and is a flirt; if aspected by Moon, loses money through women but if aspected by Venus gains through them.

12. Sun in Pisces: gets happiness through love affairs with women and is much respected by them; if aspected by Venus has a very good wife, but if aspected by Saturn the native is attached to low women.

Sun in Various Houses

13. Sun in 4th attachment with a barren woman; no happiness from love affairs.

14. Sun in 6th houses; the native is full of lust.

15. Sun in 7th house.

(i) If Sun strong by sign and 'ansha' is in the seventh house, the native would be attached to his own wife.

(ii) Sun in the 7th house: if aspected by a malefic the native would get into disfavour with women.

(iii) Sun in the 7th house: the native may have union with a barren woman, particularly if not aspected by Jupiter.

(iv) Sun in the 7th house; the native may marry a girl with very firm breasts.

(v) Sun in the 7th house if strong and aspected by lord of the 9th or 4th house or the 5th house: gain of money by marriage.

(vi) Sun in the 7th house well-aspected; the native's wife would be proud, religious, with less hair on body, her eye balls a little yellowish in tinge fond of travelling but not very talkative or generous.

16. Sun in the 8th house; the native may have enmity with some women.

17. Sun in the 9th house; there may be enmity with women of good social rank.

18. Sun in the 12th house; may marry or have liaison with a barren woman.

Sun in Combination with other Planets

19. Sun, Mercury together make one subservient to the wishes of ladies.

20. Sun, Venus together : one gets money by association with women.

21. Sun, Saturn together; devoid of conjugal happiness.

22. Sun, Moon and Saturn together: proficient in sexual matters.

23. Sun, Mars and Mercury together; devoid of happiness.

24. Sun, Mercury and Venus together: pines for love due to not having or separation from wife/beloved.

25. Sun, Mercury and Saturn together: behaves like a eunuch.

26. Sun, Saturn and Jupiter together: good wife.

27. Sun, Venus and Saturn together: not of good moral character.

28. Sun, Mercury, and Jupiter together: attached to his own wife.

29. Sun, Moon, Mars and, Saturn, not of good morals.

30. Sun, Moon, Jupiter and Saturn together: good wife.

31. Sun, Moon, Venus and Saturn together : behaves like a woman.

32. Sun, Mars, Mercury and Jupiter together: not much conjugal happiness.

33. Sun, Mars, Mercury and Saturn, together : low morals.

34. Sun, Mars, Venus and Saturn together: low morals.

35. Sun, Mercury and Jupiter, Saturn together: behaves like a eunuch.

36. Sun, Moon, Mars, Mercury and Jupiter together : lives separated from wife.

37. Sun, Moon, Mars, Mercury and Saturn together: devoid of matrimonial happiness.

38. Sun, Moon, Mars, Venus and Saturn together: low morals and attached to other people's wives.

39. Sun, Moon, Jupiter, Venus and Saturn; liked by ladies.

40. Sun, Moon, Mars, Mercury, Jupiter and Saturn together; attached to other women and suffers physical diseases.

Sun in Combination with other Planets in Various Houses

41. Sun and Venus in first house: not good for conjugal happiness.

42. Sun and Venus together in 2nd; the native marries or cohabits with a barren woman.

43. Sun and Venus in the 5th house; the native's wife suffers from some bodily defect. The native himself is strongly sexed and has much yearning and many love affairs.

44. Sun in close association with Venus and Mars in the 5th house: there may be premature death of wife.

45. Sun in the 6th house and Moon in the 12th house; not only the native's but his wife's eyesight is also impaired—at least one of the eyes.

46. Sun and Moon in the 7th house: the man is humble and is always oppressed by ladies.

47. Sun and Mars in the 7th house: suffers from separation from wife and has to undergo much distress for/through wife.

48. Sun in the 7th house with Mars and Venus; bad for wife's longevity; more than one marriage likely.

49. Sun and Mercury in the 7th house: devoid of conjugal happiness.

50. Sun and Jupiter in the 7th house: too much under influence of wife and given to lusts thereby causing a rift between himself and his father.

51. Sun and Venus in the 7th house house: not good for conjugal happiness, distress from women.

52. Sun and Venus in the 7th house aspected by malefics; wife may suffer from disease; conjugal unhappiness.

53. Sun and Saturn in the 7th house; devoid of conjugal happiness and wealth.

54. Sun and Rahu in the 7th house: the native would squander his wealth over women; loss of wealth through women.

55. Sun with Mars or Saturn or Rahu or Mandi in the 7th house: the native's wife has well-developed pudendum.

56. Sun, Moon and Venus in the 9th house house: all wealth and happiness is destroyed due to quarrel with/on account of women.

57. Sun, Mars and Venus in the 9th house: the native has much quarrels with young girls whom he seduces. His own wife may suffer or may die prematurely from ill-health.

58. Sun Mercury and Saturn in 9th house; sinful and attached to other people's wives.

59. Sun, Jupiter and Venus in the 9th house: enjoys life.

60. Sun, Moon, Mars and Venus in the 9th house: satisfied with his own wife.

61. Sun, Mars, Mercury and Jupiter in the 9th house: prosperous wife.

62. Sun, Mars, Mercury and Saturn in the 9th house attached to other persons' wives and loss of wealth thereby.

63. Sun, Mars, Jupiter and Venus in the 9th house: seduces young girls.

64. Sun, Mercury, Jupiter and Saturn in the 9th house: sinful and attached to others' wives.

65. If Sun and Venus are together in the 10th house from Moon, the native derives much prosperity and wealth through/from women.

66. If Sun is in the 12th house and Moon is in 6th, the native may lose prematurely eyesight in one eye and so does his wife.

67. If Sun, Venus and lord of the 7th house are aspected by benefics, the native's wife would be virtuous.

68. If Sun be the lord of the 7th house, strong and conjoined with a benefic in a benefic sign and ansha and aspected by a benefic, the native's wife would be virtuous.

69. If Sun be the lord of the 7th house and posited in malefic signs and malefic anṣhas and aspected by malefics, wife would be sinful.

70. Add together the longitudes of (i) Sun and Venus. If the sum total falls in a benefic sign and house and is aspected by benefics, it is conducive to matrimonial happiness. *Vice versa*.

71. The effect of Sun is more prominently shown in 22nd year or in middle age.

Aphorisms of Moon

Moon is assigned the same amount of strength in Hindu Astrology which equals that of the Ascendant (Lagna or Rising Sign). The entire system of directions in the Hindu system rotates around Moon. The position of Moon in a Nakshatra (Constellation) and in fact its longitude gives the balance of Mahadasha at birth. The basic characteristic of a person with which he is endowed with due to the various planetary positions in the birth chart, are modified due the Dashas one is passing through to a great extents. An individual takes on the qualities, the characteristics, looks etc. of the planet whose dasha he (she) is passing through. These changes in turn endow him with success or otherwise. We give below the effect of Moon in different signs, houses, Navanshas, and in conjunction with other planets:

Moons in Different Signs

1. *Moon in Aries*: the native is consumed with passion and is henpecked; if aspected by Venus he gets a good wife.

2. *Moon in Taurus*; the native is much sex-minded; if aspected by Mars passions are particularly unbridled and the native may forsake friends and relations for the sake of a woman but is much adored by the fair sex; if aspected by Jupiter good wife; if aspected by Venus much enjoyment; if aspected by Saturn secret enmity by women.

3. *Moon in Gemini*; well-versed in amorous arts, fond of female company, henpecked; if aspected by Venus gets a good wife; if aspected by Saturn does not have pleasures of life in full measure.

4. *Moon in Cancer*, amorous; if aspected by Jupiter gets a good wife; if aspected by Venus has company of good women, some of whom may be of profligate character; gets financial support from/through women.

5. *Moon in Leo*; enmity with women; if aspected by Mars has a strong wife; if aspected by Mercury the native is feminine in make-up, is liked by women and subservient to their control. He may have to serve or be subordinate to a woman some time in his life; if aspected by Venus, the native serves under a woman and is well-versed in amorous arts; if aspected by Saturn female company is liked by him.

6. *Moon in Virgo*; fond of women, attached to the wives of others; if aspected by Sun devoid of wife (there may be premature death of wife—look for other indications also; if aspected by Venus good and frequent female company; if

aspected by Saturn the native is controlled by women and/ derives money through them.

7. *Moon in Libra*; has company of more than one woman and is henpecked. If aspected by Mars has liaison with other men's wives, if aspected by Saturn much sexual indulgence.

8. *Moon in Scorpio*; attached to other people's wives; if aspected by Venus, dissipation of bodily vigour and wealth through women.

9. *Moon in Sagittarius*; If aspected by Venus the native is good-looking, amorous and has a good wife.

10. *Moon in Capricorn*; If Moon is in Capricorn, one is attached to an elder woman, or wife of a senior relation; if aspected by Mercury does not have much female company. If aspected by Jupiter company of more than one woman; if aspected by Venus liaison with another man's wife, if aspected by Saturn ungratified passions and attached to another man's wife.

11. Moon in Aquarius, if aspected by Mars; attached to other people's wives; if aspected by Mercury much liked by women and well-versed in arts of love; if aspected by Jupiter has much enjoyment of women; if aspected by Venus gets a bad wife, but is attached to other people's wives; if aspected by Saturn attached to another person's wife.

12. *Moon in Pisces*; attached to many women, henpecked; if aspected by Sun has much sexual desires and gets a pleasant-looking wife, if aspected by Mercury, is sorrounded by good women; if aspected by Jupiter, has women around him; if aspected by Venus much indulging with and adored by women; if aspected by Saturn unsatisfied lust and devoid of conjugal happiness.

Note. The above applies fully only when the sign Moon is in, the lord of the sign and Moon are all strong and the above Judgement should be modified according as the dispositor is exalted or debilitated.

Moon in Various Houses

13. If benefic Moon is posited in an even sign in the first house, the native has a good-looking wife.

14. If the Moon be waning and in dark half of the month and in an odd sign the native's wife is aggressive and overbearing.

15. Moon in any house in opposition to Mars or Saturn is not good for married happiness.

16. Moon in the 4th house conjoined with or aspected by Saturn; the native may have love affair with a person inferior in status.

17. If weak moon be in fifth and there are malefics in 1st, the 7th and 12th houses from ascendant the native marries a woman who is barren or does not enjoy conjugal happiness or his wife dies prematurely.

18. If weak Moon be in the 5th house and malefics occupy the first, 7th or 12th house there would be no married happiness.

19. Moon in the 6th house; the native is not very passionate.

20. Moon in the 7th house, the native is attached to his beloved one but his jealousy is aroused very soon.

21. If there is full Moon in the 7th house, the native's wife would be well-behaved and endowed with children.

22. A benefic Moon in the 7th house and well-aspected: the native's wife will be fair, well-proportioned in body, healthy, discriminate and talkative.

23. Moon in the 7th house (if the birth be in the dark half of the month) makes one full of lust.

24. Moon in the the 9th house: the native is much adored by ladies.

Moon's Position in Navamsha*

25. If Moon be in 'navamsha' of

(a) Venus and aspected by Mars the native is attached to others' wives.

(b) In 'navansha' of Saturn and aspected by Venus he is fond of wicked women.

(c) Taurus: one is fond of luxury and pleasure and he leads a life of enjoyment.

* Navamsha—one-ninth portion of sign. See Appendix IV.

(d) Aquarius and aspected by Mars: attached to other people's wives.
(e) Venus and aspected by Saturn; will be attached to other women.
(f) Mercury and aspected by Venus: the native undertakes work under a woman.
(g) Sun and aspected by Venus: the native would be without lust.

Moon Conjoined with other Planets

26. Moon and Mercury together: is generally liked by ladies.

27. Moon and Saturn together has love affairs with an elder woman.

28. Moon, Mars and Jupiter together: liked by ladies generally; falling in for pretty faces.

29. Moon, Mars and Venus together: husband of an ill-tempered woman.

30. Moon, Jupiter, and Saturn together: associated with an elder woman.

31. Moon, Mars, Jupiter and Venus together: not liked by ladies.

32. Moon, Mars, Mercury and Venus and Saturn together: attached to many ladies.

33. Moon, Mars, Mercury and Jupiter together: keeps concubines/has love affars with other people's wives.

34. Moon, Mars, Mercury and Venus together: has good wives.

35. Moon, Mars, Jupiter, Venus together: has good wife.

36. Moon, Mars, Venus and Saturn: husband of a wanton woman.

37. Moon, Mercury, Venus and Saturn together attached to other people's wives; his own wife very ill-tempered.

Moon with another Planet in Various Houses

38. If Moon and Venus are together in the 1st house, the native has the enjoyment of a number of damsels, some of them of loose morals.

39. Benefic Moon and Venus in the 4th house together confer home comforts and conjugal happiness.

40. If waning Moon (from the 10th to 15th house day of the dark fortnight) be conjoined with Jupiter in Virgo in the seventh house and there be a malefic in the 4th house the native would survive his wife.

41. Moon, Venus together in the 7th house: the native is attached to a number of women and has much enjoyment of sex life.

42. Moon and Saturn together in the 7th house: there is little conjugal happiness. The native would survive his first marriage partner and remarry.

43. Moon and Saturn together; unless Saturn be in his own sign and well-aspected, this is not a good combination for married happiness. Wife may be sickly or Saturnine, cold and ill-tempered and matrimonial happiness is marred. If in a male nativity, Moon be in the 7th house along with Saturn and Mars and Venus be in 'varga' of Saturn or Mars and aspected by them the native as well as his wife would be adulterous (look for other indications also to confirm this point).

44. If a weak Moon along with a malefic be in the 7th house, the native has liaison with another's wife.

45. Moon and Venus in the 9th house: the native's wife may have some love affairs.

46. Moon, Mars and Venus in the 9th house: the native is much liked by women and is under their sway so much so that he loses much wealth and vitality through them. The native is likely to survive his wife and undergoes much suffering.

47. Moon, Mars, Mercury and Saturn in the 9th house; same as above.

48. If Moon be the lord of the 7th house and conjoined with or aspected by a malefic and posited in the 'navamsha' of a malefic or hemmed in between malefics, the native's wife is sinful.

49. If Moon be the lord of the 7th house and in a friend's house or in exaltation and in benefic 'vargas' and conjoined with benefics, the wife is virtuous.

50. If there be a benefic in the 7th house from Moon and a malefic in 4th house from Moon, the native antagonises his mother for the sake of his wife.

51. Moon represents a mature person and in a male nativity if Moon be significator of adulterous intercourse it may show liaison with a woman (who may be young) but slightly elder in age than the native.

52. Moon shows its effect in 24th year. For example, if Moon be in the seventh house there is likelihood of marriage in twenty-fourth year of age.

Aphorisms of Mars

Mars and Venus are of prime importance. They control and expedite marriages in the case of women and men respectively. For example, a strong Mars in the horoscope of a girl enables her to get married* comparatively early whereas a strong Venus will endow her with an unparalleled charm to attract the opposite sex. In the case of a male horoscope, it is the other way round i.e. a strong Venus will endow him with women and a good looking wife ultimately and a strong Mars† will give him the dash and drive to seek the company of women leading to success in love.

Different effects of Mars are stated below:

1. Mars in Aries: the native is attached to a number of women. He may seduce a good woman.
2. Mars in Taurus: the native is aggressive in courtship. The native is attached to other people's wives and wholly under beloved one's control.
3. Mars in Leo; likelihood of premature death of the first consort; a handicap for conjugal happiness.
4. Mars in Libra: the person is pleasing to women folk; there is liability of the first wife dying prematurely. The native spends much money on wine and women. He is too much under the control of his lady-love.
5. Mars in Aquarius; the native is fond of drinks.
6. Mars in Aries aspected by Sun makes one endowed with

---

* See chapter 10 Female Nativity.

† Strong Mars should not be confused with Kuja-Dosha or Manglik Dosha which arises due to the placement of Mars in the 1st, 4th, 7th, 8th, or 12th, house in a horoscope.

wealth and wife; if aspected by Moon fond of damsels; aspected by Mercury he is too much devoted to erotic arts and is given to public women; if aspected by Venus a person may be entangled in a case due to women and the income fluctuates due to spending unnecessarily on women; if aspected by Saturn the native is addicted to another person's wife.

7. Mars in the house of Venus if aspected by Sun: the native is inimical to women; if aspected by Moon he is fond of a large number of women and is liked by them.

8. Mars in the house of Mercury: if aspected by Moon, the person is rather effeminate or is in charge of girls; if aspected by Venus he carries out errands of women.

9. Mars in Cancer if aspected by Venus the person is agitated due to company of women and spends away his fortune and is in many difficulties due to his being under the sway of women.

10. If Mars is in Leo and aspected by Moon, he may get money from women or is solicited by them. If aspected by Venus he is every young and has the pleasure of company of a large number of women.

11. Mars in the house of Jupiter aspected by Jupiter: the person does not have conjugal happiness. If aspected by Venus he is very much adored by young damsels.

12. Mars in the house of Saturn aspected by Sun: the person is endowed with wife and children. If aspected by Venus he gets many luxuries, and is fond of doting upon women. If aspected by Saturn he is inimical to women.

13. Mars in the 1st, 4th, 7th and 8th or 12th houses: the native is 'manglik'* and should preferably marry a person who has Mars or malefics in one of the above places.

14. Mars in the above places (vide 13 above) is unfavourable for the longevity of the partner unless malefic influences are equally strong in the other horoscope.

15. Mars and Venus in 1st: the native has a number of love affairs, is of loose morals and wastes much money thereby.

---

* 'Manglik' means having the malefic influence of Mars on his/her conjugal life.

16. Mars in 2nd; same effect as in 2 above but not so powerful.

17. Mars in the 4th house; if Mars be the indicator of liaison, it indicates union with a young woman who may be barren.

18. Mars in the 4th house from Venus; not good for married happiness.

19. Mars in the 6th house; the native is full of lust.

20. If Mars and Venus be together in the 5th house the native is devoid of conjugal happiness or marries/cohabits with a barren woman.

21. Mars in the 7th house, unless well-aspected; the native's wife would be of a furious type, her eyes getting reddish on slightest provocation her complexion pinkish with strong physique, arrogant and strongly sexed.

22. Mars in the 7th house; the native would have attachment with a number of women and would cohabit with women, even during their periods.

23. Mars in the 7th house the native's wife's breasts would be small—(not very well-developed.)

24. If Mars be in the 7th house in 'navamsha' of Venus and if lord of the seventh is in fifth, there is likelihood of premature death of the wife.

25. Mars in the 7th house in Pisces: an evil influence for longevity of wife. (Look to other aphorisms for confirmation).

26. Mars and Mercury in the 7th house; there may be premature death of first wife.

27. Mars and Jupiter in the 7th house; devoid of wife or happiness therefrom.

28. Mars and Saturn in the 7th house; devoid of conjugal happiness but if Mars and Saturn are in Cancer in the 7th house, the wife would be handsome and of good disposition and virtuous and of good morals.

29. If Mars and Venus be in the 9th house; the native has not much married happiness.

30. Mars occupying the 8th house sign from Venus; not good for married happiness.

31. Mars and Venus in the 9th house, the native may marry twice.

32. Mars and Venus in the 9th house if conjoined with or aspected by lord of the 6th house; the native has enmity with women.

33. Mars and Saturn in the 9th house; the native has love affairs with other people's wives and indulges in many sinful acts due to his craving of the sex.

34. (i) If Mars be in 12th house, (ii) there be malefics in the 7th or 8th houses from the ascendant and (iii) lord of the 7th house is in invisible half of the Zodiac; the native marries again, due to premature death of wife.

35. If Mars be in the 12th house and there be malefics in the 7th and 8th houses and the seventh house is not aspected by its lord or Jupiter and Mercury, the first wife would die prematurely unless wife's horoscope has equal malefic influences in which case there would be no married happiness.

36. If Mars be the lord of the 7th house and devoid of strength and in 'krura' 'shahtiansha', (1/60th malefic division of a sign) debilitated, combust or in an enemy's house, the wife of the native would be wicked, very coarse and sharp in speech with her husband and/or attached to another man.

37. If Mars be the lord of the 7th house and is exalted or in friendly "Vargas" conjoined with or aspected by benefics, strong and in 'Paravatansh'* or other good vargas, though cruel, she would be virtuous.

38. If Mars be the lord of the 7th house or 'navamsha' on the cusp of the 7th house in a male nativity and if it is debilitated or combust, the native marries a woman from a low family who is wicked or there is separation between the husband and wife.

39. If Mars be an important factor in Judgement of married happiness and it be in the 7th house or aspecting or associated

* When a planet is in six or more, own or exaltation or friendly 'vargas' it is called in 'Paravatansha'.

with the lord thereof; Mars gives a 'Tamasik' wife (attributes of 'Tamas' are fear, anger, want of knowledge and quarrelling nature, lethargininess, cruelty, too much anger, avarice, tendency to have double dealing, uncontrollable temper).

40. If Mars be the significator of love affairs it indicates liaison with a person of young age.

41. If Mars is strong and in its own 'trinshansha'* a person has much virility and sexual enjoyment.

42. Mars gives the effect during youth. In particular Mars show its effect in 28th year and onwards.

Mars in Combination with other Planets

43. Mars and Mercury together: associated with wicked widows and not much happiness from his own wife.

44. Mars and Venus together: attached to other's wife.

45. Mars, Mercury, Jupiter together: husband of a good wife.

46. Mars, Jupiter and Venus together: gets much benefit from fashionable ladies.

47. Mars, Venus, Saturn together: husband of a woman of wanton character.

48. Mars, Jupiter, Venus and Saturn: very fond of women.

Aphorisms of Mercury

Mercury is the planet which rules the mind. Any idea which has to take shape occurs in the mind first and then the native takes action on it. This is the reason why in many races a man is asked not to look at another man's wife. In Muslim culture, women cover their heads and face to protect them from the gaze of others. It is so because as soon as a Man looks at a woman, a desire comes in him to speak to her and then it develops into a desire to touch her and so on. The power of speech and expression also plays a definite part in ensuring success in love. A nice man is more successful in love than a strong and silent person. Most women are mislead by the smooth speakers and by the time they become wiser it is too late.

---

* 'Trinshansha' means one-thirtieth division of a sign.

We now give the effects of Mercury in various signs, houses, etc:

1. Mercury in Aries makes one fond of women. The native's wife is not good.

2. Mercury in Taurus: the native is fond of his wife.

3. Mercury in Gemini: the native may have two wives.

4. Mercury in Cancer: the native is fond of women, singing, etc. His wealth is destroyed due to enmity with women.

5. Mercury in Leo; the native is not endowed with conjugal happiness. He is not liked by women though he hankers after their company.

6. Mercury in Virgo: a person is not very strong sexually.

7. Mercury in Libra makes one addicted to public women.

8. Mercury in Scorpio: the native's wife is wicked.

9. Mercury in Aquarius; the native's wife is wicked.

10. Mercury in Pisces; the native marries a good woman.

11. Mercury in the house of Mars, aspected by Moon makes one adorable to ladies; aspected by Venus bestows company of women.

12. Mercury in the house of Venus aspected by Venus: the native is liked by young damsels.

13. Mercury in its own house aspected by Venus; the native goes to low women.

14. Mercury in Cancer aspected by Moon; the native loses his health, vitality and money due to overindulgence with women.

15. Mercury in Leo makes on devoid of shame; and if aspected by Moon the native's vitality is decreased.

16. Mercury in the house of Jupiter aspected by Venus; the person is associated with young girls and boys as their preceptor (if there are any configurations or aspects denoting adultery in nativity, such connections may be formed).

17. Mercury in the house of Saturn aspected by Mars, makes one lazy and shy; if aspected by Venus the native is attached to low women and is oversexed.

18. Mercury in the 7th house and lord of the 7th well-placed: the native is very clever in winning the favours of ladies.

19. Mercury in 7th house; the native marries a person who is intelligent, well-dressed, wealthy but who does not come from a high family and is quarrelsome.

20. Mercury in7th in the house of malefic or associated with a malefic, and aspected by a malefic the native's wife would be intelligent, fond of decoration, clever in arts, of good and refined speech, humorous but rather wanton.

21. Mercury in the 7th house: the native would be fond of other people's wives.

22. Mercury in the 7th house if in Taurus: bad for the longevity of native's wife.

23. If Mercury in the 7th house is debilitated or in an enemy's house, the native's marriage partner would be wicked.

24. If Mercury be the indicator of liaison with a woman in a horoscope, it would denote liaison with a young person, or with a prostitute or fallen woman or the wife of a teacher, particularly if Mercury be in the 4th or 7th houses.

25. Mercury in the 7th house: the native's wife's breasts are full and well-developed.

26. Mercury in the 7th house: the native's wife has a good number of children.

27. Mercury with Jupiter in the 7th house: the native enjoys a number of women. The native has a good wife.

28. Mercury and Venus in the 7th house: the native is surrounded by a number of good-looking women.

Mercury along with other Planets in other Houses

29. Mercury and Jupiter in 4th: conjugal happiness.

30. Mercury, Jupiter, Venus, Saturn together—very fond of women.

31. Mercury and Venus together: the native is endowed with wealth and wife.

32. Mercury, Venus, Saturn together; the native is fond of and attached to other people's wives.

33. If Mercury be the lord of the 7th house, strong, in friendly or exaltation 'vargas' in Aquarius the native's wife is virtuous.

34. If strong Mercury is in the 10th house from the lord of the ascendant and Moon is the 10th houe from the lord of the 7th house, the native has several wives.

35. If Mercury be the lord of the 7th house and conjoined with a 'papa' in debilitated 'ansha' in an enemy's house, or 'vargas' or combust and is in the 6th or 8th houses, hemmed in between malefics and aspected by malefics, the native's wife kills her husband inch by inch and brings misery to the whole family.

36. Mercury shows its effect particularly in 32nd year.

Aphorisms of Jupiter

Jupiter rules over conjugal bliss and the longevity of husband. It is also rules male children in the horoscope. A research was done long time back in the western countries which indicated that most proposals of marriage were given during Thursday* One who has a comfortable Jupiter in his chart will have wealth, good fortunes, success, position of responsibility and good sons. In the case of a woman Jupiter in strength will give a good husband who will be virtuous and long lived. Jupiterian persons generally have a generous, jovial, cheerful and optimistic outlook. They are always willing to help others and as such they are well respected by their friends and spouse. In angular position (1st, 4th, 7th, and 10th, houses) Jupiter protects the entire horoscope "What can other planets do to one who has an angular Jupiter". Such people have prominent 'Ears' which stand out (flanking of head). We now proceeds to give the effects of Jupiter in different signs and positions:

1. Jupiter in Aries; the native marries and has conjugal enjoyments.

2. Jupiter, in Taurus: the native is attached to one's own wife; in Scorpio has company of several women; in Capricorn he is attached to low people; in Aquarius may have liaison with the wife of some senior relation.

---

* Thursday is ruled by Jupiter.

3. Jupiter in the house of Mars; (Aries or Scorpio) aspected by Moon: endowed with conjugal happiness; if aspected by Mars: has disobedient wife; if aspected by Venus: enjoys luxury and women.

4. Jupiter in the house of Venus: (Taurus or Libra) aspected by Moon; the native is adored by young women; if aspected Mars, the native is loved by young women; if aspected by Venus has good opportunities for enjoyment; if aspected by Saturn there is no conjugal happiness.

5. Jupiter in the house of Mercury (Gemini or Virgo) aspected by Mercury; the person is endowed with wife and wealth; if aspected by Moon or Mars same as above; if aspected by Mercury: has a number of women; if aspected by Venus: the native is much loved by women and has much enjoyment.

6. Jupiter in Cancer; the native is devoid of conjugal happiness; if aspected by Moon he marries a high class woman; if aspected by Mars, marries a young wife; or associates with young unmarried girls; if aspected by Venus; has a number of women.

7. Jupiter in Leo aspected by Moon: the person becomes rich due to his wife, or shares in her property; aspected by Venus, he is liked by women; if aspected by Saturn he associates with very good women.

8. Jupiter in Scorpio; the native has marital enjoyment.

9. Jupiter is his own house (Sagittarius or Pisces) if aspected by Moon: is much liked by ladies; if aspected by Mars; there is loss of family members.

10. Jupiter in the house of Saturn if aspected by Sun: has much enjoyment; if aspected by Mercury the native is much addicted to women; if aspected by Venus; gets company of good women and luxury.

11. Jupiter in an angle conjoined with the lord of the 7th house; the native marries a woman whose breasts are well-developed.

12. Jupiter in the third house: the native is constantly harassed and efforts are made by women to dominate him.

13. Jupiter in 4th; if other combinations indicate licentious conduct, the native would carry on with a woman of priestly caste or one who is educated or inclined to be religious.

14. Jupiter in the 7th; the native's wife is virtuous.

15. Jupiter in 7th well-aspected by benefics and unaspected by malefics: the native's wife would be plump, not very tall, virtuous, colour of her eye-balls and hair slightly tinged with yellowishness.

16. Jupiter in the 7th house indicates marriage or union with a person described in 15 above.

17. Jupiter in the 7th house: the native would keep to his own wife/husband.

18. If Jupiter is in the 7th house in the navamsha of Mars or Saturn or conjoined with either of the two, the native is adulterous.

19. Jupiter in the 7th house debilitated (in Capricorn): the native marries several times and wives die one after the other.

20. Jupiter and Venus in the 7th house; has a good-looking and virtuous wife.

21. Jupiter and Saturn in the 7th house: loss of wealth due to enmity with women.

22. Jupiter in the 8th house; the native has a slovenly wife.

23. Jupiter in the 9th house; if aspected by Moon and Sun the native has a number of wives; aspected by Sun and Mercury, the native marries in a high family, aspected by Moon and Mercury enjoys luxurious couches; aspected by Moon and Venus: has liaison with another man's wife.

24. Jupiter governs 16th year of life. If Jupiter be in 12th house, and there are indications of love affair in the nativity, there is possibility of some such affair when the native is running his 16th year.

25. Jupiter and Venus together in any house: a person is fortunate in respect of conjugal happiness.

26. Jupiter indicates a person of middle age (this is for Judgement of age if Jupiter be significator or be associated with planet signifying liaison).

27. If Jupiter aspects the 7th house and Venus, wife would be virtuous.

Aphorisms of Venus

"One who commands the love of woman is better than a king". The keynote of Venus is love, harmony and rhythm. When Venus is strong and dignified it gives a good spouse, harmony in life, love of opposite sex, smoothness in life and luxuries. When Venus is tainted then laziness becomes prominent in a person. In the case of women she is likely to suffer from female health problems, difficulties in conceiving children and sickly children when they are born. In the case of men, weak and afflicted Venus will destroy his emotional life. He should be prepared to spend his time with a nagging wife. In his love life he will hook himself up with worthless women who will suck him dry and when he has lost all they will leave him for another prey.

In the chart strong Venus is desirable. For people with powerful Venus do not need to go to others but like magnet, they attract others to them. We have found that Venus in the fourth house gives a charming face and it also ensures a happy old age.

We now give the effect of the Venus in various positions:

1. Venus's is the significator of wife, love affairs and pleasures.

2. Judge in particular the following in relation to Venus:

(i) Whether it is in a friend's, enemy's, or neutral's house.
(ii) Whether it is in its own, exaltation or debilitation sign.

3. (i) Venus represents husband/wife, lust, passions, luxury and enjoyment in general.
   (ii) Put that sign as ascendant in which Venus is posited and judge all about wife/husband's affairs as if the new setting is an independent horoscope.
   (iii) Judge all about wife's wealth from the house

second from Venus, her brethren from the third house from Venus, her mother from the 4th house from Venus and so on.

4. Venus not combust is good for matrimonial happiness. *Vice versa*.

Venus in Various Signs

5. If Venus is in Aries the person has secret liaison with another man's wife; he goes to public women and gets into trouble due to women; also loses money and prosperity due to quarrels pertaining to other people's wives; in Taurus; has a number of women with him; in Gemini, the native is oversexed; in Cancer, the native may have two wives; he gets diseases due to over-indulgence in wine and women; in Leo, he is always trying to please a woman; also marries in a high aristocratic family and gets money from women; in Virgo, he is pleasant in talks with women and is addicted to women of low tastes. In Scorpio, the native is attached to some women other than his wife; the native has a quarrel with a wicked woman and loses money and wealth, due to quarrels pertaining to women; in Capricorn, he is attached to an elderly/unworthy woman and is too much under the influence of his beloved; in Aquarius, he is addicted to other women.

6. Venus in the house of Mars aspected by Sun; the native suffers due to women, his happiness and wealth are destroyed due to them. If aspected by Moon, his lust is not gratified and he is married to a low class woman.

7. Venus in its own house aspected by Sun: the native has a good wife and is henpecked. If aspected by Mars his wife and house are destroyed; he is married to an ill-tempered lady, her lust remains ungratified, and there is trouble due to women. If aspected by Saturn the native is attached to low class women.

8. Venus in the house of Mercury aspected by Moon; the native is endowed with luxuries, if aspected by Mars he wastes much money on young women and is oversexed.

9. Venus in Cancer aspected by Moon: the native has a wife who is devoted to her duty, is pure in body, comes from a high family and is rich but is of fiery temperament; aspected by Mars the native is put to much distress due to women; aspected by Mercury the native's wife is learned; aspected by Saturn he is henpecked.

10. If Venus is in Leo and aspected by Sun the native is full of lust, is adored by yong damsels and gains in wealth through women; aspected by Moon the person has to suffer much for/ on account of women; aspected by Mars derives much wealth from/or through women by whom he is much adored; also attached to other people's wives; aspected by Mercury wanders in pursuit of new love affairs, and is attached to other people's wives; aspected by Jupiter, has much enjoyment with a number of women; aspected by Saturn marries or has liaison with a widow.

11. Venus in the sign of Jupiter aspected by Mars; has enmity with women; aspected by Jupiter, much conjugal happiness.

12. Venus in the house of Saturn aspected by Sun, has congress with a number of women; aspected by Mars: there may be premature demise of wife; aspected by Jupiter, has a good life.

Position of Venus in Various Houses

13. If Venus is hemmed in between malefics in the same house or in adjacent houses it retards conjugal happiness.

14. Benefics in place of malefic in 13 above confer matrimonial happiness.

15. Malefics in the 4th, 8th or 12th houses from Venus are bad for the longevity of the wife/matrimonial happiness.

16. If the 4th and 8th houses from Venus be occupied by strong malefics the wife may die by catching fire/accident.

17. If Venus is closely hemmed in between malefics, the wife may die due to a fall or lingering disease.

18. If Venus is in the 1st house, the native is well-versed in erotic arts and much adored by ladies.

19. Venus and Saturn in the 1st house: enjoys other people's wives but is distressed.

20. If Venus is in 2nd house from Moon the person is highly passionate and enjoys luxury, wealth and women.

21. Venus in the 3rd house: henpecked.

22. Venus in the 4th house: has much home comfort and if there be indication of love affairs, it may indicate keeping a concubine in his own house.

23. Venus in the 5th house: amorous; if in conjunction with a malefic bad for matrimonial happiness.

24. Venus in the 6th house: is disliked by ladies.

25. Venus in the 7th house; gives a handsome wife.

26. When Venus is in the 7th house in 'Gandant'* and Saturn in 1st house, one may marry a barren woman.

27. Venus in the 7th house in the 'vargas' of Mars or in its own vargas; the native is of loose character.

28. Venus in the 7th house in the Navamsha of Saturn or Mars and aspected by them: the person would cohabit with other people's wives.

29. Venus in the 7th house; the native is very fond of sex indulgence.

30. Venus and Saturn in the 7th house: has congress with a number of women, some of them of inferior status.

31. Venus in 7th in the house of a benefic and aspected by a benefic: the native's wife would have beautiful eyes, be fair in complexion, well-built, having beautiful hair and fond of beautiful and luxurious articles.

32. Venus in the 7th house conjoined with 'Yam Kantak': good for matrimonial happiness.

33. Venus in 7th unassociated with malefics and if Venus be strong; wife would be rich and prosperous.

34. Venus in the 7th house if in Scorpio: bad for wife's longevity.

35. Venus, strong in the 7th house aspected by Mars: enjoys a number of women.

---

* End of 120th and beginning of 121st/degrees; end of 240th and beginning of 241st/degrees; end of 360th and beginning of 1st degrees. These are called 'gandant' degrees.

36. Venus in the 7th house: adulterous, unless well-aspected.

37. Venus in the 7th house in conjunction with a malefic; bad for matrimonial happiness.

38. Venus in the 7th house, if weak, spoils matrimonial happiness.

39. Venus in the 8th house: if strong and there are indications of love affairs, the native may have a separate home for his beloved one.

40. Venus in the 9th house in conjunction with a malefic retards matrimonial happiness.

41. Venus in the 10th house: has much sex enjoyment and gain from women, if Venus be strong gain without much effort, if weak all the same gain through women or connected with them, but with effort.

42. Venus in the 10th house from Moon: much gain from women. It brings prosperity through wife, mother sister or women in general.

43. Venus in the 11th house: the native gets money from women, poetry, drama, art, music, etc. and has a number of lady friends.

44. Venus in the 12th house; is every amorous, well-versed in arts; enjoys much luxuries and has enjoyment of women, particularly if aspected by benefics.

45. If Venus is conjoined with the lord of the 7th house, the native is excessively passionate.

46. If Venus be the lord of the 7th house and be debilitated, combust or conjoined with malefic or a debilitated planet and is in malefic 'shashtiansha' the native's wife is hard-hearted, wanton and of thieving disposition.

47. If Venus be the lord of the 7th house and be strong, in a benefic navamsha or in a friend's or exaltation navamsha, conjoined with a benefic, in its own house and benefic' shashtiansha' the native's wife is very talkative but virtuous.

48. Of the two significators of love and marriage, *i.e.* Venus and the lord of the 7th house, judge which is more prominent, and attach comparatively more value.

(a) If Venus is aspected by or conjoined with Jupiter, wife would be virtuous and handsome.

(b) If Venus be associated with a malefic or aspected by a malefic she would neither be comely in appearance nor virtuous.

49. If Venus and the lord of the 7th house are both weak and the 7th house is also weak and if they are conjoined with or aspected by malefics or hemmed in between malefics and not aspected by benefics and if malefics are in the 2nd house, 4th house, 5th house, 8th house, 9th and 12th houses (from the 7th house, from lord of the 7th house and from Venus) it is bad for conjugal happiness.

50. If Venus and the lord of the 7th house be posited in dual signs and dual 'navamshas' there may be more than one marriage.

51. If Venus and the 7th house are hemmed in between malefics or

(i) if malefics are in the 4th and 8th houses therefrom or

(ii) or in 2nd and 12th therefrom, matrimonial happiness is destroyed.

Give special attention to the above in relation to Venus.

Note. If there are benefics instead of malefics, in places referred to above good results follow.

52. If Venus and the lord of the 7th house are strong and occupy 3rd, 6th, 10th or 11th house from the ascendant they give prosperity, particularly after marriage.

53. If Venus and the lord of the 7th house are weak and occupy 'trik' positions, it is detrimental to matrimonial happiness.

54. If Venus and the lord of the 7th house are in exaltation, in their own or in friend's houses and in good vargas but in bad places such as 'trik', the good effects would not be felt.

55. As compared with 54 above if the lord of the 7th house and Venus occupy debilitated sign but are placed in good houses such as the 11th house, they would confer happiness.

56. If Venus and the lord of the 7th house are both strong and occupy good houses it is good for conjugal happiness. *Vice versa*.

57. If Venus is conjoined with a malefic and the lord of the 7th house is a malefic and in the 5th or 9th houses or in the 2nd or 10th houses, marriage would be in a distant place.

58. Judge of the wife by the lord of the 7th house/sign occupied by Venus— whichever is stronger.

If the lord of the 7th house is aspected by Jupiter she would be virtuous and handsome. If on the other hand, it is associated with or aspected by malefics she would be neither comely in appearance nor virtuous.

59. If Venus is in the 7th house or in the 3rd house, the 6th house, the 10th or 11th houses and the lord of the 2nd house similarly placed there is rise of fortune after marriage.

60. If Venus, lord of the 1st house, 2nd, and 7th houses are ill-placed, debilitated, combust or in an enemy's house or 'navamsha' or conjoined with a malefic, there is ruin of prosperity after marriage.

61. If in 60 above, the planets be in malefic 'shahshtanshas' but are conjoined with the benefics or aspected by them, there is revival of prosperity after destruction.

62. If Venus and lords of the 2nd and 7th houses be in the 6th house, the 8th or 12th houses places from ascendant it is inauspicious for the longevity of the wife.

63. If Venus and the lord of the 7th house are in malefic signs the native is full of lust.

64. If Venus and lord of the 7th house are in benefic signs and anshas conjoined with or aspected by benefics, the native has conjugal happiness and is prosperous.

65. If Venus and the 7th house are both strong, one should predict conjugal happiness.

66. If Venus and lord of the 7th house are in benefic signs and 'anshas', and the lord of the 10th house is strong the native has a good wife.

67. If Venus and lord of the 7th house are together, then the number of wives is the same as the number of planets, conjoining or fully aspecting Venus.

68. If Venus along with lords of the 2nd house, the 6th and 7th houses and malefics be in the 1st house the native is too much given to lust and has liaison with other people's wives; if aspected by benefics it is not so.

69. If Venus and the lord of 7th house from ascendant/lunar ascendant be in dual signs and 'anshas' the native will, have two wives.

70. If Venus is the lord of the 11th house strong and well-aspected, the native derives much money, or gain through women.

71. *Note.* The sign which is 7th as counted from Venus, the direction of the lord of such sign and the part of the country described by such planet, would indicate the direction and place from where the wife will come.

Venus in Association with other Planets

72. If Venus is conjoined with a malefic and is in a debilitated sign or 'ansha' and if a malefic be in the 7th house, more than one wife.

73. If Venus is conjoined with 'Gulika'* the native would have attachment with low women.

74. Venus and Saturn together, make one prosper, through a lady or profession patronised by ladies. Wealth increases under the patronage of women.

75. If Venus is in an angle with the lord of the 7th house, the native would marry a woman with full and beautiful breasts.

76. If Venus is associated with a debilitated planet or, is in a debilitated 'navamsha' the native has a bad wife. If there are good aspects the above results are modified.

77. Venus in opposition to Saturn is bad for married happiness.

78. If in a male nativity Venus and Moon are in odd signs and 'navamshas' and there is a malefic in the ascendant and

* Gulika is another name for 'Mandi'. It is a longitude which changes everyday. For calculation see some standard work.

lord of the 7th house is strong, then the native cohabits with his aunt or some lady related that way; if in the above the lord of the third house is associated with Venus and Moon the person cohabits with some woman related as sister. So judge of other relations.

Note. This would be so only if there are several strong indications of adultery in the horoscope.

Venus in 'Vargas'

79. If Venus is exalted, in its own 'vargas' or in a friend's house or attains several own benefic or exaltation 'vargas' or is in Gopuransha (more than 4 own or friends 'vargas') and in a benefic 'shastianasha' the native has a good wife.

80. If Venus is in its own 'trinshansha' it is conducive to conjugal happiness.

81. If Venus be weak and in the 'vargas' of Saturn and be aspected by Saturn, the native would be attached to a Saturnine woman (either conforming to the appearance of Saturn or elder than the native or a maid servant).

82. If Venus be in the 'varga' of Mars and be aspected by it the person would be addicted to other people's wives. If, however, there is Jupiter's aspect, the evil is mitigated.

83. If the lord of the 'navamsha' in which Venus is posited is with a benefic and is in own or exaltation 'vargas' or in 'paravatansha', the native has a number of wives (good sexual enjoyment).

84. If the lord of the'navamsha' in which Venus is posited is in debilitation, combust or in enemy's house or hemmed in between malefics or afflicted by malefic, the native may marry again.

85. Not only the 'sign' Venus is posited in but even the 'navamsha' should be considered for full appraisal of Venus.

86. Add the longitudes of Venus and lord of the ascendant. The sum total is a 'sensitive' point in relation to matrimonial happiness. The sign and house it is in and whether associated by position or aspect with benefics or malefics should be judged.

87. In the 'ashtakvarga' of Venus, find out the sign having

the maximum number of benefic dots; if wife is born with Moon in that sign she would be auspicious. *Vice versa.*

Note. Calculation of 'ashtakvarga' and 'sarvashtak varga' is advanced study. Those who have not this calculation already made in the horoscope, should if they so desire, get it done by a good astrologer. Ashtakvarga calculations are very useful for study of transits throughout the life period— and in, Judgement of dashas, antardashas, goodness or badness of planets, etc.

Aphorisms of Saturn

Life manifests as motion and Sun is the giver of life. The key word of Sun is "Life". In Mythology Saturn is the son of Sun. But it has the opposite qualities viz. Where as sun is warm (has heat), magnanimous, aristocratic, rules over high class people and helpful, Saturn is cold, calculating, rules over the labour class and "Obstruction" is the key word of Saturn. Saturn makes recluses and sours existence. The aspect of the Saturn is real bad. It fully aspect the 3rd, 7th, and 10th, houses from where it is posited, therefore Saturn in the 1st house, 5th, house and 10th house afflicts the house of marriage. This results in dissatisfaction and breakups. However, Saturn is endowed with full directional strength in the seventh house. It gets one out of one marks. The reason is that placement of Satrun is much better than its aspect. It gives a very faithful and hardworking spouse. The spouse is chaste, has discretion, and is wise. It can at times cause delay in marriage or living apart for a long time.

We now give the effect of Saturn in other positions:

1. Saturn in Taurus: the native is attached to women who are his relations; more than one wife.

2. Saturn in Taurus—the native is attached to women elder in age and has affairs with them, and does errands for other people's wives; in Gemini: the native is full of lust and is well-versed in amorous arts; in Leo; devoid of conjugal happiness; in Virgo visits public women; in Libra has liaison with women of loose character; in Capricorn attached to other people's wives; in Aquarius, fond of females and given to drink, and spends much money on them.

3. Saturn in the house of Mars aspected by Moon: the native is attached to low and unattractive women; aspected by Mars fond of females; aspected by Venus attached to other people's wives and public women.

4. Saturn in the house of Venus aspected by Sun: enjoys in other people's houses; aspected by Moon; is handsome and derives much benefit from women; aspected by Mercury; is not very potent and serves women; aspected by Venus; fond of females and given to drink.

5. Saturn in the house of Mercury aspected by Moon; gets wealth and respect from women and does work for them; if aspected by Mercury fond of dances and music and associated with women; aspected by Venus; much liked by ladies and treated as a leader and adviser in their group.

6. Saturn in Cancer aspected by Sun; devoid of conjugal happiness; aspected by Mars having liaison with a relation's wife (who is not very good); aspected by Jupiter; conjugal happiness.

7. Saturn in the house of Sun and aspected by Sun; given to drinks; aspected by Moon; enjoys a number of women; aspected by Mars; devoid of conjugal happiness; aspected by Mercury: humble and always carrying out orders of women; aspected by Venus; has enmity with women though of very good appearance himself.

8. Saturn in Sagittarius: has a good wife.

9. Saturn in the house of Jupiter aspected by Moon: has good conjugal happiness and also wealth.

10. Saturn in its own house aspected by Sun: devoid of conjugal happiness; aspected by Venus attached to other people's wives.

11. Saturn in Capricorn or Aquarius: the person is attached to another person's wife and also gets other person's wealth.

12. Saturn gives a 'tamasic' wife who may be lethargic, avaricious, cruel, cunning and a hard task-master.

13. Saturn in its own 'trinshansha'*; the native's wife would die prematurely and he would be attached to another man's wife.

---

* Trinshansha is one of the sub-divisions. See Appendix IV

14. Saturn in the 1st house: the native is always hankering for pleasure due to ungratified craving of the sex.

15. Saturn in the 6th house: the native is very lustful.

16. Saturn in the 7th house unless well-aspected or lord of the 7th house be strong in its own house: premature death of wife.

17. Saturn in the 7th house—if in Pisces: one wife would die after the other.

18. Saturn in the 7th house unless the lord is strong or the 7th house is well-aspected: as unprepossessing wife; she may be tall but lean and thin.

19. Saturn in the 7th house; not at all good for conjugal happiness.

20. When Saturn is the significator of liaison it indicates union with a low woman or who is in menses. She may be dwarfish or dark in complexion or of low status (a maid servant).

21. If Saturn is with the lord of the 7th house in an angle the native's wife's breasts are long and fallen.

22. If Saturn be the lord of the 7th house and conjoined with a malefic/in a debilitated 'navamsha' in a debilitated sign/in an enemy's house/in a 'charansha' aspected by a malefic, the native's wife is of loose character and proves a blot to the native's family.

23. If Saturn be the lord of the 7th house and is strong and aspected by Jupiter and other benefics, the native's wife is virtuous.

24. If Saturn be the lord of the 7th house and conjoined with a malefic, the native would be adulterous.

Aphorisms of Rahu and Ketu

In Hindu Astrology Rahu and Ketu has the same importance as that of the other planets. It is surprising that Western Astrology does not take them into account. They are aslo called 'The Shadow Planets'. Rahu and Ketu do not aspect other planets. They also do not receive the aspects from other planets. They show the full effect of the planet.

(i) They conjoin with, or

(ii) According to the lord of the sign they are posited in if there is no planet with them.

Rahu and Ketu are endowed with malefic effects. The keyword of Rahu is 'Secrecy' and 'constant changes'. In the 7th house Rahu gives secret love affairs particualrly in the case of women. It also casues ups an downs in relationship. Wearing of a 'Gomedak'* is recommended.

Ketu is not very nice in the house of marriage. On one side it gives a dignified and learned husband but on the ohter side it gives chronic health problems to the spouse. The same is the case if 'Ketu' is in the 5th house. It causes a number of miscarriages, abortion of at times deformity in children. One in whose horoscope Ketu† causes afflication should denote a cow to a Brahmin to reduce the negative effects.

We now give below the effects of Rahu and Ketu:

1. Rahu and Ketu are the northern and southern nodes of Moon. These are not planets but merely points of intersection, of the planes of Earth's and Moon's orbits. These keep shifting backwards.

2. Rahu and Ketu are both evil and of these two Rahu has the same attributes as Saturn and Ketu as those of Mars.

3. Rahu and Ketu do not aspect nor are aspected but give the effect of the places they are posited in or of the planets with which they are conjoined.

Note. One school of astrology advocates their being aspected.

4. Rahu or Ketu in the 1st house; not at all a good position for conjugal happiness. Rahu therein, the native gets sex urges at unsuitable times.

5. Rahu or Ketu in the 2nd house: bad for conjugal happiness.

6. Rahu or Ketu in the 7th house; the native's wife may be attached to another person (mark for other indications also) or

* A Gem for Rahu.

† See Phaldipika.

may be sickly or uncouth in appearance. If well-aspected, not so.

7. If Rahu or Ketu is conjoined with the lord of the 7th house and the sign they are posited in is aspected by a malefic, the native is adulterous.

8. Ketu in the 7th house gives a sickly wife.

9. If Rahu is in the 7th house the native is attached to another man's wife and has not much love lost between himself and his wife.

10. When Rahu or Ketu is the significator of liaison, union with a low woman is indicated. She may be of low caste or of very inferior status.

11. Rahu or Ketu if with a benefic, who is the lord of the 7th house and is strong if posited in the 5th or 9th houses is good for financial prosperity through wife.

12. Rahu in the 8th house: bad for conjugal happiness.

13. Rahu/Ketu in the 9th house: quarrels with wife's relations.

14. Rahu/Ketu in the 12th house: bad for conjugal happiness there may be a liaison with a low caste woman.

CHAPTER 9

LORDS OF HOUSES

A horoscope is conventionally divided into 12 houses. Each house has jurisdiction over certain subjects and matters. As soon as a planet moves from one house to another, its dignity, interpretation and effects undergo major changes. Keeping this in view we have created a separate chater for the Hindu astrology which deals with the different signs, rising in the first house. The first house is called Lagna, or Lagnam. It is the same as Ascendant or the Rising sign. We have also given the results when different 'Dreshkana' or decanate are rising. The effects of lords of houses when they have different strength, placements and relationship with other planets.

Lord of the 1st House

The Ascendant and its lord gives total indication of not only the native's personality, his appearance, mental attributes but also as to how he will carry on with his partner. The relationships between husband and wife depends upon the friendship, enmity* or neutrality between the lords of the first and seventh houses. We give below the effect due to the lord of the first house:

1. If Aries be on the cusp of the first house, the native has much sexual vivacity and is fond of his wife.

2. If Taurus be on the cusp of the 1st house, the native is patient and perseverant in courtship and succeeds in receiving the favours of ladies.

---

* See 'Astrology and You' by the Authors and Appendix III in the second part.

3. If Gemini be the sign on the cusp of the first house, the native falls in for every pretty face he comes across; is well-versed in the erotic arts and much activity or correspondence may be connected with his love affairs/marriage.

4. If Cancer be the sign in the 1st house, the native is submissive to women, but his married life may not be happy.

5. If Leo is the sign rising, the native has differences with his wife as the native does not like to be dictated upon by his wife and antagonises her.

6. If Virgo be rising, the native is fond of sex indulgence.

7. If Libra be on the cusp of the 1st house the native is submissive to women.

8. If Scorpio rises, the native is oversexed.

9. If Capricorn be rising the native dotes upon his beloved one and may also be attached to some women elder than himself (and who may be related also).

10. With Aquarius on the cusp of the 1st house the native indulges in unholy acts—for other women.

11. With Pisces rising the native is fond of his wife, who may be a little shy.

12. If the degree rising (ascendant) be in the 1st 'dreshkana'* and if malefics are in the 3rd 'dreshkana' in 2nd or 12th house there is likely to be disease in private parts, hampering full enjoyment.

13. If a person's ascendant is in the 2nd 'dreshkana' and there are malefics in the 1st 'dreshkana' of 2nd or 12th house, same result as in 12 above.

14. If a person's ascendant is in the 3rd 'dreshkana' and there are malefics in the second 'dreshkana' in the 2nd or 12th house same results as 12 above.

15. If there are malefics in the 1st house, 2nd and 7th houses and the 7th house lord be in debilitation or combust, loss of wife is indicated. He may even marry a third time.

16. (a) If benefics are near the 1st or 7th house: early marriage.

---

* Dreshkana is decanate. See Appendix IV

(b) If the 1st, 2nd and 7th houses are conjoined with benefic planets in benefic vargas and their lords also conjoined with and aspected by benefics—early marriage.

17. If Cancer or Leo be the sign rising and Saturn be posited in the 7th house it will give the effect of only the 7th house and not of the 8th or 6th house lordship.

18. If Taurus be rising and Mars be in the 7th house it will give the effect of lordship of the 7th house only and not of the 12th house.

19. If Scorpio be rising and Venus is posited in the 7th house, it will give the effect of lordship of the 7th house only and not of the 12th.

20. Similarly, in the above examples 17 to 19 if the planet concerned is posited in a house other than 7th it will give more the effect of the other lordship.

21. Wife/husband's sign (in which Moon would be posited) would probably be one in trine to the sign occupied by lord of the 1st or 7th houses or their 'navamsha' sign or their exaltation or depression signs or the sign containing the greatest number of benefic points in 'ashtakvarga'.

22. If the lord of the 1st, even though a malefic be posited in 7th, it would show good result and not produce any untoward effect. Similarly, if the lord of the first house owning a bad house also, it would only show good results.

23. If the lord of the 1st or 2nd house is in a debilitated sign and associated with or aspected by Venus— there is tendency to sex-practices such as cunnilinctus.

24. If any 'papa' is conjoined with the lord of the 1st house the native is attached to another man's wife.

25. If the lord of the 1st and 6th houses be conjoined with malefics, same as above; the native is too lustful.

26. If the lord of the 1st house is conjoined with or aspected by benefics owning the 7th house or posited in the 7th house, rise of fortune after marriage.

27. If the lord of the 1st house is in benefic 'anshas' and the lord of the 2nd and 7th houses are strong in 'para-vatansha' early marriage.

28. If the lord of the 1st, 2nd and 6th houses along with malefics be in the 7th house, the native is adulterous.

29. Lord of the 1st house in seventh well-aspected; the native's wife is good-looking and well-behaved.

30. If the lord of the 1st house along with a benefic be in the 7th house: the native marries from a good family.

31. If the lord of the 1st house is in the 7th house in a 'papa' rashi: the native's wife is from a low family.

32. If the lord of the 1st house is conjoined with the lord of the 7th house, the native's wife will be beautiful but if it be combust then the wife would not be good-looking.

33. If the lord of the 1st and/or 7th house, be in debilitation, combust or in the 'navamsha' of enemy and in malefic 'shashtiansha' (1/60th division) the native may have to marry a third time.

34. If the lord of the 1st house is in the 7th house conjoined with the lord of the 7th and if the 7th house or its lord be strong, good will result, otherwise, if they are weak it will not be conducive to good results.

35. If the lord of the 1st is devoid of strength and weaker than the lord of the 7th house, and associated with a malefic or in a malefic house or in a debilitated 'ansha' or descending (going down towards its debilitation sign) the native himself/herself is of inferior status than the marriage partner.

36. If the lord of the 1st house is stronger than the lord of the 7th house and ascending (*i.e.* going towards the exaltation sign) or is in exalted 'varga' or 'ansha' or in a 'kendra' or in a 'trikona' with a benefic, the native himself is superior in status to his wife's family.

37. If the lords of the 1st and 7th houses are of equal strength the status of the two (husband and wife) is equal, *i.e.* both come from families of the same standard.

38. See whether the lords of the 1st and the 7th house in a horoscope are friends or enemies. It is good for conjugal happiness if they are friends. *Vice versa.*

39. If the lord of the 1st and 7th houses are great enemies and in quincunx the husband and wife would be inimical (see for other indications as well).

40. If the lord of the 1st and 7th houses are great friends and apply to each other both (husband and wife) would be friendly. (Look to other indications also.)

41. If the lord of the ascendant has a good number of benefic points in its 'ashtakvarga' in the 7th house and if the lord of the 7th house is associated with the lord of the 1st house and is strong, good will result.

42. If the lord of the ascendant has a small number of benefic points in its 'ashtakvarga' in the 7th house and is associated with the lord of the 7th house who in its turn is weak, bad results would follow.

43. If the 7th house or the lord thereof has 'bandh'* with the lord of the first house, it is favourable for matrimonial happiness.

44. If the lord of the 1st house be in the the 8th house and a malefic in the 7th house and lord of the 2nd house also conjoined with a malefic, there would be more than one marriage.

Note. The sign and 'navamsha' occupied by the (i) lord of the ascendant, (ii) lord of the sign occupied by Moon, and (iii) lord of the 7th house.

The husband/wife will have some attributes pertaining to the lords of these or their exaltation or depression signs.

46. Add together the longitudes of the following:

(a) the lord of the 1st house and Venus, and
(b) the planets in whose signs the lords of the 1st and 7th house are posited.

The Janma-rashi (radical Moon's) of the wife would be one of the two above or in trine to them.

47. If the lord of the 1st house is in the 12th house aspected by an enemy, pleasures of life are denied to the native.

---

* Two planets are said to be in 'bandha' when they fully aspect each other or mutually exchange sings or both are in angles or trine, *i.e.* in 1,4,7,10 or in 5 and 9 as counted from ascendant.

48. Add the longitudes of (1) lord of ascendant and Venus. The longitude indicated by the sum total is a sensitive point in regard to conjugal happiness, *i.e.* if it is conjoined with benefics it is good. *Vice versa.*

49. Add the longitudes of (i) lord of ascendant and (ii) lord of the 7th house. The longitude indicated by sum total, if well-placed, well conjoined and well aspected; good for matrimonial happiness. *Vice versa.*

2nd House

Second house and its lord is an important factor as family (wife, children etc.) are judged from it. It is also important because whereas the seventh house indicate the spouse, the second house (being the 8th house as counted from the 7th house) indicate the termination of the life or relationship with the wife.

Due to this fact in some parts of Southern India, the placement of Mars in the second house is also taken in 'Kuja* Dosha' or 'Manglik' effects.

We now give below the effects of the second house and its lord:

1. If only one strong benefic planet conjoins the lord of the 2nd house; only one wife.
2. Lord of the 2nd house conjoined with a 'Papa': the native is attached to another's wife.
3. If the lord of the 2nd house is in the house of Mars or associated with or aspected by Venus, the native resorts to cunnilinctus.
4. If the lord of the 2nd house be in the 7th house or associated with a number of planets, the native will have more than one wife.
5. (i) If the lord of the 2nd house be in the 7th house and (ii) if the lord of the 7th house in the 7th house: the person would have only one wife.

---

* Kuja Dosha means break up of the first marriage unless due to other factors it is nullified.

6. If the lord of the 2nd be in the 10th house, the native would be adulterous.

7. If the lord of the 2nd house is conjoined with a weak planet (s) owning 'trik'; as many wives demise as is the number of planets that conjoin.

8. If the lord of the 2nd house is in the 7th house the wife is fond of luxuries, intent upon saving money, but if the planet be a malefic, she may be barren.

9. Lord of 2nd in the 4th/10th house; native is inclined to have amours with other people's wives.

10. If the lord of the 2nd house is weak, combust, debilitated, in a great enemy's house, in 'paparashi', 'ansha' or aspected by malefics, the wife would be from a lower family.

11. If the lord of the 'navamsha' in which the lord of the 2nd house is posited is with a benefic, and in its own or exaltation 'vargas' in 'paravatansha', the native has a number of wives or enjoys a number of ladies.

12. If there are malefics in the 2nd and 7th houses in a male nativity, they bring about sorrow by the death of the partner. If such combinations are found in the nativity of the wife also, it nullifies the effect.

13. If there are malefics in the 2nd house, the 9th and 10th house, the wife comes from a distant place.

14. If malefics in their depression or inimical houses are posited in the 7th house, the 8th and 2nd houses, it is bad for the longevity of both, husband and wife.

15. The lords of the 2nd house, the 6th and 12th houses from ascendant are not good for 7th house. (Because they become lords of the 6th house, the 8th and 12th houses, if counted from the 7th house).

16. If the lords of the 2nd, and 7th houses are strong, there would be conjugal happiness.

17. If the lords of the 2nd house, the 7th and 10th houses are in the 10th house: same as above.

18. If the lord of the 2nd house or the 7th or 10th houses be in 4th house it indicates liaison with other person's wife.

19. If the lord of the 2nd and 7th houses are in 'Gopuransha', and the lord of the 10th house is in the 7th house, the native is very lucky in love and marriage and has a number of wives.

20. If (a) planets owning the 2nd house, the 7th and 12th houses be posited in 'kendra' and 'trikona' and are aspected by Jupiter (b) benefics be posited in the 2nd house, the 7th house, the 11th house from the lord of the 7th house; conjugal happiness is indicated.

21. If the lord of the 2nd and 12th houses are in the 3rd and aspected by Jupiter or by the lord of the 9th house, a man has several wives.

Note. When Hindu astrological works were written, polygamy was common in India. Now, we should interpret the rules against the present social and legal background.

3rd to 6th Houses

We cannot separate a part from the whole so the importance of 3rd, 4th, 5th, and 6th houses in a horoscope is also considered in estimating success in a love relationship.

The 3rd house indicates the mind, the manner of thinking and communication and a person's success depends upon his ability of comprehension and expression. The 4th house is important as it indicates the atmosphere at home and happiness. Conjugal happiness is a very important part of life. The 5th house controls love life of an individual. The 6th house being the 12th from the 7th house (marriage) indicates the destruction (or loss) of marriage.

Benefic planets in the 3rd, 4th, 5th and 6th houses indicates a harmonious mind, a happy life, success in love as well as good family life.

We now give the effect of the third house to sixth house:

3rd House

1. The 'third' house being in trine to the 7th house, affects conjugal happiness according as there are benefics or malefics in the house.

2. Lord of the 3rd house in the 7th house: the native's wife

is of good temper and prosperous but if the planet be a malefic, the native's wife may have a liaison with a family member younger than the native. (Look for other confirmatory configurations also).

4th House

3. Malefics in 4th house impair happiness in general while the benefics enhance the same. Planets herein therefore play an important role.

4. If the lord of the 4th house in the 7th house be a malefic, the native's wife disobeys the native's father. If it be Mars or Venus the native's wife comes from a good family.

5. If the lord of the 4th house is in the 7th house and friendly with lord of the 7th house and conjoined with or aspected by it gain of land/property through husband/wife is indicated. This would be so if the fourth house be also strong.

5th House

6. The 5th house is the house of children, and as such interconnected with the 7th house. Benefics herein are good for the 7th house happiness. *Vice versa*.

7. If the 5th house is tenanted by the lord of the 6th house, the 7th house, 8th or 12th houses it is not good.

8. If the lords of the 5th and 7th houses are strong and aspected by malefics and conjoined with or aspected by the lord of the the 6th house then the native's wife would have a paramour (look for other indications also).

9. Lords of the 5th or 8th houses in 7th are not good for wife's longevity.

10. If the lord of the 5th house is in the 7th house (ii) the lord of the 11th house conjoined with a malefic (iii) and Venus, be weak the wife runs serious risk to health during pregnancy or delivery.

11. If the lord of the 5th and 7th houses are strong and aspected by benefics: good for conjugal happiness.

12. If the lord of the 5th house is in the 7th house the native's wife is loving, well-behaved and of even temper but if the

lord of the 5th house is in 8th, he does not enjoy conjugal happiness for long.

6th House

13. The sixth house is twelfth from the 7th house and as such planets herein affect adversely the 7th house.

14. If 6th and 8th houses from the ascendant are occupied by malefics it is unfavourable for wife's longevity/married happiness.

15. If lord of the 6th house is in the 7th house the native's wife is always opposing the husband, is very ill-tempered and always causes mental anguish to the husband. If the planet be a benefic, she may be barren or there may be abortions.

16. If the lord of the 6th house be a malefic and in 9th, the native is full of lust.

17. If the fifth and 7th houses from L/L.A.* are aspected by or conjoined with benefics it is good for married happiness.

18. If the houses referred to above are conjoined with or aspected by malefics it is bad.

7th House

This entire book in fact is devoted to the 7th house. A relationship between the native and his spouse. In the following chapter special effects (as mentioned in the Hindu System) of the Seventh House is given below:

1. The physical attributes of the wife would be according to the planet in the 7th house.

2. If there is a benefic sign in the 7th house and the same is aspected by Jupiter, the native is not adulterous.

3. Even signs on the cusp of 7th house are good for conjugal happiness. Lord of the 7th house in even sign: good for conjugal happiness.

4. If the 7th house or 'navamsha' therein is owned by a benefic, the native gets a virtuous wife. If the same is aspected by benefics good for conjugal happiness.

5. If the cusp of the 7th house is in malefic 'ansha' or

* 'L' is abbreviated form of Lagna or (Ascendant) L/A means Lunar Ascendant, *i.e.* the sign in which Moon is posited.

aspected by a malefic, the marriage would be in a distant place.

6. If the 7th house is in the 'varga' of Saturn or Mars and if Venus is aspected by Saturn or Mars, the native is addicted to other women.

7. If the 7th house itself or the lord of the house is hemmed in between malefics, the native may marry again.

8. If there are several malefics in 7th and the lord of the 7th is conjoined with malefics and if Ketu is in the 6th the native's two wives—one after the other die and he marries a third time.

9. Planets in the 7th house from lagna or Moon, if benefics, confer happiness. *Vice versa*.

10. If three or more planets be strong in the 7th house, the native will have several wives or love affairs.

11. If lord of the 'trika' is in the 7th house it spoils the house (conjugal happiness).

12. If the 7th house has malefics it is a bad augury for matrimonial happiness. If there are malefics in the 7th house and they are aspected also by malefics, there may be disease in private parts.

13. If there is 'Dhuma' in the 7th there is no marriage or delayed marriage. If there is 'Karmuk' there may be premature death of the partner, if there is 'Parivesh' the wife would be ill-tempered and ill-behaved and if 'ketu' therein, she may be barren. If there is 'Kala' there may be no marriage or wife may die prematurely. If there is a 'papa' in the 7th house the wife may have miscarriages.

14. When 'Mandi' is in 7th house, it acts like a mangal dosha (malefic influence similar to Mars). The native is very passionate but wife/husband's longevity is impaired.

15. If the 7th house is conjoined with 'Yamkantak' it is good. If the 7th house is conjoined with 'Gulika'—it is evil. Even the lord of 'Gulika' in the 7th house is bad.

16. If there is a planet in the 7th house in the sign of Venus the number of wives is the same as the number of the planet(s) which conjoin or aspect such planet.

17. If the 7th house is conjoined with or aspected by its

lord, Jupiter, Mercury or Venus it is good; if aspected by malefics, it is unfavourable.

18. If the 7th house is aspected by a malefic, wife of the native is sinful and evil-tempered. If the cusp of the 7th house is in malefic vargas the wife of the native would be inimical to the husband.

19. If the 7th house is weak and is tenanted by the lord of the 'trika' it is bad. If aspected by benefics the position is a little improved.

20. Even a benefic in an enemy's house in the 7th house is not good.

21. Also see whether the planet posited in the 7th house, is lord of a good house or a bad one.

22. Even a malefic, if strong in its own house in the 7th house, would assure conjugal happiness.

23. A malefic planet in the 7th house and owning it, if weak spoils conjugal happiness.

24. If hermaphrodite planet (Mercury of Saturn) occupies the seventh house and the 11th house is occupied by two planets, there may be more than one marriage.

25. Benefic in the 7th house are good, unless they own a 'trika' place.

26. Greater the number of planets in the 7th house or aspecting it greater the number of women with whom one will associate.

27. In 26 above if malefics aspect the 7th house, wife may die or happiness will not be ensured from such association.

28. If 'Gulika' is in the 7th house, the native will have more than one union and would be quarrelsome.

29. If a malefic occupies the 7th house and is aspected by another malefic, it is bad for longevity of wife/husband.

30. A malefic planet in the 7th house in the 'vargas' of a malefic gives a bad wife or destroys her.

Note. If the above are aspected by benefics the evil is mitigated.

31. If seventh house is tenanted by the lord of the 5th and

8th, *i.e.* Jupiter in case of Sinha Lagna (Leo Ascendant) people and Mercury in case of Kumbha Lagna (Aquarius Ascendant) people; loss of husband/wife.

32. If the seventh house lord is conjoined with the lord of 'Mandi' Rashi, it spoils conjugal happiness.

33. If the seventh house is hemmed in between malefics, it indicates premature death of wife/husband.

34. If there be a benefic in seventh house and the house be hemmed in between benefics and these benefics be not conjoined or associated with malefics, it is extremely good for conjugal happiness and prosperity.

35. Husband or wife should also be judged from the following:

(a) by the planet posited in the 7th house.
(b) by a planet aspecting the 7th house.

36. If planets of inharmonious elements are together in 7th house, they would create disease or mental unhappiness.

37. If the total number of benefic points in the 7th house exceeds 28 (out of 337) in 'Sarvashtak varga' it augurs well for conjugal happiness. *Vice versa.*

38. If the lord of the seventh house is in:

(a) first house, the native is attached to his own wife and does not fall in love with other ladies, but if it be in the first house with a malefic, the native would be adulterous particularly, if Aries or Scorpio be the ascendant.
(b) second the native's wife is wicked and though the native may have monetary gain through/by marriage, the wife may not be well-behaved.
(c) third in Taurus or Libra, then the number of wives would be according to the planets, which conjoin Venus.

39. If the lord of the seventh house is a malefic and in third the native's wife may have some liaison with some junior member in the family (look for other confirmatory indications also).

40. If the lord of the 7th house is in fourth the (i) native's wife may live separately for long periods. (ii) the native may

have a liaison with another person's wife. This is so if the lord of the seventh and seventh house itself are weak and aspected by 'papas'.

41. If the 7th house lord is in the 4th house and the two lords are friendly and conjoined or aspecting each other, acquisition of land or building through wife may be predicted.

42. If the lord of the seventh is in the fifth

(i) the native's wife may live for long, under the protection of his sons.
(ii) the wife is sickly or the native has enmity with her. If the planet be a malefic the native suffers from wasting disease due to over-indulgence.

43. If the lord of the 7th house is in the 7th house it is conducive to conjugal happiness.

44. If the lord of the 7th house is

(i) in 8th the native spends much money on other women and may not have conjugal happiness.
(ii) If the lord of 7th is in ninth, the native's wife is good-looking but if the planet be a malefic the native would be full of lust and his virility would be impaired.
(iii) If in 10th, the native marries in a family higher than his own and is under the influence of his wife. The native would have some love affairs also.
(iv) If in 11th the native's wife is good and well-behaved.

45. If lord of the 7th house is in the 11th house and lord of the 11th house in the 7th house, there may be gain through partnership.

46. If lord of the seventh house is in the 12th house the native may in his advanced age marry or have love affair with a woman of young age who may not be well-behaved.

47. If the lord of the 7th is in 12th and the 12th lord is in 7th, partnership would result in much expenditure and financial difficulties.

48. If the lord of the 7th house from lagna or from 'Janmapati' dispositor of Moon is in 12th and if the lord of the lagna and Janmapati be malefics and occupy 7th, conjugal happiness is not warranted.

49. If the lord of the 7th house is in a 'papa' rashi and is

aspected by a 'papa' or is conjoined with one and is posited in an untoward house, *i.e.* 6th, 8th or 12th the native does not have matrimonial happiness adequately. *Vice versa.*

50. If the lord of the 7th house is in the house of Mars or associated with or aspected by Venus the native resorts to cunnilinctus.

51. If the lord of the 7th house is posited in Taurus or Libra, the native is full of lust.

52. If the lord of the 7th house is exalted or retrograde in the 1st house, there would be more than one wife.

53. If the lord of the 7th house is exalted or in its own or friend's 'vargas', in angle, trine or conjoined with the lord of the 10th, same as above, *i.e.* more than one wife/several love affairs.

54. If the lord of the 7th is in 'Shubha ansha' and aspected by 'Shubha'* the native's wife comes from a good family. But if it is in a 'papa rashi' in 'papa vargas' or conjoined with a 'papa' then she comes from a bad family.

55. If the lord of the sign, in which the 7th house lord is posited is weak or in 'trika' house conjugal happiness would be impaired.

56. If the lord of the 7th is in a 'Krura' 'Shashtiansha' the native has a bad wife.

57. If the lord of the 'navamsha' in which lord of the 7th house is posited is in debilitation, combust or in enemy's sign or hemmed in between malefics or aspected by malefics the native may marry again. Judge similarly in relation to lord of the 7th house.

58. If the lord of the 7th house is in the ascendant, it is good particularly so if the lord of the ascendant also be in 7th house.

59. If the lord of the 7th house is in 'Kendra' in a shubha rashi, shubha ansha and aspected by shubha the native's wife would be virtuous.

60. If the lord of the 7th house is in an angle or a trine exalted in its own house or in friend's house or in such vargas and aspected by the lord of the 10th, the native marries several times or has the enjoyment of several women.

---

* 'Subha' means a benefic.

61. If lord of the 7th and 11th houses are both in angles, same as above—several wives.

62. If the lord of the 7th house is in 'trika' it spoils the good effect of described above; the 8th house is the worst position.

Note. The evil is enhanced if it is in 'papa' vargas and aspected by malefics. The evil is mitigated if it is in 'shubha vargas' and aspected by benefics.

63. If the lord of the 7th house is in a sign near to that occupied by the lord of 1st house there would be early marriage.

64. If the lord of the seventh is in 'trik' and/or if the lord of the 'trik' is in 7th house it impairs matrimonial happiness *but if the planet posited is benefic (though lord of trik it is not so bad.* Also the evil is not fatal if there are benefic aspects on such planet. Look to other indications also.

65. If a malefic owns the 7th house and is posited in the 6th house, the 8th house, 12th or 2nd houses from lagna it destroys the 7th house prospects.

66. If a benefic owns the 7th house and is posited in the 6th house, the 8th house, 12th or 2nd house from lagna it is incapable of giving maximum good effect.

67. If the lord of the 7th house occupy 'trika' position it will show bad results pertaining to the 7th house, if it be weak.

68. In 62 above if it be strong, the injury would be only slight.

69. If the lord of the 7th is associated with or aspected by the lord of the trika the good effect is spoiled.

70. If the lord of the 7th is associated with a debilitated planet or is in a debilitated 'navamsha' the native has a bad wife; not so if it has benefic aspect.

71. If the lord of the sign in which the 7th house lord is posited is associated with a number of planets more than one wife is indicated.

72. If the lord of the 7th house is conjoined with a malefic and/or a malefic is posited in the 7th house or if the lord of the 'navamsha' in which the lord of the 7th house is posited is a malefic the native has a bad wife.

73. If the lord of the 7th house be conjoined with Saturn,

Mars, or Rahu and be in Krura 'shashtiansha' (1/60th div.) there may be more than one wife.

74. If the lord of the 7th house be in debilitation and associated with a benefic and if there be a malefic in the 7th house, there would be more than one marriage.

75. If the lord of the 7th house along with a malefic be in the 1st house same as above.

76. In 74 and 75 above effects are modified if there are benefic aspects.

77. If the lord of the 7th house is conjoined with or aspected by a 'shubha' or is hemmed in between 'shubhas', the native has a good wife.

78. If the lord of the 7th house or the lord of the 2nd house is conjoined with weak planets who own the 6th house, the 8th or 12th houses as many wives demise as the number of the planets, which conjoin. Similarly the number of wives is in accordance with 'shubha' planets that conjoin. If only one strong planet conjoins the lord of the 7th house, there is only one wife.

79. If the lord of the 7th house is with Rahu or Ketu the native is adulterous (look for confirmatory evidence).

80. If the lord of the 7th and 11th houses are together or fully aspected by each other, are strong and in the 5th or 9th house it is good for love and marriage.

81. If the lord of the 'navamsha', in which the lord of the 7th house is posited is with a benefic and is in own or exaltation 'vargas', in Paravatansha, the native has a number of women.

82. If the lord of the 7th house is posited in a 'shubhansha' and aspected by shubha planets or is in exalted 'ansha' or strong by being in several own or exalted 'vargas', one marries in a high family.

83. If the lord of the 7th house is combust or in an enemy's 'ansha' or in association with another debilitated planet or is weaker than the lord of the 1st house, marriage would be in a lower family.

84. If the lord of the 7th house is in a debilitated ansha or otherwise debilitated the wife/husband would be from a lower family.

85. The sign, 'ansha' of the husband/wife is the same as occupied by the lord of the 7th house or the exaltation or debilitation sign of the lord of the 7th house.

86. If it is not one of the above, it is one in 'trine' to above.

87. If the lord of the 6th is associated with the lord of the 7th or 7th house or the 7th house lord is in 6th house, there may be enmity with women.

88. If the lord of the 7th house and 7th house itself are strong and/or connected with benefics or have their aspects, the wife would be virtuous.

89. If there be benefic sign in the 7th house unaspected by malefics it is good for conjugal happiness.

90. Mark the planets which exchange places with the lord of the 7th house, or are conjoined with it or are in full mutual aspect with it (they and the lord of the 7th house) or are in a square or trine to it. These planets would produce results connected with the 7th house and also connected with the house they are owners of.

91. If the lord of the 7th is conjoined with or placed in a 'Bandha' with the lords of the 6th house, the 8th or 12th houses from lagna, it is not good, 'Bandha' positions have been described above.

92. Find out the number of points the lord of the 7th has in its own ashtakvarga. If the benefic points be 4 or more it would be good; if less then 4 it is not good. (Fortunate points in Ashtakvarga are called 'Rekhas' in Northern India and Bindus in Southern India).

93. When the lord of the 7th house is very strong/stronger than the lord of the 1st house, one marries in a rich family. Look to other indications also.

94. If the lord of the 7th house is weak one marries in a poor family, and the wife may not be handsome, if there be no good aspect on 7th house.

95. If the lord of the 7th house be benefic and strong, the wife would be of a good disposition.

96. If the lord of the 7th house occupies an enemy's house

or is in depression or combust or aspected by malefics and the 7th house is also conjoined with or aspected by malefics, wife/husband will die rather prematurely or there would be no married happiness.

97. One would marry a girl living in the direction indicated below:

(a) Sign of the planet occupying or aspecting the 7th house.

(b) A sign arrived at by totalling longitudes of Venus and lord of 7th.

98. If in above the Navamsha is fixed, wife would be from a nearby place.

99. Wife or husband may come from the part of the country indicated by the following:

(a) Direction presided over by lord of 7th,

(b) Direction presided over by planet aspecting 7th house or posited therein,

(c) Direction of 'navamsha' Rashi in 7th house, and

(d) Direction of 'navamsha' of Venus.

100. For better judgement of the 7th house effects make the 7th house, the lagna and then judge about connected affairs, as if the new setting be a complete and independent horoscope. For example, 8th house would become the 2nd house. Judge from this, wife's wealth and so on.

8th to 12th Houses

The importance of the 8th house to 12th house is no less in the matters of marriage. The 8th house indicates conjugal bliss and particularly in the case of women, it rules the longevity of the husband. Malefics in the 8th house destroys the life of spouse. The 9th house controls the relationship between the native and his in-laws. The 10th house indicates the social life and parents of the spouse. The 11th house indicate friends, the love life of the spouse, children and thier married life. The twelfth house has jurisdiction over problems in marriage—ups and downs in matrimonial relationships. It also rules how an emotional link will end. Planets in the fifth house indicate successful beginning in love life but how it will end will be clearly indicated from the twelfth house.

We give now the effects of the 8th to 12th house:

1. If the lord of the 8th house is in 7th, the wife is quarrelsome. If a malefic is in 8th house there may be premature death of wife/husband, if other partner's horoscope does not have 'Mangal'* dosha.

2. If the lord of the 9th house be in third, the wife is good and the native is considerate to her, if in seventh: the native's wife is truthful, good-looking and religious.

3. If the lord of the 9th house is in the 7th house and the lord of the 7th house is in the 4th house: several wives.

4. If the lord of the 10th house is weak, the native is of vacillating mind and corrupt.

5. If the lord of the 10th house is in the 4th house the native has love affairs; if in seventh, the native has a good wife who is obedient and attached to husband. Lord of the 10th house in the 10th house: the native has illicit connection with other women.

6. If the lord of the 10th house is in the 7th house and is weak, the native is corrupt.

7. If the lord of the 10th is along with Venus in the 7th house: same result.

8. If the lord of the 10th house is aspected by Saturn or is in a sign of Mars or conjoined with Venus, the native enjoys more than one woman.

9. If the lord of the 10th house and lord of the 'navamsha' in which the lord of the 10th house is posited, are conjoined with Saturn and aspected by the lord of the 6th house: the native has the enjoyment of a number of women.

10. If the lord of the 10th house from the ascendant, Moon of Sun is in the 'navamsha' of 'Venus' the native has the

* 'Mangal' Dosha = malefic influence described in ch. 11.

patronage of a woman (may be his wife or employer or beloved) and gains thereby.

11. If lord of the tenth from Lagna/L.A. is in 'vargas' of Venus prosperity through women (wife, sister or other women).

11th House

12. If strong planets are in the 11th house, the native derives many luxuries.

13. If the lord of the 11th is in 7th, the native is long-lived and marries only once.

12th House

14. If female planets are in the 12th house, the native loses much money an account of /through women.

15. If a debilitated planet is the 12th or the 12th house is associated with Saturn 'Mandi', or Rahu the pleasures of life are denied to the native.

16. If there are malefics in the 12th house or if the lord of the 12th is associated with malefics or is in a malefic 'ansha' or aspected by malefics, the native does not have adequate opportunities to enjoy pleasures of flesh.

17. If the lord of the 12th is in 1st house, the native's virility is impaired due to over-indulgence; if in 7th: if a benefic the native suffers from wasting diseases due to over-indulgence with his own wife; if the planet be a malefic due to association with other women.

18. If the lord of the 12th house be in the 10th house, the native does not have liaison with other women.

19. If the lord of the 12th house is exalted or 'shubha' vargas and aspected by 'shubhas' one has ample opportunities for pleasure.

21. If the lord of the 12th is strong conjoined with and aspected by benefics the native enjoys life.

22. If the lord of the 12th house be a malefic but is exalted or in its own or friends' 'vargas' and the planet in whose sign lord of the 12th house is also so placed the native has opportunities to enjoy life.

23. If the lord of the 12th house is associated with or aspected by a weak lord of the 7th house in a malefic 'ansha', there is waste of money due to wife or women.

CHAPTER 10

FEMALE NATIVITIES

It was necessary to give a separate chapter for women. Most things are already covered in the preceeding and succeeding pages. It should be noted that when the original books were written, women although they enjoyed a high status in the family yet due to polygamy which existed at that time, their conjugal life was shared by other women. The most important thing is that when in a female chart the Ascendant, Sun and Moon are in odd signs and the birth is in the day time*, she is endowed with masculine temperament which may make her a lesbian† or seek unnatural satisfaction. The same is true of a man i.e. if all planets are in even sign in a male horoscope and the rising sign is Virgo then traits of homosexuality can develop. It also indicates changes in the mannerism and behaviour which will be more like that of a woman. That is why special care is needed when judgement of a horoscope of female looking men or masculine looking women is being considered. Importance to female nativity should be given in the above cases.

We give below some principles which applies to female horoscopy:

1. The general principles given in preceding aphorisms pertaining to male nativities apply *mutatis mutandis* to female nativities also, except having more than one husband simultaneously because polyandry is not in vogue. Also remarriage

---

* From Sunrise to sunset is taken as daytime.

† Relationship with other women

should not be predicted for women belonging to communities in which re-marriage is not allowed.

2. Rules about love affairs, adultery and liaisons should also be judged against the background of moral standard prevailing in a particular country, region, community or family.

3. Secret love affairs or adultery should not generally be predicted because if the standard of the community or family is orthodox morally, there may be only desire or mental attraction without any overt act.

4. When women do not follow independent career, their good fortunes pertaining to rank and wealth are transferred to their husbands.

5. All about the husband should be judged from the 7th house.

6. A woman's prosperity and happiness pertaining to the longevity of the husband should be judged from the 8th house, as well as from 7th.

7. A woman's chastity should be judged from the 4th house.*

8. Children should be judged from the 9th house. Also from fifth.

9. If Sun owns the 7th house or the 'navamsha' on the cusp of 7th, there is some abnormality about the womb affecting her fecundity.

10. If Sun and Saturn are in even signs and even navamshas and there is a malefic in the 1st house and lord of the 7th stronger than the first, the woman cohabits with a person related to her as uncle or so on. If the lord of the 3rd house is associated with Sun or Saturn she cohabits with someone related as brother. So judge of other relations.

11. In the above relationships, judge of the son from the 5th, maternal uncle or aunt from the 6th, elder brother or sister from the 11th, elder brother's wife or elder sister's husband from the 5th house and so on.

12. If Sun is in the 7th house in a female nativity the native's husband is fair, passionate, but of a fiery temperament.

---

* Students are requested not to pronounce their judgment regarding chastity of women. Astrology is not intended to break up homes, or destroy domestic peace and concord.

13. If the Sun be in the 7th and 5th house and lord thereof is afflicted: she would be barren.

14. Sun in 7th house in conjunction with Rahu, Saturn or Mars or aspected by the same, would lead to separation between the couple.

15. If Sun be the lord of the 1st house or of the sign in which Moon is posited whichever is stronger, note the 'Trinshansha' in which the ascendant or Moon is posited. She would be according to the planet presiding over Trinshansha. If the planet* presiding over 'Trinshansha' be:

(a) Mars: masculine, *i.e.* aggressive and quarrelsome.
(b) Saturn: adulterous.
(c) Jupiter: much beloved and marrying a person of high position.
(d) Mercury: behaving in a masculine fashion (may excel in sports).
(e) Venus: may have adulterous intercourse with a close relation.

16. If a girl is born when Moon's longitude is between 226° 40 minutes and 240° (*i.e.*, in Jyeshtha) and the 5th house is afflicted her marriage is likely to affect adversely her husband's elder brother.

17. If a girl is born in Ashlesha Nakshatra, *i.e.* the longitude of Moon be between 106° -40 minutes and 120° and her tenth house be also afflicted she is likely to be unfortunate to her mother-in-law. Mark for other indications also.

18. If a girl is born in 'Mool' nakshatra (*i.e.*, if Moon's longitude be between 240° and 253°-20 minutes and her 4th house be also afflicted) she is likely to prove baneful to her husband's father.

19. If a girl is born in Vishakha Nakshatra (*i.e.*, Moon's longitude is between 200° and 213°-20′and her 9th house be also afflicted) and if her husband's younger brother may not

---

* For ascertaining which planet presides over which Trinshansha see Appendix IV.

have good configuration for longevity she is likely to prove harmful for the health of her husband's younger brother.

20. Girls born in Krittika,[1] Pushya, Chitra, Ardra, Ashlesha, Jyeshtha, Shatabhisha and Moola are easily affected by evil combinations in 5th or 7th houses. A native is said to be born in a particular asterism when radical Moon is in that asterism.

21. If Moon is in Scorpio, Virgo, Taurus, or Leo in the 6th house there is some abnormality about the womb, affecting her fecundity.

22. If Moon be in the 1st or 7th house in the Navamsha of Sun, the woman is of loose conduct. If Moon be in its own house or exalted and beneficially aspected, she is virtuous but if Moon be debilitated, combust, in an enemy's house or conjoined with a 'papa' or in the 30th degree the woman is not virtuous and may become a widow (look for confirmatory evidence also).

23. If Moon be the lord of the 1st house or Moon be in Cancer note whether 'L'[2] or 'LA' is stronger and take that which is stronger and the following would be the effect according as the longitude of L/LA falls in the Trinshansha of:

(a) Mars: independent and self-willed, roaming about freely.
(b) Saturn: she would be, by her behaviour oppressive and curtail the longevity of her husband.
(c) Jupiter: endowed with many good qualities.
(d) Mercury: clever in arts and crafts.
(e) Venus: adulterous.

24. If Moon and Venus and the rising sign be in the sign or ansha of Mars or/and Saturn she would be inclined to have paramours.

25. If Moon, Mercury and Venus be weak and Saturn be of medium strength while other planets be strong, the female would be masculine in nature and temperament.

26. If Moon, 1st house and 4th be associated with benefics she will have qualities and be chaste. *Vice versa* if instead of benefics there be malefics.

---

1. For longitudes of moon referred to by these asterisms, see chapter 11.
2. L means Lagna or ascendant. L.A. means Lunar Ascendant.

27. If Moon be in the 7th house weak and aspected by 'Papas' her husband would be sickly and given to too much indulgence. But if Moon be strong and well aspected, he will be handsome though having flirtatious tendencies.

28. If Moon be in the 7th house associated with Mars and Venus she will have illicit connections and the same would be connived at or be with the approval of her husband.

29. If the dispositer of Moon and the lord of the rising sign are in even signs and aspected by benefics, the woman would be of good disposition.

30. If the above two are in odd signs and aspected by malefics, she would be of a crooked nature, uncontrollable, aggressive and not lucky.

31. If the dispositer of Moon and lords of the 1st and the 9th houses be associated by conjunction or aspect with benefics and placed in good houses without being combust or in depression it is a.good combination for being virtuous and happy.

32. If Moon is in the 7th in the 'navamsha' of Mars or Saturn in a female nativity she has adulterous intercourses with the permission of her husband. This is so if her 4th and ninth houses are also afflicted.

33. In at any time Moon be transiting in a female nativity, house other than the 3rd, 6th, 10th and 11th houses from the ascendant and be aspected by Mars, at the time of commencement of menses, the 15 days' period following is propitious for impregnation.

34. When Moon transits the 3rd, 6th, 10th and 11th houses in the husband's horoscope and is aspected by Jupiter the time is suitable for impregnation.

35. If Mars be the lord of the rising sign or 'navamsha' and Mars be debilitated or combust, the female comes from a low family, is wicked or there is constant quarrel/separation between husband and wife.

36. If Mars rules the 7th house or the navamsha therein, there is likely to be some trouble with monthly period/womb affecting fecundity.

37. If Mars and Venus occupy each other's navamsha the woman will form illicit connections with others.

38. If Mars is in the 7th house, unless exalted or very well-aspected, the husband would be cruel, lazy impolite, clever in talking and a little reddish in complexion.

39. If Mars is in the 7th house aspected by a malefic it is bad for the longevity of the husband.

40. If Mars be the ruler of L/LA* whichever is stronger, note the 'trinshansha' of the longitude. If it is presided by:

- (a) Mars: she would be wicked and ill-behaved.
- (b) Saturn: she will lead the life of a menial servant, *i.e.* in household drudgery.
- (c) Jupiter: virtuous.
- (d) Mercury: deceitful.
- (e) Venus: licentious.

Mercury

41. If Mercury be the ruler of the rising sign or the sign in which Moon is posited (whichever is stronger) and the 'trinshansha' concerned be presided over by:

- (a) Mars: she would be dishonest and treacherous.
- (b) Saturn: she would be frigid, and not with good capacity to bear children.
- (c) Jupiter: chaste.
- (d) Mercury: has many accomplishments.
- (e) Venus: voluptuous and adulterous.

Note. Jupiter's aspect modifies the evil particularly so, if it be strong by sign and house.

42. If Mercury be in the 7th house the husband is learned, wealthy, clever but deceitful.

43. If Jupiter be in the 7th house the native's husband is long-lived, wealthy and very passionate. If Jupiter is in Capricorn in 7th house and weak in navamsha also, it is unfortunate.

44. If Jupiter be the lord of L/LA whichever is stronger, the effect is as follows according as the 'trinshansha' is presided by:

- (a) Mars: endowed with many good qualities.
- (b) Saturn: not much inclined to sex intercourse.

---

* Lagna/Lunar Ascendant.

(c) Jupiter: highly virtuous.
(d) Mercury: very clever and intelligent.
(e) Venus: chaste.

45. If Venus be in the 7th, the husband is beautiful, indulging in luxuries everyday, having poetic tendencies and possessing land.

46. If Venus be the lord of L/LA note the stronger one. The effect would be according as the L/LA falls in the 'trinshansha' of:

(a) Mars: wicked and ill-behaved.
(b) Saturn: may marry again.
(c) Jupiter: endowed with good qualities.
(d) Mercury: skilled in music and arts.
(e) Venus: well-known for her good qualities and accomplishments.

47. If Saturn is in the 7th house or aspects that house marriage is delayed, but Saturn in its own house or if it be lord of the 1st house would not cause delay in marriage.

48. If Saturn owns the 6th house or the navamsha therein there is likely to be some congestion or uterine trouble.

49. If Saturn is in the 7th house, the husband is sober, behaves like and elderly man or is elderly in age and is reserved. If badly aspected he may be sinful. Also give attention to aspects it receives.

50. If Saturn be the lord of L/LA whichever is stronger and the 'trinshansha' of L/LA concerned be presided by:

(a) Mars: she would occupy a low position and waste her life in household drudgery.
(b) Saturn: addicted to a saturnine person (or to a servant).
(c) Jupiter : attached to her husband.
(d) Mercury: wicked.
(e) Venus: barren.

51. Rahu or Ketu in the 7th house: her husband may come from a low family or be low in mind/or sickly or there may be a jarring note in conjugal life.

Note. Mark for other indications also.

52. If lagna/or L.A. are in even signs the woman would be feminine in appearance and temperament but if they be in odd signs she would be masculine, *i.e.*, aggressive, domineering and quarrelsome.

53. If good planets are posited in L/LA or aspect the same, virtuous qualities would be found in a woman and she would be attractive also. But if malefics aspect or are conjoined with L/LA she would not be comely and would cause constant irritation and strife.

54. If rising sign is owned and aspected by benefics in a woman's nativity and is also well aspected at the time of coitus the time is propitious to fertility.

55. In a female nativity, if the rising sign be Cancer or the 'navamsha' be Cancer and Moon is weak it is harmful for the longevity of the husband, but if Moon be strong, she is good and virtuous.

56. All about the physical appearance of a woman should be judged from the lagna and L.A.

57. Happiness pertaining to husband should be judged from 7th from lagna and L.A., (*i.e.* seventh from the lunar ascendant).

58. If there are strong 'Raja Yogas'* or other 'yogas' indicating great prosperity and possession and if the woman does not follow an independent profession their good effects are transferred to the husband.

59. In a female nativity if the sign or 'navamsha' rising is owned by a benefic the woman is virtuous; if the same is aspected by benefics, she is handsome also.

60. When benefic planets occupy the second house the woman may predecease her husband.

61. Malefics in the 4th house incline towards clandenstine affairs.

62. Benefic in the 4th, 7th and 8th houses are good.

63. Benefics in the 4th house incline to chastity.

64. Association or happiness of a woman should be judged from the 4th house.

* 'Raj Yogas' means combinations for high position in life.

65. Benefics in 'trikonas' (5th and 9th houses) are good for prosperity. If there are malefics instead of benefics in above, judge otherwise.

66. If benefics own the 7th house and the 7th 'navamsha' the pudendum and genitals would be beautiful and fleshy (if malefics judge otherwise).

67. Malefics in 7th produce a jarring note in the marital life.

68. When the seventh house is not strong and is not occupied or aspected by benefics the husband would not have an imposing personality.

69. If the 7th house has a movable sign on the cusp and the lord of the 7th is also in a movable house, the husband would generally be away.

70. Judge of the husband by the sign, (on the cusp 7th) owner of the sign and the planet posited in or aspecting the 7th house.

71. If malefics occupy the seventh house it is bad for the longevity of the marriage partner. (If the malefic points in the two horoscopes of husband and wife are equal, the evil effects are set off). See Chapter 39.

72. If both benefics and malefics aspect the seventh house, the native may re-marry. (This would be so only where allowed by custom.)

73. If there is a weak malefic planet in the 7th house aspected by a benefic one, the native may be abandoned by her husband.

74. If a 'Papa' planet is in the 7th house or a 'Dhuma' is therein, the woman is wicked. If waning, Moon having less (than 5 digits) be therein (7th) she would be adulterous. Look for other indications also.

75. Judge of the appearance of the husband by the 7th house.

76. If the 7th house or 'navamsha' on the cusp of 7th house be owned by a benefic or be associated with a benefic, the husband would be of good appearance *vice versa*.

77. Malefic in the 7th house curtail the longevity of the husband.

78. If there are good as well as bad planets in the 7th house, she may re-marry, if it be according to the custom of the society.

79. Malefic planets in the 8th house are bad for the prosperity of the husband.

80. Malefics in the 8th house curtail longevity of the husband.

81. Give special attention to the 8th house for longevity of the husband.

82. The death of the husband is to be judged from the 8th house from ascendant or Moon, whichever is stronger.

83. Widowhood may occur in the age indicated by the lord of the navamsha in which the lord of the 8th house is posited.

84. If a malefic in the 8th in a female nativity is debilitated, in an enemy's or 'papavargas' there is liability of premature death of the husband.

85. If there is a strong benefic planet in the 9th house and the lord thereof is also strong, the woman has the good fortune of having her husband and children despite malefics in the 7th and 8th house.

CHAPTER 11

MUTUAL HARMONY

In the present chapter we have given the Hindu System of comparison of horoscopes between a boy and a girl with to marry. The learned readers would read the mathematical part of compatibility in the chapter. However, side by side with this certain practical aspects should be taken into account in order to make life easier and happier.

The horoscope of the boy and girl should be cast either through a computer software or with the help of an Ephemeris. There are many ephemeris which give the daily position of planets. Some of them differ on account of error which has occurred due to following 'Surya Sidhanta' or due to differences in the Ayanamsa. We think that it is best to follow Lahiri's Ephemeris in India which gives an accurate position of Planets. At this juncture we would also like to mention that many software programes exists which give the results of comparison of charts within minutes but many of them has errors and relying on them could be disastrous for a layman.

Proper emphasis be given to Kuja Dosha but we should also take into account that it can get cancelled if in the other chart Saturn or Rahu or Ketu etc. are situated in similar positions. It should also be noted that the mangalik dosha or Kuja dosha becomes stronger after twenty-eight years and does not get reduced as some people advocate. We should also know that some girls are born with certain configurations in their horoscopes viz., tithi, nakshatra, day of the week that with whoever she is married to, the health of the husband is affected.

There are also certain factors which indicate plurality of marriage in the case of men.

The practical aspect is that the girl should be younger (in age). The girl should not be from a higher caste. The girl should have a good family background. A girl should not be from a family where neurosis, lunacy, or chronic health problems exists. The same negative things should be avoided in a boys family. Both of them should be religious, kind hearted and generous. The boy should not be desirous of 'Sannyas'. He should be able to earn a decent livelihood. A girl should not have an extra part in her body or any type of deformity. A girl with a very high forehead should be avoided. A girl should not be very thin or very fat. A girl should be mentally and physically fit to bear children. A boy should not be feminine looking.

It is best to avoid a girl who is argumentative, quarrelsome or opinionated. A girl who is sweet submissive, and has respect for older people, should be preferred.

The boy should be able to take initiative and also a family loving person.

No sad happenings should have taken place prior to marriage in either family.

A proper timing of marriage should be selected after examining both horoscopes. In case horoscopes are not available than a good 'Muhurta' should be selected from the 'names'.

The transiting Moon should not be in the 8th or 4th houses from the radical Moon.

In a girl's chart Jupiter should not be in transit in the 8th from the Janmarashi (Natal Moon).

Jupiter or Moon should not be combust (Asta).

We now give the aphorisms of mutual harmony:

1. The judgment of mutual harmony between a male and a female rests mainly on two planks:

   (a) Equality of *malefic influence* in the two horoscopes.
   (b) Zodiacal position of Moon in one nativity *vis-a-vis* the zodiacal position of Moon in the other.

Malefic Influence

1. If Mars is in the 1st, 7th or 8th houses from the rising sign (ascendant) the nativity is allotted *malefic points* as per details given below:

(a) 192 if Mars is in Cancer.
(b) 180 if Mars is in a great enemy's sign.
(c) 168 if in an enemy's sign.
(d) 144 if in Capricorn.
(e) 108 if in Aries up to 12 degrees.
(f) 96 if in Scorpio or in Aries 13 to 30 degrees or in a neutral's house.
(g) 48 if in a friend's house.
(h) 36 if in a great friend's house.

2. If Mars be in the 2nd, 4th or 12th houses from the ascendant, the nativity is allotted the following malefic points:

(a) 48 if in Cancer.
(b) 45 if in a great enemy's house.
(c) 42 if in enemy's house.
(d) 36 if in Capricorn.
(e) 27 if in Aries, up to 12 degrees.
(f) 24 if in Scorpio or in Aries 12 to 30 degrees or in a neutral's house.
(g) 12 if in a friend's house.
(h) 9 if in a great friend's house.

3. If Saturn be in the 5th, 7th or 8th houses from the rising sign the nativity is alloted malefic points as follows:

(a) 128 if in Aries.
(b) 120 if in a great enemy's house.
(c) 112 if in an enemy's house.
(d) 96 if in Libra.
(e) 72 if in Aquarius up to 20 degrees.
(f) 64 if in Capricorn or in Aquarius from 20 degrees onwards or in a neutral's house.
(g) 32 if in a friend's house.
(h) 24 if in a great friend's house.

4. If Saturn be in the 2nd, 4th or 12th houses from the rising sign, the nativity is allotted the following malefic points:

(a) 32 if in Aries.
(b) 30 if in a great enemy's house.
(c) 28 if in an enemy's house.
(d) 24 if in Libra.
(e) 18 if in Aquarius up to 20 degrees.
(f) 16 if in Capricorn or in Aquarius 20—30 degrees or in a neutral's house.
(g) 8 if in a friend's house.
(h) 6 if in a great friend's house.

5. If Rahu be in the 1st, 7th or 8th houses from the rising sign the nativity is to be allotted malefic points as follows:

(a) if in debilitation 128.
(b) if in great enemy's house 120.
(c) if in an enemy's house 112.
(d) if in exaltation 96.
(e) if in Mool Trikona 72.
(f) if in own house or a neutral's house 64.
(g) in a friend's house 32.
(h) in a great friend's house 24.

6. If Rahu* be in 2nd, 4th or 12th from the rising sign the nativity is allotted the following malefic points:

(a) if in debilitation 32.
(b) if in a great enemy's house 30.
(c) if in an enemy's house 28.
(d) if in exaltation 24.
(e) if in Mool Trikona 18.
(f) if in own or neutral's house 16.
(g) in a friend's house 8.
(h) in a great friend's house 6.

7. If Ketu occupies an unfavourable house, the nativity is allotted the same number of malefic points as Rahu vide 5 and 6 above.

* Look to the placement of lord of the sign occupied by Rahu or Ketu.

8. If Sun occupies the 1st, 7th, or 8th houses from the rising sign the nativity is allotted the following malefic points:

(a) if Sun is in Libra 64.
(b) if in a great enemy's house 60.
(c) if in an enemy's house 56.
(d) if in Aries 48.
(e) if in Leo up to 20 degrees 36.
(f) if in Leo from 21 up to 30 degrees or in a neutral's house 32.
(g) if in a friend's house 16,
(h) if in a great friend's house 12.

9. If Sun be in the 2nd, 4th or 12th houses from the rising sign the nativity is allotted the following malefic points:

(a) if in Libra 16.
(b) if in a great enemy's house 15.
(c) if in an enemy's house 14.
(d) if in Aries 12.
(e) if in Leo up to 20 degrees 9.
(f) if in Leo from 20 up to 30 degrees, or in a neutral's house 8.
(g) if in a friend's houses 4.
(h) if in a great friend's house 3.

10. If any of the above planets or nodes of the Moon, *i.e.* Rahu, or Ketu occupy an unfavourable position in relation to Lunar ascendant (the sign in which the Moon is posited in the nativity) half of the malefic points mentioned above are to be allotted. For example, if Mars in debilitation occupies the 1st house (ascendant) the nativity is to be allotted 192 malefic points (vide Rule No.1 above). Suppose, this Mars is in the 7th house from Moon also, then the nativity is to be allotted 96 in addition to 192, due to position of Mars in relation to the ascendant, as well as from Moon. Suppose, Mars occupies an unfavourable position in relation to the Moon alone then the nativity is to be allotted 96 malefic points only in relation to Moon. Make similar calculations if Saturn, Sun, Rahu or Ketu occupy an unfavourable position from the Lunar ascendant.

11. Similarly, if any of the above planets, *i.e.* Mars, Saturn, Sun, Rahu or Ketu occupy an unfavourable position in relation to Venus in the nativity, one-fourth of the malefic points mentioned in rules 1 to 9 above are to be allotted. In example (vide 10 above) if Mars occupies say 8th position from Venus one fourth of 192, *i.e.* 48 malefic points are to be allotted in addition.

If Mars occupies such position only in relation to Venus and not in relation to rising sign or Moon then only 48 malefic points are to be allotted.

12. *If a malefic* occupies unfavourable position in relation to rising sign, Moon as well as Venus, malefic points are to be added on each of the above counts.

13. (a) All the malefic points which a nativity gets on account of unfavourable positions of Mars, Saturn, Sun, Rahu and Ketu in relation to the rising sign, the sign in which Moon is posited and the sign in which Venus is posited should be added together to form *total* malefic points.

(b) If the total malefic points in the male nativity equal to the total malefic points, (*i.e.* are more or less the same because it is not possible that they be always identically equal) the two nativities are declared as agreeing in respect of malefic points.

14. The malefic points in the two horoscopes are compared to see that combination of the planets which point to the premature demise of the partner are equally balanced in two horoscopes or not.

15. If the malefic points in one nativity are more or less the same as in the other nativity all astrological aphorisms which point to the premature death of husband/wife should be treated as eliminated or cancelled.

16. The malefic points in the two nativities are compared to see that the malefic influences in one nativity do not affect the longevity of the life partner. But to see mental agreement and conjugal happiness the zodiacal positions of Moon in the two nativities are most important.

Points of Harmony

17. Hindu system lays great stress on the sectors in which Moon in the 2 horoscopes are posited. *If the good points obtained as shown hereafter are 18 or more marriage is permissible.*

Higher the number of good* points (more than 18) better for mental agreement and conjugal happiness.

If the number of points obtained is less than 18 marriage is not fortunate.

18. The zodiac is divided into 27 divisions; each division is presided over by a fixed Star or cluster of fixed Stars after whom the division is named. The names of these 27 divisions are as given below:

0°Aries to13°-20′ Aries	Ashwini
13°-20′ Aries to 26°-40′ Aries	Bharani
26°- 40′ Aries to 10′ Taurus	Krittika
10° Taurus to 23°-20′ Taurus	Rohini
23°-20′ Taurus to 6°-40′ Gemini	Mrigshira
6°-40′ Gemini to 20° Gemini	Ardra
20° Gemini to 3°-20′ Cancer	Punarvasu
3°-20′ Cancer to 16°-40′ Cancer	Pushya
16°-40′ Cancer to 30° Cancer	Ashlesha
0° Leo to 13°-20′ Leo	Magha
13° 20′ Leo to 26°-40′ Leo	Purva Phalguni
26°-40′ Leo to 10° Virgo	Uttara Phalguni
10° Virgo to 23°-20′ Virgo	Hasta
23°-20′ Virgo to 6°-40′ Libra	Chitra
6°-40′ Libra to 20° Libra	Swati
20° Libra to 3°-20′ Scorpio	Vishakha
3°-20′ Scorpio to 16°-40′ Scorpio	Anuradha
16°40′ Scorpio to 30° Scorpio	Jyeshtha
0° Sagitt. to 13°-20′ Sagitt.	Mool
13°-20′ Sagitt. to 26°-40′ Sagitt.	Purvashadha
26°-40′ Sagitt. to 10° Capricorn	Uttarashadha
10° Capricorn to 23°-10′ Capricorn	Shravan
23°-10′ Capri. to 6°-40′ Aquar.	Dhanishtha
6°-40′ Aquar. to 20° Aquar.	Shatabhisha
20° Aquar. to 3°-20′ Pisces	Purva Bhadra
3°-20′ Pisces to 16°-40′ Pisces	Uttara Bhadra
16°-40′ Pisces to 30 Pisces	Revati

* Good points mean points of harmony.

19. For purposes of determining points of Harmony, however, the Zodiac is divided into 38 sectors as follows:

ARIES	LIBRA
0° to 13°-20'	180° to 186°-40'
13°-20' to 26°-40'	186°-40' to 200°
26°-40' to 30°	200° to 210°
TAURUS	SCORPIO
30° to 40°.	210° to 213°-20'
40° to 53°-20'	213°-20' to 266° 40'
53°-20' to 60°	226°-40' to 240°
GEMINI	SAGITTARIUS
60° to 66°-40'	240° to 253°-20'
66°-40' to 80°	253°-20' to 255°
80° to 90°	255° to 266°-40'
	266°-40' to 270°
CANCER	CAPRICORN
90° to 93°-20'	270° to 280°
93°-20' to 106°-20'	280° to 285°
106°-20' to 120°	285° to 293°-20'
	293°-20' to 300°
LEO	AQUARIUS
120° to 133°-20'	300° to 306°-20'
133°-20' to 146°-40'	306°-20' to 230°
146°-40' to 150°	320° to 330°
VIRGO	PISCES
150° to 160°	330° to 333°-20'
160° to 173°-20'	333°-20' to 346°-40'
173°-20' to 180°	346°-40' to 360°

Note. The entire 360 degrees comprising twelve signs have been divided into 38 sectors. The division into 38 sectors is not just arbitrary but very scientific. Here, however, space does not permit us to go into the reasons behind this division, but it may be stated that the division is based on the relationship of Nakshatra (fixed star or cluster of stars), sign and according as a particular sector is fiery, watery, etc.

20. Points of harmony in the two nativities (female nativity and the male nativity) would be according to the sectors in which Moons in the two nativities are.

The points of harmony would respectively be according as Moon in the female nativity is in one or the other of 38 sectors in order:

(*i*) If the Moon in the *male nativity* is in Sector I.

28, 34*, $27\frac{1}{2}$, —$18\frac{1}{2}$, $23\frac{1}{2}$, $23\frac{1}{2}$, —27, 19, 19, —$21\frac{1}{2}$, $30\frac{1}{2}$,
25, —20, 26, $16\frac{1}{2}$, —13, 11, 13, $22\frac{1}{2}$, $27\frac{1}{2}$, $22\frac{1}{2}$, —$16\frac{1}{2}$,
$24\frac{1}{2}$, 12, —12, 26, 27, $25\frac{1}{2}$, —28, 28, 27, $20\frac{1}{2}$, —20, 15,
18, —$14\frac{1}{2}$, $24\frac{1}{2}$, 25.

(*ii*) If the Moon in the *male nativity* is in Sector II.

33, 28, $27\frac{1}{2}$, —$18\frac{1}{2}$, $23\frac{1}{2}$, $13\frac{1}{2}$, —18, 27, 26, — 28, $21\frac{1}{2}$,
$23\frac{1}{2}$, — 21, 19, 27, —$21\frac{1}{2}$, 20, 6, —$15\frac{1}{2}$, $29\frac{1}{2}$, $22\frac{1}{2}$—
$16\frac{1}{2}$, $14\frac{1}{2}$, $18\frac{1}{2}$, — 20, 19, 20, 27, $29\frac{1}{2}$, 27, 26, $10\frac{1}{2}$, —11,
21, 25, —$21\frac{1}{2}$, $15\frac{1}{2}$, $24\frac{1}{2}$, .—

(*iii*) If the Moon in the *male nativity* is in Sector III.

$28\frac{1}{2}$, 29, 28, —19, 10, $18\frac{1}{2}$, —21, 21, 22, — $23\frac{1}{2}$, $26\frac{1}{2}$,
$22\frac{1}{2}$, —$17\frac{1}{2}$, 21, 22, —$16\frac{1}{2}$, $16\frac{1}{2}$, 19, — $28\frac{1}{2}$, $17\frac{1}{2}$, —$20\frac{1}{2}$,
$14\frac{1}{2}$, $19\frac{1}{2}$, $24\frac{1}{2}$, — $24\frac{1}{2}$, 18, 19, 14, — $16\frac{1}{2}$, $14\frac{1}{2}$, $13\frac{1}{2}$, 26,
—26, 28, 20, —$16\frac{1}{2}$, $18\frac{1}{2}$, $11\frac{1}{2}$.

(*iv*) If the Moon in the *male nativity* is in Sector IV.

$18\frac{1}{2}$, 19, $16\frac{1}{2}$, —28, 19, $26\frac{1}{2}$, —$18\frac{1}{2}$, $18\frac{1}{2}$, $19\frac{1}{2}$, 20, 23,
19, — $18\frac{1}{2}$, 22, 23, —21, 21, $25\frac{1}{2}$, — $23\frac{1}{2}$, $12\frac{1}{2}$, $15\frac{1}{2}$—

* For example, Moon in the male nativity is in sector I and in the female nativity, Moon is in sector II then the points of harmony would be 34.

$19\frac{1}{2}$, $24\frac{1}{2}$, $29\frac{1}{2}$, —19, $12\frac{1}{2}$, $13\frac{1}{2}$, $8\frac{1}{2}$, —14, 12, 10, $23\frac{1}{2}$, —$30\frac{1}{2}$, $32\frac{1}{2}$, $24\frac{1}{2}$, —19, 21, 14.

(*v*) If Moon in the *male nativity* is in Sector V.

$21\frac{1}{2}$, $22\frac{1}{2}$, 9—19, 28, 34, —$25\frac{1}{2}$, $24\frac{1}{2}$, $23\frac{1}{2}$, —24, 24, 12, —$11\frac{1}{2}$, $25\frac{1}{2}$, 27, —25, 26, 20, —20, $16\frac{1}{2}$, $10\frac{1}{2}$, $14\frac{1}{2}$, $27\frac{1}{2}$, $22\frac{1}{2}$, —13, 19, 20, $11\frac{1}{2}$, —17, 18, 17, 20, —$27\frac{1}{2}$, $25\frac{1}{2}$, $31\frac{1}{2}$, —26, 25, 17.

(*vi*) If Moon in the *male nativity* is in Sector VI.

$22\frac{1}{2}$, $13\frac{1}{2}$, $15\frac{1}{2}$, —$25\frac{1}{2}$, 36, 28, —20, 26, $24\frac{1}{2}$, —25, 17, 21, —$19\frac{1}{2}$, $17\frac{1}{2}$, $25\frac{1}{2}$, $23\frac{1}{2}$, 26, 12, —12, 27, $18\frac{1}{2}$, —$22\frac{1}{2}$, $20\frac{1}{2}$, $22\frac{1}{2}$, —14, 11, 12, 18, —$11\frac{1}{2}$, $24\frac{1}{2}$, 26, 12, —19, 25, $31\frac{1}{2}$, —26, 17, 26.

(*vii*) If Moon in the *male nativity* is in Sector VII.

26, 17, 19 —$16\frac{1}{2}$, 27, 20, —28, 34, $32\frac{1}{2}$ —19, 10, 13, —$22\frac{1}{2}$, $20\frac{1}{2}$, $28\frac{1}{2}$, $30\frac{1}{2}$, $33\frac{1}{2}$, 19, —13, 27, $19\frac{1}{2}$, —13, 11, 13, —21, 19, 18, 24, —$20\frac{1}{2}$, 24, $23\frac{1}{2}$, $8\frac{1}{2}$, —10, 18, $24\frac{1}{2}$, $25\frac{1}{2}$, $16\frac{1}{2}$, $25\frac{1}{2}$.

(*viii*) If Moon in the *male nativity* is in Sector VIII.

17, 26, 20—$17\frac{1}{2}$, $23\frac{1}{2}$, 25, —33, 28, 24, —$10\frac{1}{2}$, 18, 12, —$22\frac{1}{2}$, $28\frac{1}{2}$, $21\frac{1}{2}$, $23\frac{1}{2}$, $23\frac{1}{2}$, 26, —20, 26, 21, —$14\frac{1}{2}$, 16, 3, —15, 27, 26, —$22\frac{1}{2}$, $21\frac{1}{2}$, 21, $17\frac{1}{2}$, —20, 10, 17, —18, $25\frac{1}{2}$, 24.

(*ix*) If Moon in the *male nativity* is in Sector IX.

18, 26, 21, —$18\frac{1}{2}$, $23\frac{1}{2}$, $23\frac{1}{2}$, —$31\frac{1}{2}$, 25, 28, —$14\frac{1}{2}$, $21\frac{1}{2}$, 15, —$21\frac{1}{2}$, $27\frac{1}{2}$, $21\frac{1}{2}$, —$23\frac{1}{2}$, $23\frac{1}{2}$, $24\frac{1}{2}$, —$18\frac{1}{2}$, $26\frac{1}{2}$, 21, —$14\frac{1}{2}$, $21\frac{1}{2}$, 6, —12, 27, 26; 26, —$22\frac{1}{2}$, $21\frac{1}{2}$, $23\frac{1}{2}$, $17\frac{1}{2}$, —19, 10, 17, —18, 27, $25\frac{1}{2}$,.

(*x*) If Moon in the *male nativity* is in Sector X.

$22\frac{1}{2}$, $30\frac{1}{2}$, $25\frac{1}{2}$, — 22, 27, 26, —$19\frac{1}{2}$, 13, 16,—28, 35, $28\frac{1}{2}$, — $16\frac{1}{2}$, $22\frac{1}{2}$, $16\frac{1}{2}$,—$19\frac{1}{2}$, $19\frac{1}{2}$, $20\frac{1}{2}$,—20, 28, $22\frac{1}{2}$, — 19, $26\frac{1}{2}$, —$10\frac{1}{2}$—$8\frac{1}{2}$, $23\frac{1}{2}$, $23\frac{1}{2}$, $23\frac{1}{2}$,—27, 27, 28, 22,—14, $7\frac{1}{2}$, $13\frac{1}{2}$, 18, 26, $24\frac{1}{2}$.

(*xi*) If Moon in the *male nativity* is in Sector XI.

$31\frac{1}{2}$, $23\frac{1}{2}$, $26\frac{1}{2}$, — 23, 26, 19, —11, $20\frac{1}{2}$, 23, —35, 28, $28\frac{1}{2}$, — $18\frac{1}{2}$, $16\frac{1}{2}$, $25\frac{1}{2}$, $28\frac{1}{2}$, $28\frac{1}{2}$, $12\frac{1}{2}$, — 12, 28, $21\frac{1}{2}$, —18, 18, 20, — $17\frac{1}{2}$, $13\frac{1}{2}$, $13\frac{1}{2}$, $24\frac{1}{2}$, — $28\frac{1}{2}$, 25, 26, 13, —5, —15, $20\frac{1}{2}$, —25, 19, 27.*

(*xii*) If Moon in the *male nativity* is in Sector XII.

27, $24\frac{1}{2}$, $23\frac{1}{2}$,—20, 13, 22, —$15\frac{1}{2}$, $13\frac{1}{2}$, $16\frac{1}{2}$, — $28\frac{1}{2}$, 30, 28, —16, $16\frac{1}{2}$, $18\frac{1}{2}$, $21\frac{1}{2}$, $23\frac{1}{2}$, $26\frac{1}{2}$, — 26, $15\frac{1}{2}$, 19, — $15\frac{1}{2}$, 21, 26, —24, $17\frac{1}{2}$, $17\frac{1}{2}$, $9\frac{1}{2}$, —13, 15, 15, 28, —20, 20, 14, —$18\frac{1}{2}$, 20, 13.

(*xiii*) If Moon in the *male nativity* is in Sector XIII.

$20\frac{1}{2}$, 21, $17\frac{1}{2}$, —$19\frac{1}{2}$, $12\frac{1}{2}$, $21\frac{1}{2}$, —24, $23\frac{1}{2}$, $22\frac{1}{2}$, $15\frac{1}{2}$, $18\frac{1}{2}$, 15, —28, 30, $26\frac{1}{2}$, $17\frac{1}{2}$, $17\frac{1}{2}$, $23\frac{1}{2}$, — $25\frac{1}{2}$, $13\frac{1}{2}$, $17\frac{1}{2}$, —$21\frac{1}{2}$, $24\frac{1}{2}$, 31, — 25, 21, 21, $11\frac{1}{2}$, —$6\frac{1}{2}$, $5\frac{1}{2}$, $6\frac{1}{2}$, $18\frac{1}{2}$, —$25\frac{1}{2}$, $26\frac{1}{2}$, $19\frac{1}{2}$, —$11\frac{1}{2}$, $17\frac{1}{2}$, 12.

(*xiv*) If Moon in the *male nativity* is in Sector XIV.

26, 19, 21,—23, $26\frac{1}{2}$, $17\frac{1}{2}$, $20\frac{1}{2}$, $29\frac{1}{2}$, $27\frac{1}{2}$,— 20, $14\frac{1}{2}$, $15\frac{1}{2}$,— 30, 28, 34, —25, $22\frac{1}{2}$, $9\frac{1}{2}$, 10, $25\frac{1}{2}$, —$19\frac{1}{2}$,—

* Suppose, Moon in the male's nativity is in Sector XI and in the female nativity Moon is in sector xxxviii; points of harmony would be 27.

$23\frac{1}{2}$, $20\frac{1}{2}$, —$23\frac{1}{2}$, 19, 19, 27, —22, $19\frac{1}{2}$, $18\frac{1}{2}$, $5\frac{1}{2}$, —$11\frac{1}{2}$, $20\frac{1}{2}$, $25\frac{1}{2}$, $22\frac{1}{2}$, $15\frac{1}{2}$, 22.

(*xv*) If Moon in the *male nativity* is in Sector XV.

$17\frac{1}{2}$, 28, 22, —24, 28, $25\frac{1}{2}$, $28\frac{1}{2}$, $22\frac{1}{2}$, $21\frac{1}{2}$, —$14\frac{1}{2}$, $23\frac{1}{2}$, $17\frac{1}{2}$, —$26\frac{1}{2}$, 34, 28—19, 17, $15\frac{1}{2}$, —$17\frac{1}{2}$, $25\frac{1}{2}$, $18\frac{1}{2}$, —$21\frac{1}{2}$, $29\frac{1}{2}$, $16\frac{1}{2}$, —$9\frac{1}{2}$, 27, 27, 28, —23, 20, $20\frac{1}{2}$, $12\frac{1}{2}$, —$19\frac{1}{2}$, $13\frac{1}{2}$, $16\frac{1}{2}$, —$14\frac{1}{2}$, $25\frac{1}{2}$, 22.

(*xvi*) If Moon in the *male nativity* is in Sector XVI.

11, $21\frac{1}{2}$, $15\frac{1}{2}$, —21, 25, $23\frac{1}{2}$, —$30\frac{1}{2}$, $24\frac{1}{2}$, $23\frac{1}{2}$, 17, 26, $20\frac{1}{2}$, —$16\frac{1}{2}$, 24, 18—28, 26, $24\frac{1}{2}$, —$17\frac{1}{2}$, $25\frac{1}{2}$, $17\frac{1}{2}$, —18, 26, 13, —13, $28\frac{1}{2}$, 27, $28\frac{1}{2}$, —26, 24, $23\frac{1}{2}$, 16, —$17\frac{1}{2}$, $11\frac{1}{2}$, $15\frac{1}{2}$, —$16\frac{1}{2}$, $27\frac{1}{2}$, $24\frac{1}{2}$ —

(*xvii*) If Moon in the *male nativity* is in Sector XVII.

9, 19, $15\frac{1}{2}$, —21, 26, 27, —34, $24\frac{1}{2}$, $24\frac{1}{2}$, —18, 27, $20\frac{1}{2}$, —$16\frac{1}{2}$, $22\frac{1}{2}$, $16\frac{1}{2}$, —$25\frac{1}{2}$, 28, 27, —20, $27\frac{1}{2}$, $18\frac{1}{2}$, —19, 27, 12,—13, 27, 26, $27\frac{1}{2}$, —25, 25, $24\frac{1}{2}$, $17\frac{1}{2}$, —21, $8\frac{1}{2}$, $17\frac{1}{2}$, —$18\frac{1}{2}$, 26, $26\frac{1}{2}$.

(*xviii*) If Moon in the *male nativity* is in Sector XVIII.

13, 6, $18\frac{1}{2}$, —$23\frac{1}{2}$, 20, 13, —21, 27, $25\frac{1}{2}$, —$20\frac{1}{2}$, 12, 26, —$22\frac{1}{2}$, $8\frac{1}{2}$, $14\frac{1}{2}$, —$14\frac{1}{2}$, —$24\frac{1}{2}$, 27, 28, —21, 21, $27\frac{1}{2}$, —28, 12, $25\frac{1}{2}$, —27, 12, 11, 20, —$17\frac{1}{2}$, 19, $18\frac{1}{2}$, $16\frac{1}{2}$—18, 26, $18\frac{1}{2}$, —$19\frac{1}{2}$, $9\frac{1}{2}$, $20\frac{1}{2}$.

(*xix*) If Moon in the *male nativity* is in Sector XIX.

$22\frac{1}{2}$, $14\frac{1}{2}$, $27\frac{1}{2}$, —$22\frac{1}{2}$, 19, 10, —14, 20, $18\frac{1}{2}$, —20, $11\frac{1}{2}$, $25\frac{1}{2}$, —$25\frac{1}{2}$, $11\frac{1}{2}$, $17\frac{1}{2}$, —$16\frac{1}{2}$, 19, 20, —28, 28, $34\frac{1}{2}$, —$23\frac{1}{2}$, $7\frac{1}{2}$, $20\frac{1}{2}$, —27, 12, 11, 20, —$24\frac{1}{2}$, 26, $25\frac{1}{2}$, $24\frac{1}{2}$, —19, 26, $19\frac{1}{2}$, —$12\frac{1}{2}$, 5, $13\frac{1}{2}$.

(*xx*) If Moon in the *male nativity* is in Sector XX.

$26\frac{1}{2}$, $29\frac{1}{2}$, $15\frac{1}{2}$, —$10\frac{1}{2}$, $15\frac{1}{2}$, 25, —27, 27, 27, — 27, 26, $11\frac{1}{2}$, —$11\frac{1}{2}$, $25\frac{1}{2}$, $26\frac{1}{2}$, —$25\frac{1}{2}$, $26\frac{1}{2}$, 19, —27, 28, 18, — 8, $22\frac{1}{2}$, $17\frac{1}{2}$, —21, 27, 26, 19, —$23\frac{1}{2}$, $23\frac{1}{2}$, 23, 26, —22, 19, 28, —$19\frac{1}{2}$, $19\frac{1}{2}$, $11\frac{1}{2}$.

(*xxi*) If Moon in the *male nativity* is in Sector XXI.

$22\frac{1}{2}$, $22\frac{1}{2}$, $19\frac{1}{2}$, —$14\frac{1}{2}$, $9\frac{1}{2}$, $17\frac{1}{2}$, $19\frac{1}{2}$, 20, 21, — 20, 21, $16\frac{1}{2}$, — 17, $\frac{1}{2}$, $19\frac{1}{2}$, $17\frac{1}{2}$, —$16\frac{1}{2}$, $17\frac{1}{2}$, $26\frac{1}{2}$, —$34\frac{1}{2}$, 20, 28, — 17, 17 $20\frac{1}{2}$, —27, 20, 19, 12, — $16\frac{1}{2}$, $16\frac{1}{2}$, 16, 30,— $25\frac{1}{2}$, 26, 21, —14, 12, $5\frac{1}{2}$.

(*xxii*) If Moon in the *male nativity* is in Sector XXII.

$19\frac{1}{2}$, $19\frac{1}{2}$, $16\frac{1}{2}$, —$21\frac{1}{2}$, $16\frac{1}{2}$, $23\frac{1}{2}$, — $14\frac{1}{2}$, $13\frac{1}{2}$, $13\frac{1}{2}$, — 19, 20, $15\frac{1}{2}$, — $24\frac{1}{2}$, $26\frac{1}{2}$, $24\frac{1}{2}$, —18, $19\frac{1}{2}$, 28, —$24\frac{1}{2}$, 10, 18, — 28, 28, $31\frac{1}{2}$, —$24\frac{1}{2}$, $16\frac{1}{2}$, $18\frac{1}{2}$, $11\frac{1}{2}$, —14, 14, 14, 28, —28, $26\frac{1}{2}$ $21\frac{1}{2}$, — 21, 19, $12\frac{1}{2}$,

(*xxiii*) If Moon in the *male nativity* is in Sector XXIII.

$26\frac{1}{2}$, $17\frac{1}{2}$, $20\frac{1}{2}$, —$25\frac{1}{2}$, $30\frac{1}{2}$, $22\frac{1}{2}$, —11, 17, $20\frac{1}{2}$, — 26, 19, 20, — $26\frac{1}{2}$, $24\frac{1}{2}$, $30\frac{1}{2}$, — 27, 26, 11, —$7\frac{1}{2}$, $23\frac{1}{2}$, 17, — 27, 28, 30, —$16\frac{1}{2}$, $18\frac{1}{2}$, $18\frac{1}{2}$, $25\frac{1}{2}$, 28, 28, 28, 14, —12, 21, $7\frac{1}{2}$, —27, 20, 27.

(*xxiv*) If Moon in the *male nativity* is in Sector XXIV.

15, $19\frac{1}{2}$, $26\frac{1}{2}$, —$31\frac{1}{2}$, $24\frac{1}{2}$, $25\frac{1}{2}$, —13, 4, 5, — $10\frac{1}{2}$, 22, 26, —34, $24\frac{1}{2}$, $19\frac{1}{2}$, — 13, 12, 25, —$21\frac{1}{2}$, $18\frac{1}{2}$, $21\frac{1}{2}$, — $31\frac{1}{2}$, 31; 28, —16, $18\frac{1}{2}$, $19\frac{1}{2}$, $19\frac{1}{2}$, —22, 23, 23, —28, — 26, 19, 12, —$11\frac{1}{2}$, 22, 22.

(*xxv*) If Moon in the *male nativity* is in Sector XXV.

13, 20, $24\frac{1}{2}$—20, 14, 15,—23, 16, 13,—8, 17, $22\frac{1}{2}$,—24, 19, $10\frac{1}{2}$,—$15\frac{1}{2}$, 14, 28,—28, 23, 28,—$23\frac{1}{2}$, $16\frac{1}{2}$, 15,—28, 28, 27, $25\frac{1}{2}$,—$16\frac{1}{2}$, $17\frac{1}{2}$, 16, 21,—$29\frac{1}{2}$, $22\frac{1}{2}$, $15\frac{1}{2}$,—15, 24, 27.

(*xxvi*) If Moon in the *male nativity* is in Sector XXVI.

26, 19, 18,—$12\frac{1}{2}$, 19, 12,—19, 28, 27,—21, 11, 16,—20, 18, 26,—$29\frac{1}{2}$, 27, 14,—14, 27, 22,—$17\frac{1}{2}$, $14\frac{1}{2}$, $17\frac{1}{2}$,—28, 28, 27, 33,—26, $23\frac{1}{2}$, 25, 9,—$17\frac{1}{2}$, $24\frac{1}{2}$, $31\frac{1}{2}$,—31, 22, $30\frac{1}{2}$.

(*xxvii*) If Moon in the *male nativity* is in Sector XXVII.

27, 20, 19,—$13\frac{1}{2}$, 20, 11,—18, 27, 26,—$20\frac{1}{2}$, $11\frac{1}{2}$, $16\frac{1}{2}$,—21, 19, 27,—$28\frac{1}{2}$, 26, 13,—13, 26, 21, $16\frac{1}{2}$, $14\frac{1}{2}$, $17\frac{1}{2}$,—27, 27, 28, 34,—25, $24\frac{1}{2}$, $25\frac{1}{2}$, $9\frac{1}{2}$,—$16\frac{1}{2}$, $23\frac{1}{2}$, $30\frac{1}{2}$,—$31\frac{1}{2}$, $22\frac{1}{2}$, 30.

(*xxviii*) If Moon in the *male nativity* is in Sector XXVIII.

$24\frac{1}{2}$, 27, 14,—$9\frac{1}{2}$, $11\frac{1}{2}$,18,—24, 27, 27,—$21\frac{1}{2}$, $22\frac{1}{2}$, $8\frac{1}{2}$,—$11\frac{1}{2}$, 27, 28,—$29\frac{1}{2}$, $27\frac{1}{2}$, 21,—21, 18, 13,—$9\frac{1}{2}$, 22, $17\frac{1}{2}$,—$25\frac{1}{2}$, 33, 34, 28,—19, 17, 15, $16\frac{1}{2}$,—$13\frac{1}{2}$, $23\frac{1}{2}$, $29\frac{1}{2}$,—$30\frac{1}{2}$, $31\frac{1}{2}$, 21.

(*xxix*) If Moon in the *male nativity* is in Sector XXIX.

26, $28\frac{1}{2}$, $15\frac{1}{2}$,—14, 17, 21,—$20\frac{1}{2}$, $22\frac{1}{2}$, $27\frac{1}{2}$,—$28\frac{1}{2}$, 26, 12,—$5\frac{1}{2}$, 21, 22,—26, 23, $17\frac{1}{2}$,—$25\frac{1}{2}$, $22\frac{1}{2}$, $17\frac{1}{2}$,—12, 25, 20,—$15\frac{1}{2}$ 23, 24, 18,—28, 25, 24, $15\frac{1}{2}$,—$18\frac{1}{2}$, $18\frac{1}{2}$, $24\frac{1}{2}$, $28\frac{1}{2}$, $29\frac{1}{2}$, 19.

(*xxx*) If Moon in the *male nativity* is in Sector XXX.

26, 28, 11$\frac{1}{2}$, —11, 19, 24$\frac{1}{2}$, —25, 22$\frac{1}{2}$, 22$\frac{1}{2}$, — 25, 24, 13, — 5$\frac{1}{2}$, 19$\frac{1}{2}$, 21, —25, 24, 19, —27, 23$\frac{1}{2}$, 17$\frac{1}{2}$, —12, 26, 20, —15$\frac{1}{2}$, 23$\frac{1}{2}$, 24, 16, —26, 28, 27, 28, —21, 18$\frac{1}{2}$, 25$\frac{1}{2}$, —29$\frac{1}{2}$, 28$\frac{1}{2}$, 20.

(*xxxi*) If Moon in the *male nativity* is in Sector XXXI.

24, 26, 10$\frac{1}{2}$, —10, 18, 24$\frac{1}{2}$, —25, 22$\frac{1}{2}$, 23$\frac{1}{2}$, —27, 25, 13, —4$\frac{1}{2}$, 18$\frac{1}{2}$, 20, —25, 24, 19, —27, 23$\frac{1}{2}$, 17$\frac{1}{2}$, —12, 26, 20, —15$\frac{1}{2}$, 23$\frac{1}{2}$, 23$\frac{1}{2}$, 15, —25, 27, 28, 21, —21, 18$\frac{1}{2}$, 25$\frac{1}{2}$, —30$\frac{1}{2}$, —29$\frac{1}{2}$, 22$\frac{1}{2}$.

(*xxxii*) If Moon in the *male nativity* is in Sector XXXII.

21, 10, 25, — 23$\frac{1}{2}$, 20, 13, — 12, 17, 17$\frac{1}{2}$, —21, 13, 27, — 18$\frac{1}{2}$, 4$\frac{1}{2}$, 11$\frac{1}{2}$, —16$\frac{1}{2}$, 19, 18, —26, 27, 32$\frac{1}{2}$, —27, 12, 25, —21$\frac{1}{2}$, 8$\frac{1}{2}$, 8$\frac{1}{2}$, 15$\frac{1}{2}$, 25$\frac{1}{2}$, 30, 30, 28, —20, 25, — 20$\frac{1}{2}$, 25$\frac{1}{2}$, 14$\frac{1}{2}$, 22$\frac{1}{2}$.

(*xxxiii*) If Moon in the *male nativity* is in Sector XXXIII.

21,10, 25, —29$\frac{1}{2}$, 26, 19, —13, 20, 18$\frac{1}{2}$, 12$\frac{1}{2}$, 4$\frac{1}{2}$, 18$\frac{1}{2}$, — 24$\frac{1}{2}$, 11$\frac{1}{2}$, 18$\frac{1}{2}$, —16$\frac{1}{2}$, 19, 18, —20, 21, —26$\frac{1}{2}$, —27, 12, 25, —25, 16$\frac{1}{2}$, 15$\frac{1}{2}$, 22$\frac{1}{2}$, —17$\frac{1}{2}$, 22, 20$\frac{1}{2}$, 18$\frac{1}{2}$, —28, 33, 27$\frac{1}{2}$, —17, 6, 14.

(*xxxiv*) If Moon in the *male nativity* is in Sector XXXIV.

15, 20, 27, — 31, 24$\frac{1}{2}$, 27, —21, 11, 11, —7, 14$\frac{1}{2}$, 18$\frac{1}{2}$, 25$\frac{1}{2}$, 19$\frac{1}{2}$, 12$\frac{1}{2}$, —10$\frac{1}{2}$, 8$\frac{1}{2}$, —24, —26, 20, 26, — 26$\frac{1}{2}$, 22, 18, —21$\frac{1}{2}$, 23$\frac{1}{2}$, 22$\frac{1}{2}$, 22$\frac{1}{2}$, — 17$\frac{1}{2}$, 18$\frac{1}{2}$, 18, 23$\frac{1}{2}$, — 33, 28, 19, 7$\frac{1}{2}$, 16, 16.

(*xxxv*) If Moon in the *male nativity* is in Sector XXXV.

$16, 24, 19\frac{1}{2}, —23\frac{1}{2}, 30\frac{1}{2}, 29\frac{1}{2}, —23\frac{1}{2}, 16, 17, —11, 18,$
$12\frac{1}{2}, —18\frac{1}{2}, 24\frac{1}{2}, 15\frac{1}{2}, —14\frac{1}{2}, 14\frac{1}{2}, 18\frac{1}{2}, — 20\frac{1}{2}, 25,$
$22, —22\frac{1}{2}, 24\frac{1}{2}, 11, —11, 31\frac{1}{2}, 29\frac{1}{2}, 28\frac{1}{2}, — 23\frac{1}{2}, 23\frac{1}{2},$
$23, 21, —28\frac{1}{2}, 19, 28, —16\frac{1}{2}, 21\frac{1}{2}, 18.$

(*xxxvi*) If Moon in the *male nativity* is in Sector XXXVI.

$14\frac{1}{2}, 22\frac{1}{2}, 17\frac{1}{2}, —20, 27, 26\frac{1}{2}, —27\frac{1}{2}, 19, 19\frac{1}{2}, —17, 24,$
$18\frac{1}{2}, —17\frac{1}{2}, 23\frac{1}{2}, 15\frac{1}{2}, —18, 19, 22, —15, 20\frac{1}{2}, 16\frac{1}{2}, —$
$21, 24, 10\frac{1}{2}, 17\frac{1}{2}, 32\frac{1}{2}, 32\frac{1}{2}, 31\frac{1}{2}, —30\frac{1}{2}, 31\frac{1}{2}, 32\frac{1}{2},$
$26\frac{1}{2}, —18\frac{1}{2}, 9, 18, —28, 33, 28\frac{1}{2}.$

(*xxxvii*) If Moon in the *male nativity* is in Sector XXXVII.

$24\frac{1}{2}, 16\frac{1}{2}, 19\frac{1}{2}, —22, 26, 17, —17, 27, 27\frac{1}{2}, —25, 18, —$
$20, —18\frac{1}{2}, 16\frac{1}{2}, 26\frac{1}{2}, —29, 27, 11, —4, 20, 13\frac{1}{2}, —18, 18,$
$21, —25\frac{1}{2}, 23\frac{1}{2}, 23\frac{1}{2}, 32\frac{1}{2}, — 32\frac{1}{2}, 30\frac{1}{2}, 31\frac{1}{2}, 15\frac{1}{2}, —$
$7\frac{1}{2}, 17\frac{1}{2}, 23, —33, 28, 33.$

(*xxxviii*) If Moon in the *male nativity* is in Sector XXXVIII.

$26, 28, 11\frac{1}{2}, —14, 19, 27, —27, 27, 28, —25\frac{1}{2}, 27, 12, —$
$12, 24\frac{1}{2}, 24\frac{1}{2}, —27, 27, 21, —13, 13, 5, —9\frac{1}{2}, 27, 21, —27,$
$32\frac{1}{2}, 32\frac{1}{2}, 23\frac{1}{2}, —23\frac{1}{2}, 22\frac{1}{2}, 24\frac{1}{2}, 22\frac{1}{2}, —14\frac{1}{2}, 16\frac{1}{2},$
$20\frac{1}{2}, —30\frac{1}{2}, 34, 28.$

Note. The number of harmonious points between a male nativity and a female nativity have been given above arranged in 38 paras according as Moon in the *Male* nativity is one or other of the 38 sectors.

In each para while looking up the number of harmonious

points, it should be carefully noted in which sector is Moon in the *Female nativity.* The 38 figures given under *each* para are, accordingly as the Moon in the *female nativity* is in one the other, of 38 sectors in order.

CHAPTER 12

TIMING OF EVENTS

Timing of Events

In the judgement of the timing please note that native should be of a marriageable age. Secondly whether in his chart, marriage is indicated and if yes then at around what age otherwise it would be like a barren tree which remains without fruits and flowers, season after season.

If the person is older and married then when indication comes for marriage or romance then it will cause a love affair, a child birth or some other happy events related to his children. The events would differ according to the age of the person. The dashas of planets which rule the 7th house or which is posited in the 7th house can indicate marriage in young age but in old age they may show the effect of 'Marakesh'. All factors should be considered when arriving at a timing of events.

We give below some aphorisms about the Timing of Events:

1. So far we have stated principles which bring about matrimonial happiness or success in love affairs, fruition of desire, and events that bring joy or sorrow in relation to conjugal life. Now we give principles which deal with timing of events.

Directions*

2. Any planet whose mahadasha is in progress if benefic and friendly to the 7th house lord would produce good results pertaining to the 7th house, if it be posited in the 7th house from the 7th house lord.

---

* Those who are not conversant with Hindu system of directions are advised to read Appendix II.

3. The same will be the result if in 2 above dasha of the 7th lord is in progress and the antardasha of the other planet is running.

4. In the beginning, a planet gives the effect of the house it is in; then of the positional strength, *i.e.* rashi, ansha and vargas. Then of planets associated with or aspecting it.

5. (a) If the 7th house is well or badly tenanted ?
   (b) If the lord of the 7th house is well placed by sign and house or is otherwise?
   (c) If the 7th house is well-aspected or badly aspected? what would be the effects if some of the features above are good and some are bad ? The effects of a good planet's dasha would be to confer conjugal happiness, that of the evil planet would be to curtail it.

6. When during the mahadasha of Sun there is antardasha of Moon, Mercury, Jupiter or Venus one may marry.

7. Even an exalted Sun if posited in debilitated navamsha would bring about loss of conjugal happiness and money during its dasha.

8. If Sun is weak and has crossed 10th degree of Aries and is proceeding towards Libra, its 'dasha' will not be good unless it is well placed by sign and house and is lord of a good house.

9. Attach great importance to the 'navamsha' position of the planet whose mahadasha or antardasha is in progress. If a planet is debilitated in sign but exalted in navamsha it is not so bad. Vargottgam Planets give very good results.

10. If Moon is in the 7th house and there is antardasha of a benefic in Moon's mahadasha it promotes the 7th house affairs. A malefic does otherwise.

11. Moon's dasha is good for 7th house if the Moon is in the bright half of the month, from 10th day to full Moon day. It is fairly good if between full Moon day and first five days of the dark half.

12. If the Moon is debilitated or weak or going towards debilitation rashi, its dasha is not good. Moon is deemed to go

towards the debilitation rashi when its longitude is between 3° Taurus and 3° Scorpio.

13. If Moon is in the 7th house and if it fulfils the conditions in Aphorism 11 above, it is good for the 7th house prosperity.

14. If Moon is in the 7th house and is described by conditions in 12 above it brings about adverse conditions pertaining to 7th house.

15. The particular period presided over by Moon are Bright half of the month, Rohini,* Hasta, Shravan, Cancer (Sign), when Moon or Jupiter is therein, effects of Moon come into fruition.

16. When Mars is in the 7th house the sub-periods of benefics show good results, those of malefics otherwise.

17. During its dasha and antardasha Mars would give more the results of 7th house ownership than of 2nd, if Libra be the ascendant.

18. Mars would not show bad results during its dasha and antardasha, if the rising sign be Aries or Scorpio.

19. Mars would in its dasha/antardasha primarily give the effect of the 12th house ownership and not so much of the 7th house ownership when Taurus is the rising sign, *i.e.* it would give more the effect of ownership of 'trika' than of an angle, and as such show evil results.

Note. But in 18 and 19 above if Mars be posited in Aries or Scorpio, it would give more the effect of the house it is posited in.

20. Mercury would show more the effect of the 10th house lordship than of 7th if Sagittarius be the rising sign. Its dasha/antardasha would be good if Mercury is posited in a good house.

21. Mercury during its dasha and antardasha gives more the effect of the 7th house lordship than of the 10th house, when Pisces is the rising sign.

Note. But if Mercury be posited in Gemini or Virgo, it will give more the effect of the house it is posited in.

---

* For ascertaining longitudes of these see Chapter 8.

22. Jupiter during its dasha and antardasha gives more the effect of the 7th house lordship than of the 10th house when Gemini is the ascendant.

23. Jupiter gives more the effect of the 4th house lordship than of the 7th house when Virgo is the ascendant, but during its dasha/antardasha, the 7th house effect may be felt.

Note. This above must be kept in view when judging its dasha and antardasha. But if Jupiter be posited in Sagittarius or Pisces, it will give more the effect of the house it is posited in.

24. Venus gives primarily the effect of the 7th house lordship during its dasha and antardasha and not so much of 2nd lordship when Aries is the rising sign.

25. Venus would during its dasha/antardasha give more the effect of the 12th house ownership than of the 7th house when Scorpio is the rising sign. This is with regard to comparative value in assessing its value as lord of and angle and 'Trik'. If, however, Venus is posited in Taurus or Libra it will give more the effect of the house it is posited in. But whatever be the rising sign, it will bring about fruition of matrimonial/love affairs if well- placed and well-aspected radically in its dasha and antardasha. If ill-placed and ill-aspected, judge otherwise. Evil effects would be felt.

26. Note the following: (i) Venus, (ii) lord of the seventh house, (iii) planet occupying 7th and (iv) planet aspecting 7th house. If Venus be conjoined with or aspecting any of the other three mentioned above and be strong, beneficial effects would come to pass in the Dasha or Antardasha of Venus. But if the above be malefics and Venus also be weak ill effects would be felt during the major/minor period of Venus.

27. Note the following: (i) navamsha occupied by Venus, (ii) the rashi occupied by Venus, (iii) the rashi occupied by the lord of the 7th house and (iv) the 'navamsha' occupied by the lord of the 7th house.

If the lords of the above 4 be in some 'bandh', during the dashas and antardashas of the above four matters pertaining to love/marriage would gain prominence.

28. Note the planet ruling the asterism in which Venus is posited. The marriage of the native may be ccomplished during the dasha or antardasha of the planet.

29. When Leo is the ascendant, Saturn would during its dasha and antardasha give more the effect of the 7th house lordship than of the 6th house.

30. Saturn would give more the effect of the 8th house lordship than of the 7th house during its dasha and antardasha, if Cancer be the rising sign.

Note. But if Saturn is posited in Capricorn or Aquarius it will give more the effect of the house it is posited in.

31. When Saturn is along with a malefic, the person indulges in secret sins, is devoid of conjugal happiness but has illicit connections with women of lower status. This should be judged during the period of its antardasha assessing well, its strength as well as of the lord of the major period. If Saturn is, however, exalted or very strong or aspected by Jupiter, etc. the effect would be favourably modified.

32. If Saturn is in the 7th house, during its dasha, there is great friction with wife or due to her. It would not be bad if Saturn be the lord of the 1st house or of the 7th house.

33. In aphorisms above, during the dasha and antardasha of the various planets when it owns two houses 7th and one more, if the other house comes after 7th, the planet concerned will show its 7th house effect in the 1st half. But if the other house owned is from 1st to 6th it will give the 7th house ownership results only in the latter half of its sub-periods.

34. In Aphorisms 16 to 27 when a planet is described as giving effect primarily of one house lordship the effect of the other house lordship is also present but is not so important.

35. Rahu or Ketu in the 7th house are good if conjoined therein with a lord of the 1st, 5th or 9th houses.

36. Rahu or Ketu by themselves in 7th house effect adversely during their dashas and antardashas.

37. Rahu if posited in the 12th house, ascendant, the 2nd or 6th houses from ascendant destroys the 7th house happiness during its dasha and antardasha.

38. When Rahu is associated with a debilitated planet the person does not have conjugal happiness during its (Rahu's) antardasha.

39. If Rahu is conjoined with the 7th house lord Rahu would show the result of the 7th house lord—good or bad as the latter may be.

40. *Note.* In 39 above, the 7th house lord though good and auspicious by itself will cause evil during the concluding portion of its dasha.

41. In aphorisms 17, 18, 19, 20, 21, 22, 23, 28, 27 if the planet concerned is in its own house and in the 7th house, it will give more the effect of the 7th house but if posited in its own house other than the 7th house it will give more the effect of the other house. (This has also been explained in notes above).

42. If 'Mandi' be in the 7th house, the lord of the 7th house gives bad results during its dasha/antardasha.

43. When the dasha or antardasha of the planet owning the 'navamsha' occupied by the lord of the 1st house is in progress prospects of marriage may be fulfilled.

44. If the lord of the 2nd house from lagna occupies the 12th house, its antardasha may not be very fruitful to mature marriage prospects, particularly if it be weak.

45. Lord of the 2nd if inimical to lord of the 7th house would not show very happy results.

46. Whenever there is antardasha of a planet who is the lord of the 2nd, 6th, 12th houses from lagna it is bad for 7th house prospects. If such an antardasha synchronises with Saturn's unfavourable transit through 7th house, it is worse (See Transits).

47. If the lord of the 5th or 9th houses is in association with the lord of the 7th house its dasha and antardasha would be good for love/marriage.

48. Planets owning the 6th house if weak would bring about annihilation of love/marriage, giving rise to enmity, hindrance, etc. during their periods.

49. The sub-period of a weak planet in the 6th house from

the rising sign would be bad for love/marriage.

50. The lord of the 22nd decanate from the 7th house cusp would give a set back to love/marriage and if the lord of the major sub-period be also unfavourable may bring about serious illness to wife/husband. This would particularly be so, if the former be weak.

51. Dashas and antardashas of planets very friendly to the lord of the 7th house show good results. Particularly so, if they are lords of good houses and well-placed by sign and house.

52. Fruition of prospects of love/marriage may be expected in the dasha/antardasha of planet owning the 7th house and well-placed.

53. The marriage of the native may occur during the periods presided over by a planet occupying or aspecting the 7th house.

54. Results similar to 53 above may be expected during the antardasha of a planet who occupies a sign 7th from that indicated in 53 above. (If the latter planet's Dasha is in progress).

55. If the 7th house lord is a benefic and (i) exalted (ii) in its own Mooltrikona (iii) or in its own house its good effects would respectively be (i) full, (ii) three quarters and (iii) half in its dasha/antardasha.

56. When 7th house lord is a malefic combust or debilitated its dasha antardasha will be fully bad. But if it be in its own house it will be 50% bad, and still less bad if it be in Moolatrikona or exalted.

57. If the 7th house lord is a 'Shubha' its dasha may not be so good for the native's prosperity and health though good for matrimonial prospects.

58. If the 7th house lord is a 'malefic' its dasha would be better generally for the prosperity. If strong it would show good effects with regard to matrimonial matters. If weak and afflicted bad results follow.

59. The 7th house lord would bring about the fruition of the 7th house prospects in the dasha or the antardasha of the planets who are associated with the 7th house lord in any manner.

60. The 7th house lord gets strengthened if associated in any way with the lord of the 5th or 9th. Its position would be doubly strong if associated with the lords of both the 5th and the 9th. Excellent results follow.

61. The the 7th house lord though a *papa* itself would during its dasha give good results in the antardasha of the planet specified in 60 above *i.e.,* of the lords of 5th or 9th, if the same are conjoined with the 7th house lord.

62. When the lord of the 7th house is weak there will be distress connected with the beloved, separation from wife, intrigue with wicked women, diseases in private parts, etc.

63. The dasha of the 7th house lord would be better if it is the second, 4th, or 6th dasha but bad if it be 3rd or 5th or 7th.

64. The first dasha is of the planet, who presides over the major period at birth-time. Then others follow in the following order: Sun, Moon, Mars, Rahu, Jupiter, Saturn, Mercury, Ketu, Venus.

65. If the 7th house lord is a benefic and debilitated or posited in 6th, 8th, or 12th from ascendant it will give bad results. But it would give extremely bad results, if it be a malefic instead.

66. Destruction of the 7th house happiness should be predicted in the dasha and antardasha of the planet who is a "Great enemy" of the 7th house lord.

67. Malefics in the 7th house or associated with lord of the the 7th house or Venus, if weak, show very evil results.

68. Benefics in the 7th house or associated with the lord of the 7th house or Venus if strong are productive of very good results.

69. Marriage may be accomplished when there is dasha of lord of the sign, and 'navamsha' occupied by the lord of the 7th house.

70. Dasha of a planet posited in the 7th house would prove baneful if the planet is combust or defeated by enemies or debilitated or in the 'Shad-vargas' of the enemy.

71. The the 7th house lord gives particularly evil results if it owns 22nd decanate from the lagna, (this is possible only in nativities with cancer as ascendant.)

72. If the 7th house lord is a 'papa', its dasha or antardasha in the period or sub-period of another 'papa' is not auspicious.

73. In the sub-period of the 7th house lord, if it be a malefic, there would be strong opposition with wife/husband or her death, if the major period be also evil and there be indications of premature death of partner.

74. If the 7th house lord is fully strong, on its highest exaltation point, its dasha would be fully auspicious.

75. If the 7th house lord is in its exaltation sign, its dasha would be auspicious.

76. If the 7th house lord is devoid of strength its dasha or antardasha would be unfavourable.

77. If the 7th house lord is in depression or inimical sign or 'ansha' its dasha would be highly unfavourable.

78. If the 7th house lord is ascending—going towards the exaltation points, its dasha on antardasha would be gradually 'beneficial.

79. If the 7th house lord is descending—going down towards its debilitatioin point, its dasha or antardasha would be gradually deteriorating.

Note. If more than one feature as described above be present the result would be mixed according as the particular feature is strong or weak.

80. Dasha or antardasha of malefics posited in the 8th will not be much good for the 7th house prosperity.

81. Dasha or antardasha of malefics in 2nd would also be not favourable.

82. As benefics by ownership, posited in the 9th, 10th and 11th house would be good for matrimonial happiness, their dasha/antardasha would confer hapiness.

Relative Position of Lords of Major and Minor Periods

83. When the 'dashanath' and 'antardashanath' are in mutual 6th, 8th position there is friction with wife/husband if the nativity shows such a tendency and planets whose dasha/antar are in progress have bearing on the 7th house.

84. (a) If the 7th house lord is 'antardashanath' and is in 12th from 'dashanath' it would not do good; but if it be in 2nd, 11th, 3rd, 4th, 5th, 9th or 10th from dashanath it would be good.

(b) If the 7th house lord is the mahadashanath, antardasha of a planet 12th from it (*i.e.*, posited in a sign just preceding the sign in which mahadashanath is posited) would not do good.

85. When the dasha of the 7th house lord is in progress any planet's antardasha who is inimical to it will be inauspicious.

86. Similar are the results when there is, antardasha of 7th house lord, in its enemy's mahadasha.

87. When one planet is in 7th from one another if there is antardasha of a malefic, there would be trouble pertaining to 7th house. If it be a benefic and strong, there would be happiness.

88. If of the two—dashanath and antardashanath one is benefic and ther other is malefic, during the 1st half the effect of antardashanath would be felt and during the latter half that of the dashanath, or alternatively mixed effects would be felt or only of that planet which is overwhelmingly stronger.

89. Venus if strong confers company of young damsels, marriage and other pleasures in its dasha and antardasha.

CHAPTER 13

TRANSITS (HINDU SYSTEM)

As in the Western System so also in the Hindu System Transits are important. Hindu Astrologers in the past used to predict marriages, child birth etc. based just on the transit of Jupiter in 2nd, 5th, 7th, 9th, or 11th house from the Janma Rashi (Natal Moon). Secondly, Transit of Sun in the Zodiacal Signs of the planets whose Mahadasha or Antardasha is in progress also gives the eventful months.

The effect of Transits in the Hindu System is at times slightly different viz., Jupiter's transit on the Moon is adverse in the Hindu System and may cause health problems related to chronic headaches or blood disorders, whereas in the Western Astrology it is mentioned to give very good results. Another difference is that the transit of Saturn is not that bad compared to its Aspect in the Hindu System. In Western Astrology Rahu and Ketu are not considered at all but in the Hindu system these are full fledged Planets and the transit of Rahu on Moon causes mental anguish of the worst type. The same is the case when Rahu transits the cups of the 1st house or the radical Sun. This time it effects the body like can cause confinement due to sickness, or imprisonment or kidnapping.

We are giving below the effects and results of other Transits:

1. Firm results and permanent effects are produced by dashas and antardashas while others by transits.

2. Transits should be judged against the background of prevailing dasha and antardasha.

3. Sometimes transits accelerate good or bad effect. The

planets are increasingly effective in their influence (as transiting planets) in the following order:

Moon, Mercury, Venus, Sun, Mars, Jupiter, Rahu and Saturn.

The goodness or badness of these should be determined according to the following aphorisms.

4. A planet during transit, if exalted, in friendly house and good place from ascendant and Moon would show good results.

5. A planet during transit, if debilitated, in enemy's house or combust would show bad results.

6. A transiting benefic would not be so good, if it is aspected by malefics.

7. A transiting malefic, would not be so bad if it is aspected by benefics.

8. Effect of transit in the 7th from any radical position is marked, when it is in exact opposition (*i.e.*, at an exact distance of 180 degrees).

9. Sun and Mars show their effect as soon as they enter a Zodiacal sign.

10. Mercury shows its effect throughout.

11. Moon and Saturn show their effect when they are beyond 20° in a sign.

12. Jupiter and Venus show their effect when they are in the middle of the sign.

13. If in the judgment of transiting influence, some planets be found to have good attributes as well as bad, the effects are set off, the balance good or bad is the result.

14. Fruition of the 7th house matters—matrimonial—may be expected when Sun, Moon and Jupiter transit it.

15. When the 7th house lord's dasha or antardasha is evil, particularly bad results would be shown during the month, or months Sun transits, the 7th house or the 7th house lord's depression or inimical signs.

16. When Jupiter, Moon and Venus transit the signs of the planet, owning the 'navamansha lagna' fruition of love/ marriage may occur.

17. If Moon be stronger than the 'lagna' substitute

(ascendant) lord of the sign containing the Moon' in place of the lord of the 1st house in aphorism above and then judge.

18. When Jupiter by transit arrives at a sign trine to the 7th, 7th house affairs prosper.

19. When Jupiter in its transit arrives at the radical position occupied by the lord of the 7th house or in trine thereto, there would be fruition of matrimonial happiness.

20. Add the longitudes of the lords of the 1st and the 7th houses. When Jupiter arrives in this sign or in trine thereto, there would be prospects of matrimonial alliance.

21. Add together the longitudes of the lord of the 1st house, 7th house and Venus. When Jupiter arrives at this position, there would be fruition.

22. If Jupiter passes through a sign triangular to the navamsha, occupied by the lord of the 7th house, marriage may be accomplished.

23. It is helpful for love/marriage when the lords of the 1st and 7th/Venus arrive at a conjunction or aspect each other.

24. There is fruition of matrimonial happiness when Venus, lord of ascendant or lord of the 7th transit 7th house.

25. When Venus/lord of the 7th house transits the first house or the sign occupied by lord of the 1st house there would be prospects of a matrimonial alliance.

26. When Saturn in its transits arrives at the sign and 'navamsha' occupied by the lord of second and 6th from ascendant it is unfavourable for 7th house.

27. Saturn transiting 7th house from ascendant or from radical Moon brings trouble to husband or wife or affairs connected with him/her if the nativity is weak.

28. When lord of the 'Mandi' sign (in which 'Mandi' is posited) transits the 7th house it portends matrimonial unhappiness or illness of husband/wife.

29. When lord of 22nd decanate from 7th house cusp transits 7th house it brings ill-health to husband/wife or matrimonial trouble.

30. When Venus transits the sign or 'navamsha' occupied

by lord of seventh or the sign trine to it there may be fruition of love/marriage.

31. Marriage should be predicted when suitable dasha and antardasha are current and when lord of the ascendant transits the seventh house or conjoins with or aspects the lord of the seventh.

32. When the lord of the 1st house and the 7th are conjoined together in transit or aspect each other, there would be prospect of matrimonial alliance.

33. Lord of the 1st coming by transit to the 7th house: marriage may be accomplished.

34. Marriage may be accomplished when Venus or the lord of the 7th by transit comes to a sign triangular to the sign or 'navamsha' occupied by lord of the 1st house.

35. Marriage may be indicated when Jupiter transits the sign on the cusp of 7th house or in trine to it or transits over or in trine to the radical position of lord of the 7th.

36. (a) When Venus, the lord of the 1st and 7th houses from ascendant or the lord of the house occupied by the radical Moon, transits the 7th house, the influence is helpful for love/marriage.

(b) When they transit the house occupied by the lord of the 7th: similar result.

(c) When they transit the 5th or 9th house: similar result.

37. If there is enmity between the lord of the 1st and the 7th house there would be conjugal friction when they transit 7th and 1st houses respectively.

38. If there is friendship, natural and temporal between the lords of the 1st and 7th, 7th house affairs prosper when they transit 7th and 1st houses respectively.

39. If the lord of the 7th is strong, 7th house affairs prosper when the lord of the 1st, is in transit, conjoined with it.

40. When the lord of the 1st house transits the sign or navamsha occupied by the lord of the 7th or radical Venus or in trine to it, there may be success in love/marriage.

41. When Venus or lord of the 7th transits the sign or 'ansha'

occupied by the lord of the 1st or in trine to it, the time is propitious for love/marriage.

42. Whenever the lord of the 2nd house transits the 7th house it creates trouble pertaining to the 7th house (unless the 7th house be also its own sign). Not so bad if it be a benefic and a friend of lord of 7th.

43. If a planet owns or is posited in the 7th house or aspects it and if it be a benefic it would promote the happiness of the 7th house when it transits the ascendant.

Note. In above, if it be a malefic it would destroy the happiness when it transits the 1st house.

44. When the lord of the 7th house transits the sign and navamsha occupied by lord of the 1st, there would be a prospect of matrimonial alliance.

45. When lord of the 8th house transits seventh or the sign and 'ansha' occupied by the lord of the 7th or Venus it destroys matrimonial happiness.

46. When lord of 'Mandi' does so (vide above) the same result.

47. When lord of the 22nd Decanate from 7th house cusp transits as above (vide above) the same result.

48. If the prevailing transits are good as well as evil for matrimonial happiness the judgment should be arrived at weighing the two kinds of influences.

49. Transits should always be judged against the background of dasha and antardasha.

Lords of Major and Minor Periods and Transits

50. If an auspicious planet during its dasha or antardasha transits the 7th from ascendant or radical Moon it augments 7th house prospects. Malefics do the reverse.

51. Mark the house as counted from the ascendant and from the Moon, the 7th house lord during its dasha or antardasha if transiting it, will show the effect pertaining to the house of the transit.

52. If a dashanath (planet whose major period is current) is exalted, in a friend's house or in its own house *during its transit,* it would strengthen the 7th house prospects if in such

condition it transits the 7th house, (if it be strong radically also).

53. If a dashanath is in its sign of debilitation or in an enemy's house, it would during its transit through 7th house produce unfavourable results, if it be weak in radical horoscope also.

54. Same as above is the result if the dashanath gets combust in the 7th house during transit.

55. If the dasha or antardasha of the 7th house lord is in progress and its gets combust or transits its enemy's house or its depression sign, it would show infavourable results.

56. If the dasha or antardasha of the 7th house lord is in progress it would show good results when it transits a sign which is its own or exaltation sign or when it gets retrograde.

57. When the dasha or antardasha of the 7th house lord is good, particularly good effects will be shown during the month the Sun transits the sign which are the 7th house lord's own signs or its exaltation sign.

APPENDICES

APPENDIX I

CALCULATION OF DIRECTIONS IN WESTERN ASTROLOGY

The radix (or the planetary positions and rising sign at the time of the birth) show the possibilities or rather the probabilities in regard to events that are likely to occur in the native's life. The Directions as they are technically called show the 'time' at which a particular event, warranted by the nativity, would occur. In other words, if the horoscope answers the question 'what' the Directions answer the question 'when' ?

The horoscope of birth never changes. It is the constant factor. If we compare a multistoreyed sky scraper to the life of a person, we may compare the birth horoscope or the *radix* to the ground floor. The progressed horoscope (position of planets and ascendant and M.C. for the 2nd year) is the second storey. The progressed horoscope for the 3rd year is the third storey. The progressed horoscope for the 60th year would be the 60th storey and so on.

I have imported the analogy of the multistoreyed building to show that just as dimensions of upper storey are conditioned by the dimensions or space occupied by the ground floor— in the same way the *progressed* horoscope for a particular year is conditioned by the *dimensions* or limitations of the radix (birthchart).

The upper storey may be more beautiful or more airy or better furnished but you cannot conceive a 5,000 sqr. feet, hall on a subsequent storey—if the total area of the ground floor is only 500sq.feet. Now, how to make progressed horoscope:

One system called the Arabic system is that you calculate the ascendant and position of planets for 24 hrs. after birth and this will be the progressed horoscope for the second year. Calculate the horoscope for 48 hrs, after birth (or 3rd day) and it would be progressed horoscope for the 3rd year and so on. Here the period of one day or 24 hrs, is reckoned as equal to one year of life.

Some astrologers keep the Ascendant and M.C. and *other angles* of birth chart fixed and calculate only the positions of planets 24 hrs, after birth, or 48 hrs after birth, etc.

Others calculate ascendants and M.C. etc. also along with planetary position and call the new calculations progressed ascendant, progressed M.C., progressed Sun, progressed Moon and so on.

Now reverting to the example horoscope in the introduction, we have taken the following birth data:

Date of birth :	11-12-1915.
Time of birth :	1-30 P.M. I.S.T.
Place of birth :	New Delhi.

Suppose, we want to calculate directions for 23rd year; then working as follows:

11th	Dec.	1915	1st year begins at	1-30	I.S.T.
12th	Dec.	1915	2nd year begins	,,	,,
13th	Dec.	1915	3rd year begins	,,	,,
31th	Dec.	1915	21st year begins	,,	,,
1st	Jan.	1916	22nd year begins	,,	,,
2nd	Jan.	1916	23rd year begins at	1-30	I.S.T.

We know that to know directions for 23rd year, we have to calculate a *new* horoscope called the progressed horoscope, for the 23rd year as if the person was born on 2nd January 1916 at 1.30, L.S.T. at New Delhi.

Since, readers are already familiar with various steps

explained in introduction, I shall not go through the elaborate process of explaining each step. The chart for 2nd Jan, 1916 Indian Standard Time 1.30 P.M. for New Delhi would be as follows:

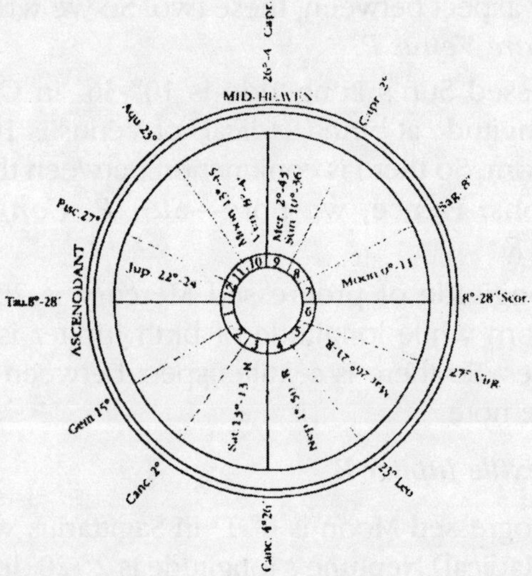

Position of Planets			Declination		
Sun	9 - 10 - 36		23	South	2
Moon	8 - 0 - 11		24	South	53
Mars	4 - 29 - 48	R	14	North	53
Mercury	9 - 20 - 43		23	South	59
Jupiter	11 - 22 - 24		4	South	10
Venus	10 - 8 - 4		19	South	55
Saturn	3 - 13 - 13		22	North	19
Herschel	10 - 13 - 45		17	South	20
Neptune	4 - 1 - 50	R	19	North	28
Ascendant	1 - 8 - 28				
M.C.	9 - 26 - 4				

Now, we have to go carefully through the aspects which the radical positions of planets (positions at birth) form with the progressed positions:

(i) The progressed Ascendant is 8°-28′ Taurus and progressed Venus is 8°-4′ Aquarius so there is the square aspect between, these two. So we write—*Asc. P. square Venus P.*

(ii) Progressed Sun's Longitude is 10°-36′ in Capricorn and longitude at birth (Radical) of Venus is 10°-40′ in Capricorn. So there is conjunction between these two positions. Hence, we note—*Sun P. Conjunction Venus R.*

(iii) The longitude of progressed Mercury is 20°-40′ in Capricorn while longitude of birth Jupiter is 19°-48′ in Pisces. So there is sextile aspect between the two and we note:

Mercury P. Sextile Jupiter R.

(iv) The progressed Moon is 0°-1′ in Sagittarius while the birth (Radical) Neptune's longitude is 2°-20′ in Leo. So the aspect between these two is Trine. Hence, we write:

Moon P. Trine Neptune R.

(v) We should not forget that Moon's longitude was 0°-1′ at 1-30 P.M. Indian Standard Time on 2nd January, 1916 but the 23rd year of the native would correspond to the influences and aspects of planets from 1-30P.M. on 2nd January to 1-30 P.M. on 3rd January, 1916. Now as Moon is very swift-moving, it would advance a little less than 15° during the next 24hrs. (see Ephemeris for the year). Therefore, when it passed 12° in Sagittarius it formed sextile aspect with Radical Herschel, so we write towards the close of the year there would also be:

Moon P. Sextile Herschel R.

(vi) Similarly, when moon comes up to about 8° in

Sagittarius it would be forming sextile aspect with progressed Venus and we may note that after sixth months are over there would be the effect of:

Moon P Sextile Venus P.

These examples would suffice to show how longitudinal directions are computed. To mark parallels we have to note in two columns the declinations of Radical as well as of Progressed planets as shown here under:

DECLINATIONS

Planets	*Radical*	*Progressed*
Sun	22°-56′	23°-2′
Moon	13°-11′	24°-43′
Mars	14°-57′	14°-53′
Mercury	23°-32′	23°-59′
Jupiter	5°-16′	4°-10′
Venus	24°-21′	19°-55′
Saturn	22°-6′	22°-19′
Herschel	17°-37′	17°-20′
Neptune	19°-21′	19°-28′

In the comparative table drawn above I have not entered the direction of the declination, *i.e.* whether it is Northern or Southern, because to determine parallel aspect between two planets, it is immaterial whether both are in the same or in different directions.

It would be seen at a glance that the following aspects are formed:

(1) Sun P Parallel Mercury R.

(2) Moon P Parallel Venus R.

(3) Mercury P Parallel Venus R.

(4) Venus P Parallel Neptune R.

(5) Venus P Parallel Neptune P.

The effect of each direction can be looked up in chapter 6. I have dealt herein only with those directions which have a hearing on love affairs and marriage. Others have been omitted, as being outside the scope of the subject-matter of this book.

But before closing this point I want to emphasise one point. That is of *Transits*.

In Direction we have taken one day or 24 hours equal to one year of life but if we have to ascertain Transit effects for the 23rd year, we have to look to the year 11th December, 1937 to 11th Dec. 1938 when the native would be *actually* running 23rd year.

In the words of Raphael, "When the places of evil Directions are excited or aspected by evil planets the results are very powerful and evil; good directions and good transits produce very beneficial results. Evil directions and good transits and good directions and bad transits have little or no effect; they nullify each other."

The major planets, Herschel, Saturn, Jupiter and Mars excite the places of directions by *transit* if they form square or opposition or conjunction or sextile or trine or parallel aspect with the place of direction. Sun if transiting such a planet's place or in parallel with one of the lords also excites it. As planets in retrograde motion become slower they act as more powerful agents of excitement.

For looking up transits you must have the ephemeris of the year for which the actual effects are to be judged. For example, you want to know what would be the transit effect in the 23rd year of the native. So you should have the ephemeris for the years 1937 and 1938 to know the effect for 23rd year (11th December, 1937 to 11th December, 1938). Looking up ephemeris for 1938 you would see that Jupiter would be in Aquarius 9° in January 1938.

Then transiting the place of progressed Venus (Square Ascendant) it would excite progressed position of Venus favourably. The above would suffice to show how transits excite places of Direction or points which are very sensitive

Besides exciting sensitive points transits act independently also by transiting radical places of planets and cusps of angles.

The other kind of Directions formed by the rotation of the earth on its axis, is called 'Primary Directions'. Those who are conversant with their calculations can apply the same. They are too complicated and require the use of Logarithms, of sines, cosines, tangents and calculations of Right Ascension, Semi Arcs, etc. and as such are not being explained here. Those interested are referred to standard works on the subject.

APPENDIX II

DASHA-ANTARDASHAS OR DIRECTIONAL SYSTEM IN HINDU ASTROLOGY

One important detail, which the reader must acquaint himself with, is the finding of dashas and antardashas. The 'dasha' or the major period is also called mahadasha by some people. Similarly, the antardasha or the minor period is also called or 'bhukti' or antar. In some books minor periods are referred to as sub-periods.

1. The following are the duration of Mahadasha assigned to each planet including Rahu and Ketu:

Name	*Duration*
Sun	6 yrs.
Moon	10 yrs.
Mars	7 yrs.
Rahu	18 yrs.
Jupiter	16 yrs.
Saturn	19 yrs.
Mercury	17 yrs.
Ketu	7 yrs.
Venus	20 yrs.

2. During the mahadasha or major period of any one planet, all the nine have their minor periods. Thus, in the mahadasha of Sun, there will be 9 minor periods of Sun, Moon, Mars, Rahu, Jupiter, etc. in the order given above. In the mahadasha

of Moon there will be 9 minor periods of Moon, Mars, Rahu, Jupiter, etc. in the order given above. So in the mahadasha of Mars, there will be minor periods of Mars, Rahu, etc. The point to remember is, *All the nine planets have their minor periods in any one major period,* the first minor period being of the planet whose major period is current.

The other minor period follows in succession in the order given below:

Note. In this appendix Rahu and Ketu have been again and again referred to as planets. They are in fact not planets but for convenience of treatment of the subject, one general term 'planet' has been used.

3. The following are durations of minor periods in the major period of each of the following planets:

Minor periods in the major period of Sun

Planets	*Duration*		
	y.	*m.*	*d.*
Sun	0	3	18
Moon	0	6	0
Mars	0	4	6
Rahu	0	10	24
Jupiter	0	9	18
Saturn	0	11	12
Mercury	0	10	6
Ketu	0	4	6
Venus	1	0	0
Total	**6 years**		

Minor periods in the major period of Moon

Planets	*Duration*		
	y.	*m.*	*d.*
Moon	0	10	0
Mars	0	7	0
Rahu	1	6	0
Jupiter	1	4	0
Saturn	1	7	0
Mercury	1	5	0
Ketu	0	7	0
Venus	1	8	0
Sun	0	6	0
Total	**10 years**		

Minor periods in the major period of Mars

Planets	Duration		
	y.	m.	d.
Mars	0	4	27
Rahu	1	0	18
Jupiter	0	11	6
Saturn	1	1	9
Mercury	0	11	27
Ketu	0	4	27
Venus	1	2	0
Sun	0	4	6
Moon	0	7	0
Total	**7 years**		

Minor periods in the major period of Rahu

Planets	Duration		
	y.	m.	d.
Rahu	2	8	12
Jupiter	2	4	24
Saturn	2	10	6
Mercury	2	6	18
Ketu	1	0	18
Venus	3	0	0
Sun	0	10	24
Moon	1	6	0
Mars	1	0	18
Total	**18 years**		

Minor periods in the major period of Jupiter

Planets	Duration		
	y.	m.	d
Jupiter	2	1	18
Saturn	2	6	12
Mercury	2	3	6
Ketu	0	11	6
Venus	2	8	0
Sun	0	9	18
Moon	1	4	0
Mars	0	11	6
Rahu	2	4	24
Total	**16 years**		

Minor periods in the major period of Saturn

Planets	*Duration*		
	y.	*m.*	*d.*
Saturn	3	0	3
Mercury	2	8	9
Ketu	1	1	9
Venus	3	2	0
Sun	0	11	12
Moon	1	7	0
Mars	1	1	9
Rahu	2	10	6
Jupiter	2	6	12
Total	**19 years**		

Minor periods in the major period of Mercury

Planets	*Duration*		
	y.	*m.*	*d.*
Mercury	2	4	27
Ketu	0	11	27
Venus	2	10	0
Sun	0	10	6
Moon	1	5	0
Mars	0	11	27
Rahu	2	6	18
Jupiter	2	3	6
Saturn	2	8	9
Total	**17 years**		

Minor periods in the major period of Ketu

Planets	*Duration*		
	y.	*m.*	*d.*
Ketu	0	4	27
Venus	1	2	0
Sun	0	4	6
Moon	0	7	0
Mars	0	4	27
Rahu	1	0	18
Jupiter	0	11	6
Saturn	1	1	9
Mercury	0	11	27
Total	**7 years**		

Minor periods in the major period of Venus

Planets	*Duration*		
	y.	*m.*	*d.*
Venus	3	4	0
Sun	1	0	0
Moon	1	8	0
Mars	1	2	0
Rahu	3	0	0
Jupiter	2	8	0
Saturn	3	2	0
Mercury	2	10	0
Ketu	1	2	0
Total	**20 years**		

4. Now, what remains is to determine the first major period in each nativity, because the commencement and duration of the first major period depends upon the longitude of Moon at the time of birth.

Thus, if the longitude of Moon be in any of the sectors given below, the commencement of the dasha would be of the corresponding planet whose name has been given against it:

	If the moon be in			The mahadasha or major period will be of
(a)	Aries	0° to 13°-20′	..	
	Leo	0° to 13°-20′	..	KETU
	Sagitt.	0° to 13°-20′	..	
(b)	Aries	13° - 20′ to 26°-40′		
	Leo	13° - 20′ to 26°-40′		VENUS
	Sagitt.	13° - 20′ to 26°-40′		
(c)	Aries	26° - 40′ to Taurus 10°		
	Leo	26° - 40′ to Virgo 10°		SUN
	Sagitt.	26° - 40′ to Capr. 10°		
(d)	Taurus	10° to 23°-20′	..	
	Virgo	10° to 23°-20′	..	MOON
	Capri.	10° to 23°-20′	..	

(e)	Taurus	23°-20′ to Gemini 6°-40′	
	Virgo	23°-20′ to Libra 6°-40′	MARS
	Capri.	23°-20′ to Aquar. 6°-40′	
(f)	Gemini	6°-40′ to 20°	
	Libra	6°-40′ to 20°	RAHU
	Aquar	6°-40′ to 20°	
(g)	Gemini	20° to Cancer 3°-20′	
	Libra	20° to Scorp. 3°-20′	JUPITER
	Aquar.	20° to Pisces 3°-20′	
(h)	Cancer	3°-20′ to Cancer 16°-40′	
	Scorpio	3°-20′ to Scorpio 16°-40′	SATURN
	Pisces	3°-20′ to Pisces 16°-40′	
(i)	Cancer	16°-40′ to Cancer 30°	
	Scorpio	16°-40′ to Scorpio 30°	MERCURY
	Pisces	16°-40′ to Pisces 30°	

5. Thus, suppose, a person is born at a time when Moon has just completed 16°-40′ in Pisces, his mahadasha or major period of Mercury would just commence, but suppose he is born when Moon is in 20° Pisces, he will be born in Mercury mahadasha but will not have the full quota of Mercury, because full quota of Mercury mahadasha extends from 16°-40° to 30° Pisces and since his Moon is at 20° Pisces— out of the full quota of 13°-20° the Moon had already travelled 3°-20° .

20° - 0°	Position of Moon at birth.
16° - 40°	Commencement of Mercury Mahadasha.
3° - 20°	Distance already travelled.
10° - 0°	Balance distance (deducting 3°-20′ from 13°-20′)

So the Moon was 3°-20′ ahead of the commencing point of the Mercury mahadasha. So by rule of three if the 13°-20′ constitute 17 years the balance (from 20° Pisces to 30° Pisces) or 10° would constitute

$$\frac{17\text{ Yrs.} \times 10^\circ}{13^\circ\text{-}20'} = 12 \text{ Years } 9 \text{ months.}$$

some detailed ready reckoner tables are available to find the balance Mahadasha according to the longitude of Moon. An abridged ready reckoner is being given below :

Table to find balance of Major period according to the longitude of Moon at the time of birth

Long. of Moon		Moon in Aries, Leo, Sagitt. Balance of Dasa				Moon in Taurus Virgo Capri. Balance of Dasa				Moon in Gemini Libra, Aquar. Balance of Dasa				Moon in Cancer Scorpio, Pisces. Balance of Dasa			
			y	*m*	*d*		*y*	*m*	*d*		*y*	*m*	*d*		*y*	*m*	*d*
0	0	**Ketu**	**7**	**0**	**0**	Sun	4	6	0	Mars	3	6	0	Jupiter	4	0	0
0	20		6	9	27		4	4	6		3	3	27		3	7	6
0	40		6	7	24		4	2	12		3	1	24		3	2	12
1	0		6	5	21		4	0	18		2	11	21		2	9	18
1	20		6	3	18		3	10	24		2	9	18		2	4	24
1	40		6	1	15		3	9	0		2	7	15		2	0	0
2	0		5	11	12		3	7	6		2	5	12		1	7	6
2	20		5	9	9		3	5	12		2	3	9		1	2	12
2	40		5	7	6		3	3	18		2	1	6		0	9	18
3	0		5	5	3		3	1	24		1	11	3		0	4	24
3	20		5	3	0		3	0	0		1	9	0	**Saturn**	**19**	**0**	**0**
3	40		5	0	27		2	10	6		1	6	27		18	6	9
4	0		4	10	24		2	8	12		1	4	24		18	0	18
4	20		4	8	21		2	6	18		1	2	21		17	6	27
4	40		4	6	18		2	4	24		1	0	18		17	1	6
5	0		4	4	15		2	3	0		0	10	15		16	7	15
5	20		4	2	12		2	1	6		0	8	12		16	1	24
5	40		4	0	9		1	11	12		0	6	9		15	8	3
6	0		3	10	6		1	9	18		0	4	6		15	2	12
6	20		3	8	3		1	7	24		0	2	3		14	8	21
6	40		3	6	0		1	6	0	**Rahu**	**18**	**0**	**0**		14	3	0
7	0		3	3	27		1	4	6		17	6	18		13	9	9
7	20		3	1	24		1	2	12		17	1	6		13	3	18
7	40		2	11	21		1	0	18		16	7	24		12	9	27
8	0		2	9	18		0	10	24		16	2	12		12	4	6
8	20		2	7	15		0	9	0		15	9	0		11	10	15
8	40		2	5	12		0	7	6		15	3	18		11	4	24
9	0		2	3	9		0	5	12		14	10	6		10	11	3
9	20		2	1	6		0	3	18		14	4	24		10	5	12
9	40		1	11	3		0	1	24		13	11	12		9	11	21

Long. of Moon	Moon in Aries, Leo, Sagitt. Balance of Dasa				Moon in Taurus Virgo Capri. Balance of Dasa				Moon in Gemini Libra, Aquar. Balance of Dasa				Moon in Cancer Scorpio, Pisces. Balance of Dasa			
		y	*m*	*d*		*y*	*m*	*d*		*y*	*m*	*d*		*y*	*m*	*d*
10 0		1	9	0	**Moon**	**10**	**0**	**0**		13	6	0		9	6	0
10 20		1	6	27		9	9	0		13	0	18		9	0	9
10 40		1	4	24		9	6	0		12	7	6		8	6	18
11 0		1	2	21		9	3	0		12	1	24		8	0	27
11 20		1	0	18		9	0	0		11	8	12		7	7	6
11 40		0	10	15		8	9	0		11	3	0		7	1	15
12 0		0	8	12		8	6	0		10	9	18		6	7	24
12 20		0	6	9		8	3	0		10	4	6		6	2	3
12 40		0	4	6		8	0	0		9	10	24		5	8	12
13 0		0	2	3		7	9	0		9	5	12		5	2	21
13 20	**Ven.**	**20**	**0**	**0**	Moon	7	6	0	Rahu	9	0	0	Saturn	4	9	0
13 40		19	6	0		7	3	0		8	6	18		4	3	9
14 0		19	0	0		7	0	0		8	1	6		3	9	18
14 20		18	6	0		6	9	0		7	7	24		3	3	27
14 40		18	0	0		6	6	0		7	2	12		2	10	6
15 0		17	6	0		6	3	0		6	9	0		2	4	15
15 20		17	0	0		6	0	0		6	3	18		1	10	24
15 40		16	6	0		5	9	0		5	10	6		1	5	3
16 0		16	0	0		5	6	0		5	4	24		0	11	12
16 20		15	6	0		5	3	0		4	11	12		0	5	21
16 40		15	0	0		5	0	0		4	6	0	**Merc.**	**17**	**0**	**0**
17 0		14	6	0		4	9	0		4	0	18		16	6	27
17 20		14	0	0		4	6	0		3	7	6		16	1	24
17 40		13	6	0		4	3	0		3	1	24		15	8	21
18 0		13	0	0		4	0	0		2	8	12		15	3	18
18 20		12	6	0		3	9	0		2	3	0		14	10	15
18 40		12	0	0		3	6	0		1	9	18		14	5	12
19 0		11	6	0		3	3	0		1	4	6		14	0	9
19 20		11	0	0		3	0	0		0	10	24		13	7	6
19 40		10	6	0		2	9	0		0	5	12		13	2	3
20 0		10	0	0		2	6	0	**Jup.**	**16**	**0**	**0**		12	9	0
20 20		9	6	0		2	3	0		15	7	6		12	3	27
20 40		9	0	0		2	0	0		15	2	12		11	10	24
21 0		8	6	0		1	9	0		14	9	18		11	5	21
21 20		8	0	0		1	6	0		14	4	24		11	0	18
21 40		7	6	0		1	3	0		14	0	0		10	7	15

Long. of Moon	Moon in Aries, Leo, Sagitt. Balance of Dasa	Moon in Taurus Virgo Capri. Balance of Dasa	Moon in Gemini Libra, Aquar. Balance of Dasa	Moon in Cancer Scorpio, Pisces. Balance of Dasa
	y m d	*y m d*	*y m d*	*y m d*
22 0	7 0 0	1 0 0	13 7 6	10 2 12
22 20	6 6 0	0 9 0	13 2 12	9 9 9
22 40	6 0 0	0 6 0	12 9 18	9 4 6
23 0	5 6 0	0 3 0	12 4 24	8 11 3
23 20	5 0 0	**Mars 7 0 0**	12 0 0	8 6 0
23 40	4 6 0	6 9 27	11 7 6	8 0 27
24 0	4 0 0	6 7 24	11 2 12	7 7 24
24 20	3 6 0	6 5 21	10 9 18	7 2 21
24 40	3 0 0	6 3 18	10 4 24	6 9 18
25 0	2 6 0	6 1 15	10 0 0	6 4 15
25 20	2 0 0	5 11 12	9 7 6	5 11 12
25 40	1 6 0	5 9 9	9 2 12	5 6 9
26 0	1 0 0	5 7 6	8 9 18	5 1 6
26 20	0 6 0	5 5 3	8 4 24	4 8 3
26 40	**Sun 6 0 0**	5 3 0	8 0 0	4 3 0
27 0	5 10 6	5 0 27	7 7 6	3 9 27
27 20	5 8 12	4 10 24	7 2 12	3 4 24
27 40	5 6 18	4 8 21	6 9 18	2 11 21
28 0	5 4 24	4 6 18	6 4 24	2 6 18
28 20	5 3 0	4 4 15	6 0 0	2 1 15
28 40	5 1 6	4 2 12	5 7 6	1 8 12
29 0	4 11 12	4 0 9	5 2 12	1 3 9
29 20	4 9 18	3 10 6	4 9 18	0 10 6
29 40	4 7 24	3 8 3	4 4 24	0 5 3
30 0	4 6 0	3 6 0	4 0 0	0 0 0

Note. These tables give 'balance' of Mahadasha according to the position of Moon. But in the above tables, longitudes of Moon have been given at intervals of 20 minutes (or 1/3 of a. degree). For determining the period of Mahadasha at intermediary points, the next table should be employed.

Table-B

Proportional Parts for Dasa of Planets

(To be deducted from the balance of Dasa for increase by minutes of longitude of Moon).

	Ketu		*Venus*		*sun*		*Moon*		*Mars*		*Rahu*		*Jupiter*		*Saturn*		*Merc.*		
m	d	m	d	m	d	m	d	m	d	m	d	m	d	m	d	m	d		
1	0	3	0	9	0	3	0	5	0	3	0	8	0	7	0	9	0	8	1
2	0	6	0	18	0	5	0	9	0	6	0	16	0	14	0	17	0	16	2
3	0	9	0	27	0	8	0	14	0	9	0	24	0	22	0	26	0	23	3
4	0	13	1	6	0	11	0	18	0	13	1	2	0	29	1	4	1	1	4
5	0	16	1	15	0	14	0	23	0	16	1	11	1	6	1	13	1	8	5
6	0	19	1	24	0	16	0	27	0	19	1	19	1	13	1	21	1	16	6
7	0	22	2	3	0	19	1	2	0	22	1	27	1	20	2	0	1	24	7
8	0	25	2	12	0	22	1	6	0	25	2	5	1	28	2	8	2	1	8
9	0	28	2	21	0	24	1	11	0	28	2	13	2	5	2	17	2	9	9
10	1	1	3	0	0	27	1	15	1	1	2	21	2	12	2	26	2	17	10
15	1	17	4	15	1	11	2	8	1	17	4	2	3	18	4	8	3	25	15
20	2	3	6	0	1	24	3	0	2	3	5	12	4	24	5	21	5	3	20

Example. Thus, for example, we have to find Mahadasha or major period of a planet when the Moon is at 29 degrees 48 minutes in Aquarius. From table 1 column 4 we find that at 29-40 Aquarius the balance would be 4 years 4 months 24 days, years of Jupiter Mahadasha. But herein longitude of Moon is 29-48, *i.e.*, 8 minutes more than 29-40. So looking up we find that for 8 minutes of Moon's arc, we should deduct 1 month 6 days. Doing so, the balance would be 4 years 3 months 18 days.

6. We shall now revert to the example horoscope and calculate the major and minor periods. Readers are reminded that the whole basis of major periods and minor periods is the nakshatra division of the Zodiac, (*i.e.*, division according to the 27 clusters of stars) and as such major and minor periods can be calculated on the basis of the longitude of Moon in the sidereal or fixed zodiac only. Readers are therefore referred

to the longitude of Moon as calculated in the sidereal or fixed Zodiac.

Calculation of minor periods

7. Now attention is invited to para 5 of this appendix. Since the total major period of Mars is of 7 years' duration and the balance is 4 years 2 months and 6 days it follows that duration already undergone (prior to birth, *i.e.* during gestation and previous life; this is how the matter is viewed in Hindu Astrology) was 2 years 9, months and 24 days.

Normally, the various minor periods in the major period of Mars are of the following duration :

Planets	duration y.	m.	d.
Mars	0	4	27
Rahu	1	0	18
Jupiter	0	11	6
Saturn	1	1	9
Mercury	0	11	27
Ketu	0	4	27
Venus	1	2	0
Sun	0	4	6
Moon	0	7	0
Total	**7**	**0**	**0**

Now, since 2 years, 9 months and 24 days are already gone, the minor periods of Mars, Rahu and Jupiter comprising 2 years, 4 months and 21 days and 5 months 3 days of Saturn had already elapsed before birth, (*i.e.* first three minor periods and part of 4th minor period).

So the balance of minor period of Saturn would be (deducting 5 months 3 days from 1 year 1 month and 9 days) 8 months and 6 days only.

Having calculated the minor periods in the first major period, we set down the antardashas (minor periods) as follows :

Table of minor periods in the major period of Mars

Name of Planet	*Duration*			*Till the age of*		
	y.	*m.*	*d.*	*y.*	*m.*	*d.*
Balance of Saturn minor Period in the major Period of Mars	0	8	6	0	8	6
Mercury	0	11	27	1	8	3
Ketu	0	4	27	2	1	0
Venus	1	2	0	3	3	0
Sun	0	4	6	3	7	6
Moon	0	7	0	4	2	6

No deduction on account of period already undergoneor balance period, crops up in case of succeeding dashas. So the tables follow in the following order :

Table of antardashas in the major period of Rahu

Name of Planet	*Duration*			*Till the age of*		
	y.	*m.*	*d.*	*y.*	*m.*	*d.*
Rahu in Rahu	2	8	12	6	10	18
Jupiter in Rahu	2	4	24	9	3	12
Saturn in Rahu	2	10	6	12	1	18
Mercury in Rahu	2	6	18	14	8	6
Ketu in Rahu	1	0	18	15	8	24
Venus in Rahu	3	0	0	18	8	24
Sun in Rahu	0	10	24	19	7	18
Moon in Rahu	1	6	0	21	1	18
Mars in Rahu	1	0	18	22	2	6

Table of antardashas in the major period of Jupiter

Name of Planet	Duration			Till the age of		
	y.	m.	d.	y.	m.	d.
Jupiter in Jupiter	2	1	18	24	3	24
Saturn in Jupiter	2	6	12	26	10	6
Mercury in Jupiter	2	3	6	29	1	12
Ketu in Jupiter	0	11	6	30	0	18
Venus in Jupiter	2	8	0	32	8	18
Sun in Jupiter	0	9	18	33	6	6
Moon in Jupiter	1	4	0	34	10	6
Mars in Jupiter	0	11	6	35	9	12
Rahu in Jupiter	2	4	24	38	2	6

Table of antardashas in the major period of Saturn

Name of Planet	Duration			Till the age of		
	y.	m.	d.	y.	m.	d.
Saturn in Saturn	3	0	3	41	2	9
Mercury in Saturn	2	8	9	43	10	18
Ketu in Saturn	1	1	9	44	11	27
Venus in Saturn	3	2	0	48	1	27
Sun in Saturn	0	11	12	49	1	9
Moon in Saturn	1	7	0	50	8	9
Mars in Saturn	1	1	9	51	9	18
Rahu in Saturn	2	10	6	54	7	24
Jupiter in Saturn	2	6	12	57	2	6

Table of antardashas in the major period of Mercury.

Name of Planet	Duration			Till the age of		
	y.	m.	d.	y.	m.	d.
Mercury in Mercury	2	4	27	59	7	3
Ketu in Mercury	0	11	27	60	7	0
Venus in Mercury	2	10	0	63	5	0
Sun in Mercury	0	10	6	64	3	6
Moon in Mercury	1	5	0	65	8	6
Mars in Mercury	0	11	27	66	8	3
Rahu in Mercury	2	6	18	69	2	21
Jupiter in Mercury	2	3	6	71	5	27
Saturn in Mercury	2	8	9	74	2	6

Once this chart is prepared you can know at a glace, what is the dasha (major period) and antardasha (minor period) at any period in life.

APPENDIX III

FRIENDSHIP AND ENMITY OF PLANETS

Permanent

1. (a) Moon, Mars and Jupiter are friends of Sun. Saturn and Venus are Sun's enemies, Mercury is neutral to Sun.
   (b) Moon's friends are Sun and Mercury. All others are its neutrals. It has no enemy.
   (c) Mars's friends are Jupiter, Moon and Sun. Its neutrals are Saturn and Venus. Mercury is its enemy.
   (d) Mercury's friends are Sun and Venus. Mars, Jupiter and Saturn are its neutrals. Moon is Mercury's enemy.
   (e) Jupiter's friends are Moon, Mars and Sun. Saturn is its neutral. Mercury and Venus are Jupiter's enemies.
   (f) Friends of Venus are Saturn and Mercury. Its neutrals are Mars and Jupiter. Moon and Sun are enemies of Venus.
   (g) Saturn's friends are Venus and Mercury. Jupiter is his neutral. Sun, Moon and Mars are Saturn's enemies.

The above is the permanent relationship of friendship, neutrality and enmity.

Temporal

2. (a) Planets in the 2nd, 3rd, or 4th or in 10th, 11th or 12th house from each other are friends.
   (b) Planets in positions other than those mentioned in *(a)* above are enemies. This is in regard to temporal friendship and enmity.

Five Kinds of Relationship

3. (a) Planets which are friends permanently as well as in temporal positions are great friends.
   (b) A planet which is a friend permanently but an enemy in temporal position is neutral.
   (c) If a planet is neutral permanently but a friend in regard to temporal position, is a friend.
   (d) If a planet is neutral permanently but enemy in regard to temporal position it is an enemy.
   (e) If a planet is an enemy permanently but friend in temporal position it becomes a neutral.
   (f) If a planet is an enemy permanently and also an enemy by temporal position it becomes a great enemy.
4. The following are the friends of Rahu and Ketu.
   Friends: Mercury, Venus, Saturn.
   Enemies: Sun and Moon.
   Neutrals: Others.
5. (a) Rahu's exaltation sign is Gemini, debilitation sign is Sagittarius and Moola trikona is Aquarius. Its own house is Virgo. Some astrologers consider Taurus as its own sign.
   (b) Ketu's exaltation sign is Sagittarius, debilitation sign is Gemini; Moola trikona is Leo and own house is Pisces. Some astrologers consider Scorpio as its own sign.

APPENDIX IV

SUB-DIVISIONS (VARGAS)

One unique system of finding the 'goodness' or 'badness' of a planet, usually employed in Hindu Astrology is to consider how a planet is placed in the various 'Vargas'. 'Varga' literally means one division or class or category. The following are the ten vargas:

(i) *Rashi*: Full sign consisting of 30 degrees.

(ii) *Hora*: A sign is divided into two halves first fifteen degrees (0-15) one division, the second 15 degrees (16-30) is the second division. The first half in odd signs, Aries Gemini, Leo, Libra, Sagittarius, etc. is presided over by Sun, the latter half by Moon. In even signs Taurus, Cancer, etc. the first half is presided over by Moon, the second by Sun.

(iii) *Dreshkana*: A sign is divided into three divisions. First 10 degrees (0-10) are presided over by the lord of the sign itself, the middle ten degrees (11-20) by the lord of the fifth sign and last 10 degrees (21-30) by the lord of the ninth sign. Thus, in Aries the three lords are, lord of Aries (Mars) lord of Leo (Sun) lord of Sagittarius (Jupiter) and so on.

(iv) *Trinshansha*: A sign is divided into five parts, in the following manner: in odd signs (Aries, Gemini, Leo, Libra, Sagittarius and Aquarius).

				Presided over by
(a)	0° - 5°	..	..	Mars.
(b)	6° - 10°	..	..	Saturn.
(c)	10° - 18°	..	..	Jupiter.
(d)	18° - 25°	..	..	Mercury.
(e)	25° - 30°	..	..	Venus.

In even signs (Taurus, Cancer, Virgo Scorpio, Capricorn and Pisces)

			Presided over by
(a) 0 - 5°	..	..	Venus.
(b) 6 - 12°	..	..	Mercury.
(c) 13 - 20°	..	..	Jupiter.
(d) 21 - 25°	..	..	Saturn.
(e) 26 - 30°	..	..	Mars.

(v) *Saptamansha*: A sign is divided into 7 divisions:

(a) 0° to 4°-17'-8".
(b) 40°-17' to 8°-34'-17".
(c) 8°-34' to 12°-51'-25".
(d) 12°-51' to 17°-8'-34".
(e) 17°-8' to 21°-25'-42".
(f) 21°-25' to 25°-42'-51".
(g) 25°-42' to 30°.

(1) In odds signs the lords are lords of the seven signs as counted from the sign itself. Thus, in Aries the lords are Aries, Taurus, Gemini, Cancer, Leo, Virgo and Libra.

(2) In even signs the lord of the seven signs are counted from the 7th sign onwards. Thus, in Taurus the lords of the seven divisions would be lords of Scorpio, Sagittarius, Capricorn, Aquarius, Pisces, Aries, Taurus. We have counted from Scorpio because Scorpio is seventh from Taurus.

(vi) *Navamsha*: A sign is divided into nine divisions:

(a) 0° to 3°-20'.
(b) 3°-20' to 6°-40'.
(c) 6°-40' to 10°
(d) 10° to 13°-20'.
(e) 13°-20' to 16°-40'.
(f) 16°-40' to 20°
(g) 20° to 23°-20'.
(h) 23°-20' to 26°-40'.
(i) 26°-40' to 30°.

The nine divisions in each of the signs are allotted as under:

	In Aries, Leo and Sagittarius	In Taurus, Virgo and Capricorn	In Gemini, Libra, and Aquarius	In Cancer, Scorpio and Pisces
	(1)	(2)	(3)	(4)
(1)	Aries	Capricorn	Libra	Cancer
(2)	Taurus	Aquarius	Scorpio	Leo
(3)	Gemini	Pisces	Sagitt.	Virgo
(4)	Cancer	Aries	Capricorn	Libra
(5)	Leo	Taurus	Aquarius	Scorpio
(6)	Virgo	Gemini	Pisces	Sagitt.
(7)	Libra	Cancer	Aries	Capricorn
(8)	Scorpio	Leo	Taurus	Aquarius
(9)	Sagitt.	Virgo	Gemini	Pisces

The sub-divisions are presided over by the lords of the signs, in whose jurisdiction a planet falls.

Thus, a planet in the jurisdiction (9th division) of Aries would be presided over by Mars, in that of Taurus by Venus and so on. If a planet is in the 9th division which is the same as the sign, it is called *Vargottam* and is considered as good as in it own sign. Thus if Sun be in Scorpio sign and the 9th division. It is in, also belongs to Scorpio Sun is deemed as strong if in its own sign, though the sign may not be owned by it. This is called 'Vargottam'.

(vii) *Dwadashansha*: A sign is divided in 12 divisions.

1- $2\frac{1}{2}°$, $2\frac{1}{2}°$-5°, 5°-$7\frac{1}{2}°$ and so on.

Each of the twelve divisions are allotted to signs as counted from the sign itself. Thus, the twelve sub-divisions in Aries are allotted to Aries, Taurus, Gemini, and so on. 12 sub-divisions in Taurus are allotted to Taurus, Gemini, Cancer and so on.

(viii) *Dashamansha*: A planet is sub-divided into 10 divisions.

(a) 1°-3°.

(b) 3°-6°.
(c) 6°-9° and so on.

In the case of odd signs the ten divisions are allotted to ten signs counted from the sign itself. Thus, in Aries to Aries, Taurus, etc. up to Capricorn.

In the case of even, signs they are allotted to ten signs as counted from the ninth sign onwards.

Thus, if a planet is in Taurus, the 10 sub-divisions would be allotted to Capricorn, Aquarius, Pisces, etc. (we have counted from Capricorn because Capricorn is ninth from Taurus).

(ix) *Shodashansh*: A sign is divided into 16 divisions—Each division constituting 1°-52′-30′. In odd signs the first 4 divisions are presided by Brahma, Vishnu, Hara and Ravi (gods of Hindus) and the remaining are allotted to twelve signs, counted from the sign itself. In even signs the order is reversed.

(x) *Shashti-anshas*: A sign is sub-divided into 60 divisions each constituted by 30′ (thirty minutes of arc or half a degree). In the case of an odd sign the following division are malefic. 1, 2, 8, 9, 10, 11, 12, 15, 16, 30, 31, 32, 33, 34, 35, 39, 40, 42, 43, 44, 48, 51, 52, 59 and the rest are deemed benefic. In case of even signs, the above are deemed benefic the rest are deemed malefic.

To find whether and how far a planet is good or bad we examine how it is placed in the above 10 categories or 'Vargas'.

(a) A planet in its own *sub-division* or in its *exaltation sub-division* is deemed strong.
(b) A planet in its great friend's or friend's sub-division is deemed good.
(c) A planet in its enemy's house, sub-division or great enemy's house/sub-division or in its depression sign/vargas is deemed malefic.
(d) A planet in sub-divisions owned by benefics is deemed good.
(e) A planet in sub-divisions owned by malefic is deemed malefic.

Attach 100 per cent value to a planet's position the sign and the ninth division. Attach 50 per cent value to its position in 1/2 WF division, 1/3rd division, 1/5th division, 1/7th division, and 1/12th division, and attach 25 per cent value to a planet in its 1/10th division, 1/16th division and 1/60th division. Ready reckoners for ascertaining 'Varga' position in any degree in the Zodiac are available. If one is purchased, much trouble can be saved.

If out of the ten Vargas, a planet is placed in:

(a) Two own or of great friend's, it is deemed in Parijatansh.
(b) If there are three such 'Vargas', it is in 'Uttamansh'.
(c) If there are four such Vargas it is in Gopuransh.
(d) If a planet is in 5, 6, 7, 8, 9 or 10 such Vargas it is called in 'Sinhasanansh', 'Paravatansh', Devalokansh, 'Brahma Lokansh','Airavatansh' and 'Vaisheshik anshȧ' respectively.

APPENDIX V

PRECESSION OF THE EQUINOXES OR AYANANSHA

Table of *precession of the Equinoxes on 1st January*

Year				*Deg.*	*Min.*
1900	..	..	..	22	27
1901	..	..	..	22	28
1902	..	..	..	22	29
1903	..	..	..	22	30
1904	..	..	..	22	31
1905	..	..	..	22	31
1906	..	..	..	22	32
1907	..	..	..	22	33
1908	..	..	..	22	34
1909	..	..	..	22	34
1910	..	..	..	22	35
1911	..	..	..	22	36
1912	..	..	..	22	37
1913	..	..	..	22	38
1914	..	..	..	22	39
1915	..	..	..	22	40
1916	..	..	..	22	41
1917	..	..	..	22	42
1918	..	..	..	22	43
1919	..	..	..	22	43
1920	..	..	..	22	44
1921	..	..	..	22	45
1922	..	..	..	22	46
1923	..	..	..	22	46
1924	..	..	..	22	47
1925	..	..	..	22	48

1926	..	..	..	22	49
1927	..	..	..	22	50
1928	..	..	..	22	50
1929	..	..	..	22	51
1930	..	..	..	22	52
1931	..	..	..	22	53
1932	..	..	..	22	54
1933	..	..	..	22	55
1934	..	..	..	22	56
1935	..	..	..	22	57
1936	..	..	..	22	58
1937	..	..	..	22	59
1938	..	..	..	22	59
1939	..	..	..	23	0
1940	..	..	..	23	1
1941	..	..	..	23	2
1942	..	..	..	23	2
1943	..	..	..	23	3
1944	..	..	..	23	4
1945	..	..	..	23	5
1946	..	..	..	23	5
1947	..	..	..	23	6
1948	..	..	..	23	7
1949	..	..	..	23	8
1950	..	..	..	23	9
1951	..	..	..	23	10
1952	..	..	..	23	11
1953	..	..	..	23	12
1954	..	..	..	23	13
1955	..	..	..	23	14
1956	..	..	..	23	14
1957	..	..	..	23	15
1958	..	..	..	23	16
1959	..	..	..	23	17
1960	..	..	..	23	17
1962	..	..	..	23	19.6
1964	..	..	..	23	21.2

1966	..	..	..	23	22.9
1968	..	..	..	23	24.6
1970	..	..	..	23	26.3
1972	..	..	..	23	27.9
1974	..	..	..	23	29.6
1976	..	..	..	23	31.3
1978	..	..	..	23	33.0
1980	..	..	..	23	34.7
1982	..	..	..	23	36.3
1984	..	..	..	23	38.0
1986	..	..	..	23	39.7
1988	..	..	..	23	41.4
1990	..	..	..	23	43.0
1992	..	..	..	23	44.7
1994	..	..	..	23	46.4
1996	..	..	..	23	48.1
1998	..	..	..	23	49.7
2000	..	..	..	23	51.4
2002	..	..	..	23	53.1
2004	..	..	..	23	54.8
2006	..	..	..	23	56.4
2008	..	..	..	23	58.1
2010	..	..	..	23	59.1
2012	..	..	..	24	01.5
2014	..	..	..	24	03.1
2016	..	..	..	24	04.8
2018	..	..	..	24	06.5
2020	..	..	..	24	08.2
2022	..	..	..	24	09.8
2024	..	..	..	24	11.5
2026	..	..	..	24	13.2
2028	..	..	..	24	14.9
2030	..	..	..	24	16.6
2032	..	..	..	24	18.2

Motion of Ayanansha

10	years	00	08.38
100	years	01	23.8

GLOSSARY OF ASTROLOGICAL AND TECHNICAL TERMS

Affliction (i) When a planet is weak by being debilitated or in detriment, it is a said to be afflicted.

(ii) (a)If a planet is conjoined with a malefic or parallel with a malefic planet or forming opposition, square or unfavourable aspect with a planet it is deemed to be afflicted.

(b) If a planet is in square or opposition aspect with a benefic even then it is called afflicted.

Note : If a planet be weak, in detriment or in debility and conjoined with a malefic and also forming square, semi-square or opposition with a malefic (more exact the aspect greater the affliction) the planet would be called very much afflicted. If, however, there be only one of the above circumstances present and there be good aspects (trine or conjunction or sextile) from strong Jupiter or other planets the affliction would not be considered so severe. Individual judgment must determine in each case the extent of affliction.

Airy Signs Gemini, Libra and Aquarius are called Airy signs.

Angles The ascendant, cusps of the 4th, 7th and 10th Houses are called Angles. The signs in which these four cusps are situate are called angular signs. The Ist, 4th, 7th and 10th houses are called angular houses. When planets are in angle they are considered more powerful than in other houses. Their order of strength is the 10th, 1st, 7th and 4th houses 'Kendra'.

Antipathy — Planets which have dissimilar attributes react adversely on each other and are considered as being antipathetic, *i.e.*, opposite of sympathetic.

Applying — When a planet is so moving as to form an exact aspect, it is called as applying. For example, Saturn is in 12° Leo and Sun is in 10° Taurus. Here Sun is proceeding towards forming an exact square aspect. After two days Sun will have attained 12° Taurus and would have exact square aspect.

When the process is reverse, i.e. suppose instead of being in 10° Taurus, Sun is in 14° Taurus, as Sun's motion is faster than Saturn's the distance between Sun and Saturn's exact aspect would gradually go on increasing, so the planets are said to be separating (from an exact aspect).

Aquarius — Eleventh sign of the Zodiac. Any planet having a longitude 300°-330° would be deemed to be in Aquarius.

Aries — First sign of the Zodiac. Any planet having a longitude of 0°-30° would be in Aries.

Ascendant — The point of the Zodiac which touches the Eastern Horizon as viewed from the place of birth at the time of birth. This is also called rising sign or cusp of the 1st House. The sign in which the ascendant is situated is called ascendant.

Ascending — A planet going eastwards towards the Midheaven from 4th house upwards is called Ascending planet.

Aspects — (a) Two planets are said to be in aspect with each other when the distance between them, *i.e.*, between their longitudes consists of the number of degrees noted below:

(i) When they are in the same degree the aspect is called 'Conjunction'.

(ii) When the distance is 60 degrees they are said to be in 'Sextile'.

(iii) When the distance is 90 degrees between two planets, the aspect is called 'square'.

(iv) When they are 120 degrees apart they are said to be in 'Trine'.

(v) When the distance between them is 180 degrees they are described as being in 'opposition'.

(vi) When their declination is in the same degree whether north or south or there is difference of less than one degree in their declinations they are said to be in 'Parallel'.

(b) It is, however, seldom that the distance between two planets is exactly 60,90,120 or 180 degrees. Some margin is therefore allowed. This margin is technically called "Orb". For example, if the distance between two planets is 61 degrees or 59 degrees this is not exact" sextile yet it is treated as sextile. What margin or Orb should be allowed, in respect of each kind of aspect ? This is being explained below:

(i) The orbs of the planets when applying should be six degrees and when separating 8 degrees in case of Mars, Mercury, Jupiter, Venus, Saturn, Herschel and Neptune.

(ii) The orb of the Sun when applying may be taken as 12 degrees and when separating 17 degrees.

(iii) The orb of the Moon when applying may be taken as 8 degrees, when separating 12 degrees.

(iv) The above orbs are in respect of major aspects, *i.e.* conjunction, and opposition.

(a) Divide them by 2/3 and you have orbs of trine and square.

(b) Halve them and you have orbs for sextile.

(v) For parallels do not allow an orb of more than 1 degree or one degree and a half.

(c) There are other aspects also for which please refer to introduction.

(d) (i) Square and opposition are bad aspects.

(ii) Trine and Sextile are good aspects.

(iii) Conjunction of parallel with a benefic planet is good.

(iv) Conjunction or parallel with a malefic planet is bad.

(v) Sesqui-quadrate (135 apart); Inconjunct or quincunx (150° apart) are not deemed good.

(vi) Quintile (72° apart) and Bi-quintile (144° apart) are good but weak aspects.

Barren signs Gemini, Leo, Virgo.

Benefics Jupiter and Venus.

Benefic Aspects See Aspects.

Bestial The following signs are called bestial because their names pertain to beasts: Aries, Taurus, Leo, Sagittarius and Capricorn.

Bi-Corporal Signs	—Gemini, Sagittarius and Pisces.
Birth time	Time of birth.
Biquintile	Aspect between two planets 144° apart. This is a slightly beneficial but weak aspect.
Cadent	The third, sixth, ninth and 12th houses in a horoscope.
Cancer	This is fourth sign in the Zodiac comprising 30 degrees from 90° to 120°.
Capricorn	This is the tenth sign in the zodiac comprising 30 degrees from 270° to 300°.
Caput Draconis	English name for Rahu-north node of the Moon.
Cardinal Points	Cusps of 1st, 4th, 7th and 10th houses.
Cardinal signs	Aries, Cancer, Libra, Capricorn.
Cauda Draconis	Ketu (a point 180° distant from Rahu)—Southern node of the Moon.
Colours of	Sun—Golden or orange, Moon-Silvery, Mercury—Greenish, Venus—White with bluish tinge, Mars—Red, Jupiter—Yellow, Saturn—Black, Uranus—Blue, Neptune—Indigo.
Combust	When a planet comes within $8\frac{1}{2}$ degrees of Sun, the planet loses part of its power and individual qualities because the rays emitted by it get mixed and burnt up with Sun's rays. A combust planet is considered weak.
Common Signs	Gemini, Virgo, Sagittarius, Pisces.
Converse Motion	This is caused by the diurnal motion of Earth on its axis.
Configurated	The relative position of planets in a horoscope.
Conjunction	See aspects.
Constellation	Groups of fixed stars in the Zodiac.
Culmination	When a planet arrives at Midheaven.

Cusps	The beginning of any house (see preliminary pages of this book).
Daily Motion	The average motion of a planet perday.
Debility	A planet in a sign opposite to one it is in exaltation is deemed to be in debility. This is a weak position.
Decanate	One-third of a sign—from 0° to 10° First decanate; 10° to 20° Second decanate; 20° to 30° Third decanate.
Declination	The distance any planet is north or south of equator.
Degree	One thirtieth part of a sign and 1/360th of a circle.
Degree Rising	The exact degree on the cusp of the first house or Ascendant.
Descendant	The cusp of the 7th house or 180° distance from Ascendant.
Descension	The going down of any planet from the meridian above to that below Earth.
Detriment	If a planet is in a sign opposite to one, it owns, it is deemed to be in detriment. Sun in Aquarius, Moon in Capricorn, Mars in Libra or Taurus, Mercury in Sagittarius or Pisces, Jupiter in Gemini, or Virgo, Venus in Aries or Scorpio, Saturn in Cancer or Leo are deemed to being detriment. This is a weak position.
Dignity	When a planet is in its sign and triplicity it is called essentially dignified. When in an angle it is called accidentally dignified. When in both, it is essentially as well as accidentally dignified. A planet in dignity is deemed strong.
Direct Motion	When a planet is moving forward this is direct motion. Sun and Moon have direct motion. Other planets have retrograde motion also.

Directions (Primary) — The measuring of the space between the planets (mutually) as well as from ascendant and Midheaven to ascertain when they will form an aspect— and consequently at what period of life its effect would be felt.

Directions (Secondary) — The aspects formed by Planets (mutually as well as with Ascendant and M.C.) in the days succeeding the birth. Each day between the birth and the time the aspect is formed is reckoned, as one year of life. Thus, if in a horoscope Moon forms a trine with Jupiter 15 days after birth, the good effect will be felt when the native completes 15 years of his life. (See Appendix.II)

Dispositor — The lord of the sign in which a planet is. Suppose, Moon is in Taurus. Then Venus is the dispositor of Moon. Suppose, Moon is in Gemini, then Mercury is the dispositor of Moon.

Diurnal Arc — It is the length of time, during which that part of the Zodiac in which a planet is situate is above the earth. This is measured in degrees.

Earth Signs — Taurus, Virgo, and Capricorn are earthy signs.

Ecliptic — The imaginary belt which Sun appears to move in. In fact it is the path traversed by Earth in going round Sun in one year. This is also called Zodiac. This path is not exactly circular but elliptic.

Elevated — A planet on the cusp of the 10th house is most elevated and a planet on the cusp of the 4th house is least elevated. Thus, more distant a planet is from the cusp of the 4th house more elevated it is.

Essential Dignity — See dignity.

Exaltation — Sun in Aries, Moon in Taurus, Mars in Capricorn, Mercury in Virgo, Jupiter in Cancer, Venus in Pisces, Saturn in Libra are deemed to be in exaltation. To be in exaltation is a position of strength.

Fall — Same meaning as in Debility.

Feminine sign — Taurus, Cancer, Virgo, Scorpio Capricorn, Pisces.

Fiery Signs — Aries, Leo and Sagittarius are called Fiery Signs.

Fixed Signs — Taurus, Leo, Scorpio, Aquarius.

Fruitful Signs — Cancer, Scorpio, Pisces.

Gemini — Third sign in the Zodiac comprising 30 degrees from 60° to 90°.

Geocentric — As related to the centre of the earth of viewed from the centre of the earth as viewing base.

House — The division of the Zodiac into twelve parts. The length of all the 12 houses is equal for a birth occurring on the equator or 0° latitude but as we go to the North or South of Equator due to the earth being inclined on its axis and also due to the Zodiac being elliptic and not circular, the 12 'houses' become of unequal measure.

While making a horoscope one must therefore have Table of Houses for the latitude of birth. Houses are reckoned from the Eastern Horizon towards the left hand in the order of the signs, the Ascendant being the first house. See Introduction and the chart given therein.

Human Signs	Gemini, Virgo, Aquarius and first 15° of Sagittarius.
Interception	When a sign comes between two cusps, it is deemed intercepted.
Jupiter	One of the seven planets. (presiding over Thursday).
Latitude	On the earth, as given in geographical maps—distance in degrees north or south of Equator, in heavens—distance in degrees north or south of the ecliptic line or Zodiac.
Leo	The fifth sign of the Zodiac comprising 30° from 120° to 150°.
Libra	The seventh sign of the Zodiac comprising 30° from 180° to 210°.
Lights	·Sun, Moon.
Local Time or Local Meantime	This is reckoned as follows: Suppose, the plate of birth is India (where the Indian Standard Time has been fixed on the basis of 82°-30′ of Longitude East of Greenwich), and Indian Standard Time is 4 P.M. What would be the Local Mean Time at a city in India with logitude 70° ? Deducting 70° from 82°-30′ we get 12°-30′ At the rate of 4 minutes for each degree and 4 seconds for each minute of are, we get 50 minutes; deducting 50 minutes from 4 P.M. we get 3-10 P.M. This would be the local Mean time.
Longitude	On each as given in Geographical maps it is the distance east or west from Greenwich meridian. In heavens it is the distance from 0° or beginning of Aries (The point where Sun appears to be on the spring Equinox, when day and night are equal).

Lords	See Ruler.
Malefics	Mars, Saturn and Herschel.
Mars	One of the seven planets (presiding over Tuesday).
Masculine signs	Aries, Gemini, Leo, Libra Sagittarius, Aquarius.
Mercury	One of the seven planets (presiding over Wednesday).
Meridian.	On earth 0° Longitude or Longitude of Greenwich; in heaven— Celestial longitude passing over cusp of 10th house is called upper meridian; that passing over the cusp of the 4th house is called lower meridian.
Midheaven	Cusp of the 10th House—the meridian above the earth.
Moon	One of the seven planets (presiding over Monday).
Mutable signs	Gemini, Virgo, Sagittarius, Pisces.
Nadir	Cusp of the 4th House.
Nativity	Horoscope or birth chart giving position of planets, rising sign or ascendant and cusps of the Houses.
Neptune	One of the new planets discovered during last century.
Node	That part of the ecliptic where a planet passes out of north into south latitude is its South node; that where it passes out of south into northern Latitude is its North node. Northern node of Moon is called Rahu, Southern Node is called Ketu.
Northern signs	Aries, Taurus, Gemini, Cancer, Leo and Virgo.
Opposition	See aspects.
Orbs	See aspects.
Oriental	From the 4th house Eastward to the 10th is

	Oriental. But the Sun and Moon are Oriental between the 10th to 1st House and Occidental from the 4th to 7th house. Places other than Oriental are Occidental.
Own House	Sun in Leo, Moon in Cancer, Mars in Aries or Scorpio, Mercury in Gemini or Virgo, Jupiter in Sagittarius or Pisces, Venus in Taurus or Libra, Saturn in Capricorn or Aquarius is deemed to be in its own sign or own House. Thus, Sun is owner of Leo, Moon of Cancer and so on. This is a strong position. Some modern astrologers assign rulership of Aquarius to Herschel and that of Pisces to Neptune.
Parallels	See Declination; when two planets have the same Declination whether north or south or one north and the other south, they are parallel.
Pars Fortunae	This is an imaginary point as much distant from the cusp of the 1st House, as the Moon is from the Sun. In dark fortnight the Pars Fortunae is in anywhere from the 7th to 1st house (above earth). In bright fortnight it is anywhere from 1st to 7th (below earth).
Pisces	The twelfth sign of the Zodiac comprising 30 degrees from 330° to 360°.
Planets	Sun, Moon, Mars, Mercury, Jupiter, Venus, Saturn, Herschel and Neptune.
Progressed	Position of planets progressed for computing directions.
position	Direction. In primary Direction, the progress is 59′ 8″ for each year of life. In Secondary Directions, it is the actual progress at the rate of one day (24 hours) for one year of life.
Radical Places	Places of planets at the time of birth.

Precession of the Equinoxes — When Sun is exactly on the equator, the day and night are quite equal. This happens twice in the year—in spring and autumn. Suppose, Sun is at a longitude 'x' in Spring 1955. This happens next year when Sun is 50′—25′ (of arc) before the longitude 'x'. This point is always preceding, at the above rate. Therefore, this phenomenon is called 'Precession'.

Quincunx — Planets 150° apart.

Quintile — Planets 72° apart.

Radical — Places of Planets at the time of birth.

Retrograde — The backward motion which the planets appear to have at times, on account of the position and motion of earth.

Rising sign — The Ascendant or sign in which the cusp of the first house is.

Ruler — Sun is the Ruler of Leo. Moon of Cancer, Mars of Aries and Scorpio, Mercury of Gemini and Virgo, Jupiter of Sagittarius and Pisces, Venus of Taurus and Libra, and Saturn of Capricorn and Aquarius.

Ruling Planet — Ruler of the Ascendant (the sign in which the cusp of the 1st house is) is called, the Ruling planet. But if it be weak and another strong planet be on or very near the cusp of the 1st House, such planet would be called the Ruling planet.

Sagittarius — The ninth sign of the Zodiac comprising 30° from 240° to 270°.

Saturn — One of the seven planets (presiding over Saturday).

Scorpio — Eighth sign in the Zodiac comprising 30° from 210° to 240°.

Semi-Sextile — See aspects.

Semi-Square — See aspects.

Separation	When the distance between two Planets is increasing after having formed an exact aspect. (Also see applying).
Sesqui-quadrate	See Introduction.
Sidereal Time	Angular distance of the first point of Aries. If we convert the hours, minutes and seconds on the basis of 15 degrees for each hour, it would give the right ascension of the Meridian cusp in time.
Signs	Twelve parts of the Zodiac each comprising 30°. The 12 signs in order are Aries, Taurus, Gemini, Cancer, Leo, Virgo, Libra, Scorpio, Sagittarius, Capricorn, Aquarius and Pisces.
Southern signs	Libra, Scorpio, Sagittarius, Capricorn, Aquarius, Pisces.
Square	See aspects.
Standard Time	Time by the watch prevalent in a particular country. Indian Standard time is 5 hours 30 minutes ahead of G.M.T. This is since 1903. Before that, Madras time was the Indian Standard Time for India.
Stationary	When a planet due to Earth's motion appears to be stationary. This is either when a planet changes from Direct motion to Retrograde motion or *vice versa*.
Succedent Houses	The 2nd, 5th, 8th, and 11th houses.
Sun	One of the seven planets (presiding over Sunday).
Taurus	Second sign of the Zodiac comprising 30° from 30° to 60°
Transit	The passage of any planet over radical place of any planet, part of fortunae or cusps of the 1st, 4th, 7th, or 10th Houses or over any sensitive point.
Trine	See aspects.

Triplicities	The division of 12 signs into four-groups, Fiery, Earthy, Airy and Watery.
Tropical sign	Cancer, Capricorn.
Uranus	Also called Herschel, one of the planets discovered in the last century by a scientist named Herschel.
Venus	One of the seven planets presiding over Friday.
Violent sign	Aries, Libra, Scorpio, Capricorn and Aquarius.
Virgo	Sixth sign of the Zodiac comprising 30° from 150° to 180°.
Watery Signs	Cancer, Scorpio and Pisces.
Zodiac	The imaginary path round the earth through which the Sun appears to travel. Also called Ecliptic.

The words marked with an asterisk have the same meaning as in English.

Sanskrit names for English terms have been given below:

The following words are used in the Hindu Astrology and as such a separate list is given.

Afflicted. When a planet is weak or very weak and aspected by or is conjoined with malefics it is considered as afflicted. A planet combust or in great enemy's house and devoid of strength is also considered as afflicted.

**Angles*. Kendra.

Ansha. Literally means degree, (also portion, a part) but is generally used as abbreviated form of 'Navansha' or see Appendix IV.

Antipathy. See "friends, enemies and neutrals." Appendix III.

**Applying*. Itthashala.

**Aquarius*. Kumbha.

**Aries*. Mesh.

**Ascendant*. Lagna.

Aspects. See Introduction.

Bandha. When two planets mutually aspect each other or

exchange places with each other or both are in angles or trine they are deemed in 'bandha'.

Benefics. Shubh Graha.

**Birth Time.* Janma Kala, Janma Samay, Ishtam.

**Cadent.* Apokalima.

**Cancer.* Karka.

**Capricorn.* Makar.

**Cardinal Points.* Kendras.

Combust. Asta. Moon is combust when it is within 12° of Sun. Mars is combust when within 17° from Sun. If Mercury is direct it becomes combust within 14° from Sun. But when Mercury is retrograde it is combust within 12° from Sun. Jupiter becomes combust when within 11° from Sun. If Venus is direct it becomes combust when within 10° from Sun but if Venus be retrograde it becomes combust when within 8° from Sun. Saturn becomes combust when within 15° from Sun. These are the normal distances. If planets have very wide latitude at the moment they would not become cumbust at the exact degrees specified above. But for practical purposes the above distances may be taken.

**Common Signs.* Dwiswabhava.

Conjunction. (Yuti). Two planets are said to be conjoined together when they are in the same sign irrespective of the distance intervening between them.

**Constellation.* Nakshatra. These are clusters of fixed stars. Each having jurisdiction over 13° 20 minutes. Their Sanskrit names are:

Ashvini, Bharani, Krittika, Rohini, Mrigashiras, Ardra, Punarvasu, Pusya, Aslesa, Magha, Purvaphalguni, Uttaraphalguni, Hasta, Chitra, Svati, Visakha, Anuradha, Jyestha, Mula, Purvasadha, Uttarasadha, Sravana, Sravistha (Dhanistha), Shatabhisaj, Purvabhadrapada, Uttarabhadra-pada and Revati.

**Daily Motion.* Gati.

Dasha. See Appendix II. This is also called Mahadasha.

Dashanath. Planet whose major period is current.

**Debility.* Neech.

**Decanate.* Dreshkana.

**Declination*. Kranti.

**Degree*. Ansha.

**Degree rising*. Lagna Spashta.

**Dispositor*. The lord of the house in which a planet is placed in. For example, if, Sun is in Scorpio, because Mars, is the lord of Scorpio, Mars is the Dispositor of Sun.

**Descendant*. Saptam.

Detriment. In an enemy's house.

Dignity. Strong.

Direct motion. Margi.

Directions. See Appendix I & II. In Sanskrit they are called Dashas, Antardashas, (Bhuktis) Pratyantardashas, etc.

**Ecliptic*. Bhagan or Krantivritta.

Enemy. See Appendix III.

**Exaltation*. Uchcha.

**Fall*. Neech.

**Feminine Signs*. Stri Rashi.

**Fiery Signs*. Agni Rashi.

**Fixed Signs*. Sthira Rashi.

Friend. See Appendix III.

**Gemini*. Mithun.

**Geocentric*. Bhugarbha.

Gopuransha. See Appendix IV.

Gulika. Mandi.

* *Heliacal Rising and Setting*. When a planet is not combust (see meaning above) it is said to rise out of Sun's circle of invisibility, *i.e.* visible. When it is combust, it is set *i.e.*, not visible.

**House*. Bhava, Griha, Sthana.

Hora. See Appendix IV.

Janmapati. Dispositor of Moon.

**Jupiter*. Guru, Brihaspati.

Kendra. Angles.

Kona. 5th or 9th house.

Lagna. Ascendant.

**Leo*. Sinha.

**Libra*. Tula.

**Lights*. Sun and Moon.

**Local time*. Sthaniya Kal or Samay.

Lunar Ascendant. Chandra Lagna. Lunar ascendant is that rashi in which Moon is situated at the time of birth. In Hindu astrology, judgment is arrived at by treating the rising sign as ascendant and counting from there; also by treating Lunar ascendant as the 1st house succeeding sign as the second house and so on. In this book, we have used the abbreviated form L A for Lunar ascendant.

**Longitude*. Ansha.

**Lord*. Swami, Nath. The planet which owns the sign is called the lord. Thus, if Cancer or rather some degree of Cancer is on the cusp of the 7th house, Moon would be called lord of the 7th house, in that particular horoscope.

Malefics. See Chapter 8, Aphorism 7 onward.

Major Period. See Appendix II.

Mahadasha. This is also called Dasha. This means major period of a planet.

Mandi. Also called Gulika. This position is considered very evil. Its calculation is rather complicated. See some standard work.

**Mars*. Mangal, Kuja.

** Masculine Sign*. Purusha Rashi.

Minor Periods. See Appendix II.

**Minute*. Minute of time or one 60th part of an hour. Another meaning of minute is 1/60th part of a degree. This is called minute of arc or just a minute. In Sanskrit it is called 'Kala'.

**Moon*. Chandra.

**Nativity*. Janma Kundali. Janma Patra.

Navamsh. See Appendix IV.

Neutral. See Appendix III.

Opposition. When two planets are in two signs which are mutually the 7th house from each other they are called in opposition, irrespective of the distance in degrees.

**Own house*. Sva Rashi, Swagrihi.

**Papa*. Malefic

**Pisces*. Meena.

**Planets*. Sun, Moon, Mars, Mercury, Jupiter, Venus, Saturn, Rahu and Ketu.

Prishthoday Rashi. These are signs which rise with their hinder parts first. Aries, Taurus, Cancer, Sagittarius, and Capricorn are Prishthoday rashis.

Rashi. Sign.

Precesion of Equinox. Aynansha. See Appendix V.

**Retrograde*. Vakri.

Rising and Setting. In relation to place of birth a planet is said to rise when it is in the 1st house, and it is described as setting when it is in the 7th house, *i.e.* in the eastern horizon and western horizon respectively. In relation to visibility due to nearness with Sun see Heliacal Rising and Setting.

**Sagittarius*. Dhanu.

Saptamansha. See Appendix IV.

**Saturn*. Shani.

**Scorpio*. Vrishchik.

Seconds. As one 60th part of a minute of Arc it is called vikala in Sanskrit). As 1/60th part of minute of time it is the same as in English.

*Separation. Isarapha.

Shirshoday. These are the signs which rise with their heads first. These are Leo, Virgo, Libra, Scorpio, Aquaries, and Gemini.

* *Sign*. Rashi.

* *Standard time*.

Strong. Bali or Balawan. See Appendix IV.

Succeeding Houses. Panaphar.

**Sun*. Ravi, Surya.

**Taurus*. Vrishabh.

**Transit*. Gochar.

Trikona. 5th, 9th houses.

Trik. Sixth, 8th or 12th house.

Trinshansha. See Appendix IV.

Upachay. 3rd, 6th, 10th and 11th houses.

Vargas. See Appendix IV.

Vargottam. When the sign and the 'navansha, a planet is in, are the same, the planet is called in 'Vargottam' For example, if Sun be in 29th degree of Sagittarius, it would be in the sign Sagittarius as well as Sagittarius 'navansha', hence in Vargottam.

* *Venus.* Shukra.

* *Virgo.* Kanya.

Weak. Balaheen or Nirbal.

* *Zodiac.* Bhagana, Kranti Vritta.

---

* *Note.* Certain technical words require very long explanations and have therefore been omitted. For them readers are requested to refer to some standard work on Hindu astrology.